MW00634868

WHAT YOUR COLLEAGUES ARE SAYII

These exceptional books are overflowing with worthwhile activities. Going well beyond sharing ideas, they illuminate how manipulative(s) can be used to support mathematical thinking. A particularly important feature of this book is the ongoing discussion of making connections among representations. With such intentionality and engagement in multiple representations, we can ensure that every child become confident and competent in mathematics.

Jennifer Bay-Williams
Professor and Author
University of Louisville, KY

I expected to like this book, but I flat out *love* it! Whether you are a veteran teacher, a new teacher just starting your journey, or a parent trying to help your child at home, this book is a wonderful and practical resource. While manipulatives are clearly the star here, solid instructional strategies supported by just the right amount of research provide a strong supporting cast. Each chapter features a manipulative and includes ideas for organization, classroom management, distance learning, homemade alternatives, and multiple lessons highlighting the use of the manipulative. This is a book you will use all year long!

Donna Boucher
Math Coach's Corner

Every math teacher knows that using manipulatives is a good idea. Now, with *Mastering Math Manipulatives*, every math teacher can now how to use them best. It unpacks how different manipulatives work, provides rich tasks for using them, and teaches how to maximize their effectiveness. It includes virtual manipulatives! This is a must-have for every math teacher!

John SanGiovanni
Mathematics Supervisor
Howard County Public Schools, MD

I highly recommend *Mastering Math Manipulatives*. Manipulatives play a vital role in developing a solid conceptual understanding of the math. Not only do the authors share wonderful ideas of how to use a variety of manipulatives; they also share reasons why that manipulative is effective for the given topic as well as ways to further develop that concept. This resource is great for those who are new to using manipulatives as well as those who are experienced in using them.

Kevin Dykema
Mathematics Teacher, Mattawan Middle School
President-Elect, National Council of Teachers of Mathematics, 2021–2023

Sara Delano Moore and Kimberly Rimbey have written a robust and immensely helpful guide to using manipulatives for profound student learning. In short, they have done all the deep, hard work laying out for us the intellectual and pedagogical queries we need to examine when considering using particular manipulatives—or even in deciding to use manipulatives at all! And they have done so with insight on matters of attitude and mindset, the availability of student support, fair accessibility, the role of the virtual, and more. Practical. Readable. Concrete. This is a winner of a guide.

James Tanton
Founder of the Global Math Project

Sara Delano Moore and Kimberly Rimbey masterfully show us why something we know works actually works—that manipulatives are powerful and essential tools to help children learn mathematics. This book serves as a guide to help teachers in their classrooms and in their PLCs effectively make judicious use of manipulatives. Moore and Rimbey empower teachers to use sound learning theories to select the most appropriate manipulative for a particular topic and task. Mathematics educators can use this book to sharpen their mathematical knowledge for teaching and mathematics leaders can use this book as a reference for building curriculum framework documents and engaging in deep collegial coaching conversations. The best part? Students will benefit from a much deeper understanding of *why* the mathematics works as it does. Every mathematics teacher needs a highly dog-eared version of this book in their professional library!

Paul Gray
President, NCSM: Leadership in Mathematics Education, 2021–2023

I thought I was aware of most everything I needed to know about the use of manipulatives in teaching mathematics at the elementary level—but Sara Delano Moore and Kimberly Rimbey proved me wrong. *Mastering Math Manipulatives: Hands-On and Virtual Activities for Building and Connecting Mathematical Ideas* makes a significant contribution in several ways: First, it consistently links the various representations in a useful visual that reminds the reader what mental connections students should be making from this experience. The use of multiple representations is critical to support all students particularly those with special needs in mathematics as per the new IES Practice Guide. The book also is practical and full of "I can use this tomorrow" examples across multiple content areas. An important read.

Karen S. Karp
Professor and Author
Johns Hopkins University, MD

It's always so gratifying to find a book filled with the answers to the questions we have asked over and over again. There is widespread belief in the power of concrete materials but the questions I hear are "Which manipulatives are best?", "Where and when do I fit them in?", "How do I best use them?", and "Why are there essential tools for learning?" This wonderful book answers each of these questions with clarity and classroom tested examples. Whether you teach, coach, or administrate in Grades 4 to 8, there is no doubt that the ideas and activities found in this book will strengthen the teaching and significantly enhance the learning of mathematics of your students.

Steve Leinwand
Principal Researcher
American Institutes for Research, Washington DC

As a mathematics coach and consultant I have visited dozens of math closets, those dusty corners of every school where you can find the tools you need to unlock hands-on, student-centered learning in your classroom. *Mastering Math Manipulatives* takes you to those places, yes, but it also takes you to the future with connections to virtual manipulatives, exploring the strengths and limitations of each. In this book you will find seasoned, practical advice and the kind of targeted lessons and directions you need to feel confident enough to dust off those tools and put them to good use. As I like to say, "Put your pencils down and get thinking!"

Kimberly Morrow-Leong
Mathematics Education Specialist and Fifth-Grade Teacher

We educators spend a great deal of time researching, exploring, and consolidating all the elements that combine to support students as they develop and connect mathematical understandings. It is very exciting to have this uniquely comprehensive resource that unites what is critical and necessary for rich and engaging mathematics instruction, explicitly connecting the research base and mathematics concepts and processes with essential math manipulatives. Distinct and detailed visuals and clearly articulated activities are presented in a consistent format that is accessible to new and experienced teachers.

Kathleen M. Morris
Administrative Coordinator, Elementary/Title I Mathematics
Prince William County Public Schools, VA

What a tremendous resource for teachers of mathematics! Sara Delano Moore and Kimberly Rimbey provide helpful tips and practical strategies for incorporating hands-on and virtual manipulatives into daily lessons. This book identifies a wealth of versatile manipulatives that can be used across grade levels and math domains, offers tips for planning and management, and shares sample lessons. And it includes critical discussions about making connections between varied representations to deepen students' understanding of the math skill or concept. The organization of the book is easy to follow and allows teachers to jump in and out as needed to find just what works for their students. If you are looking for useful tips and effective strategies for incorporating hands-on and virtual manipulatives into your math teaching, this is the book for you!

Sue O'Connell
Author, Speaker, Consultant/Quality Teacher Development

Mastering Math Manipulatives is the perfect support to help teachers move beyond using manipulatives for play during recess. This book provides additional ideas and strategies for supporting students who are struggling by helping them learn and grow mathematically. The practical examples included in the book are helpful for preservice teachers as well.

Cindy Beaman
Math Coordinator
Grand Island Public Schools, NE

Hands-on strategies are essential for student learning, and often natural for teachers in other contents. However, when it comes to math, the connection of hands-on tools to content and activity often seems fuzzy at best. There is finally the resource to connect the tool, the task, and the conceptual understanding together! These manipulatives-based activities provide the foundation for understanding that is essential for mathematics to make sense instead of being memorized. This book is a must for every teacher of mathematics!

Nanci Smith
Author, Consultant, and Associate Professor, Mathematics Department Chair,
and Director of Masters of Education Program
Arizona Christian University
Glendale, AZ

This book is a great resource for assisting educators in teaching mathematics for understanding. It offers preservice teachers a foundation for their future teaching by giving them opportunities to learn math concepts more deeply and conceptually by using physical (or virtual) manipulatives. In-service teachers will find this book a valuable resource to enhance their mathematics curriculum. I applaud the authors for addressing issues of access to manipulatives (physical and virtual) as well as providing helping parents and caregivers understand the importance of manipulatives and how they can assist their children at home.

Shelly M. Jones
Professor, Central Connecticut State University
New Britain, CT

Mastering Math Manipulatives
Grades K-3
The Book at a Glance

Each chapter focuses on a different manipulative and begins with an introduction to the featured manipulative including images and descriptions and information about homemade and virtual alternatives. The introduction is followed by a set of activities intended to illuminate the range of usefulness for each tool. Each activity includes:

Materials and Organization include everything that you'll need to gather and think about ahead of time.

Mathematical Purpose centers on the math students will encounter through this activity.

Activity Resources include downloadable activity sheets and recording sheets you'll use during the lesson as well as brief demonstration videos.

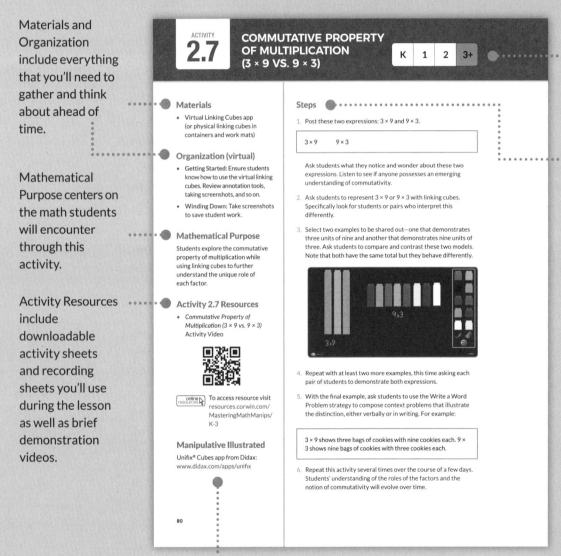

Grade-Level Bands indicate the grade levels that the activity generally addresses. The darker the color, the more relevant it is to that grade.

Steps are provided for each activity, including guiding questions and illustrated examples.

Manipulative Illustrated names the exact tool used in the activity and the URL for any virtual tools used.

The following text appears within the illustrated activity page (image 1):

ACTIVITY 2.7

COMMUTATIVE PROPERTY OF MULTIPLICATION
(3 × 9 VS. 9 × 3)

K 1 2 3+

Materials
- Virtual Linking Cubes app (or physical linking cubes in containers and work mats)

Organization (virtual)
- Getting Started: Ensure students know how to use the virtual linking cubes. Review annotation tools, taking screenshots, and so on.
- Winding Down: Take screenshots to save student work.

Mathematical Purpose

Students explore the commutative property of multiplication while using linking cubes to further understand the unique role of each factor.

Activity 2.7 Resources
- *Commutative Property of Multiplication (3 × 9 vs. 9 × 3)* Activity Video

To access resource visit resources.corwin.com/MasteringMathManips/K-3

Manipulative Illustrated

Unifix® Cubes app from Didax: www.didax.com/apps/unifix

80

Steps

1. Post these two expressions: 3 × 9 and 9 × 3.

   3 × 9   9 × 3

   Ask students what they notice and wonder about these two expressions. Listen to see if anyone possesses an emerging understanding of commutativity.

2. Ask students to represent 3 × 9 or 9 × 3 with linking cubes. Specifically look for students or pairs who interpret this differently.

3. Select two examples to be shared out—one that demonstrates three units of nine and another that demonstrates nine units of three. Ask students to compare and contrast these two models. Note that both have the same total but they behave differently.

4. Repeat with at least two more examples, this time asking each pair of students to demonstrate both expressions.

5. With the final example, ask students to use the Write a Word Problem strategy to compose context problems that illustrate the distinction, either verbally or in writing. For example:

   3 × 9 shows three bags of cookies with nine cookies each. 9 × 3 shows nine bags of cookies with three cookies each.

6. Repeat this activity several times over the course of a few days. Students' understanding of the roles of the factors and the notion of commutativity will evolve over time.

Why This Manipulative?

Because of their ability to snap together, linking cubes provide an excellent means for unitizing. This is especially important when exploring the commutative property of multiplication since the changing role of the factors is central in helping students develop conceptual understanding. For example, although 3 × 9 and 9 × 3 result in the same product (27), they do not behave the same since one is centered on units of three while the other uses units of nine.

Developing Understanding

As with Activity 2.6, be sure to distinguish the roles of the factors. One factor tells the unit size while the other reveals the number of units. Although the order of the factors in a number sentence does not necessarily indicate which factor is the multiplier and which is the multiplicand, students must realize that the roles switch with the commutative property. In U.S. classrooms, we generally consider the first factor as the multiplier and the second as the multiplicand. For this activity, you will find it helpful to make this distinction so that all students are referencing the same numbers when they talk about their findings.

As with the previous activity in this chapter, asking students to attend to context will make a huge impact on their understanding. When working with symbolic symbols, students may not internalize the need to know that although the product is the same either way, the two expressions do not represent the same situation. Context makes a huge difference in understanding what's going on with the factors.

Featured Connection

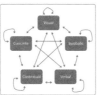 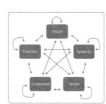

Source: Lesh, Post, & Behr (1987).

In this activity, students first engage in the Build the Equation strategy to connect from symbolic to concrete representations. This is the first step to building understanding of what the symbols are "saying" when looking at commutative pairs. To further build understanding, students use the Create a Word Problem strategy to highlight the connection between physical, verbal, and contextual representations. After creating a concrete representation of the commutative property, creating a word problem helps students verbalize a context in which the order of the factors matters. In doing so, students must make a distinction between the roles of the factors, an important idea in multiplication.

Why This Manipulative? focuses on the specific features of the selected tool and why its unique characteristics make it useful for illustrating the math concept.

Developing Understanding provides insight and guides you to think about ways in which you will develop student understanding throughout the activity.

Featured Connection provides further explanation for how to connect the concrete representations to other modes of mathematical representation including visual, symbolic, verbal, and contextual.

MASTERING MATH MANIPULATIVES

Grades K-3

MASTERING MATH MANIPULATIVES

Hands-On and Virtual Activities for Building and Connecting Mathematical Ideas

Grades K–3

Sara Delano Moore

Kimberly Rimbey

A JOINT PUBLICATION

FOR INFORMATION:

Corwin

A SAGE Company

2455 Teller Road

Thousand Oaks, California 91320

(800) 233–9936

www.corwin.com

SAGE Publications Ltd.

1 Oliver's Yard

55 City Road

London, EC1Y 1SP

United Kingdom

SAGE Publications India Pvt. Ltd.

B 1/I 1 Mohan Cooperative Industrial Area

Mathura Road, New Delhi 110 044

India

SAGE Publications Asia-Pacific Pte. Ltd.

18 Cross Street #10–10/11/12

China Square Central

Singapore 048423

President: Mike Soules

Associate Vice President and Editorial Director: Monica Eckman

Publisher: Erin Null

Content Development Editor: Jessica Vidal

Senior Editorial Assistant: Caroline Timmings

Production Editor: Rebecca Lee

Copy Editor: Melinda Masson

Typesetter: Integra

Proofreader: Rae-Ann Goodwin

Indexer: Integra

Cover/Graphic Designer: Scott Van Atta

Marketing Manager: Margaret O'Connor

Printed in the United States of America.

Library of Congress Control Number: 2021942195

This book is printed on acid-free paper.

21 22 23 24 25 10 9 8 7 6 5 4 3 2 1

CONTENTS

Visit the companion website at
resources.corwin.com/MasteringMathManips/K–3
for downloadable resources.

ACTIVITIES (BY TOPIC)

VIDEO LIST (BY ACTIVITY NUMBER)

ABOUT THE AUTHORS

Sara Delano Moore serves as Vice President for Content and Research and chair of the Mathematics Advisory Board at ORIGO Education. A fourth-generation educator, Sara emphasizes in her work the power of deep understanding and multiple representations for learning mathematics. Her interests include building conceptual understanding to support procedural fluency and applications, incorporating engaging and high-quality literature into mathematics and science instruction, and connecting mathematics with engineering design and computational thinking in meaningful ways. Prior to joining ORIGO Education, Sara served as a classroom teacher of mathematics and science in the elementary and middle grades, a mathematics teacher educator at the University of Kentucky, director of the Kentucky Center for Middle School Academic Achievement, and director of mathematics and science at ETA hand2mind. She has authored numerous articles in professional journals and is a co-author of the *Mathematize It!* series of books. She is also a contributing author to *Visible Learning for Mathematics*, as well as co-authoring the Grade 3–5 and Grade 6–8 volumes of the *Teaching Mathematics in the Visible Learning Classroom* series. Sara earned her BA in natural sciences from the Johns Hopkins University, her MSt in general linguistics and comparative philology from the University of Oxford (UK), and her PhD in educational psychology from the University of Virginia. She lives in Kent, Ohio.

Kimberly Rimbey serves as the chief learning officer at KP® Mathematics and also as the mathematics director for the Buckeye (AZ) Elementary School District. A lifelong teacher and learner, her heart's work centers on equipping teachers and helping them fall in love with teaching and learning over and over again. Kim's interests include high-quality professional learning models, building conceptual understanding through multiple representations and meaningful discourse, and building pedagogical content knowledge that goes beyond the theoretical and into the classroom. Always a teacher at heart, Kim has served as the executive director of curriculum and instruction for Buckeye Elementary School District, chief learning officer for the Rodel Foundation of Arizona, and the mathematics program area coordinator for the Paradise Valley (AZ) Unified School District. That said, everything Kim has done in her career is based on what she learned during her 18 years as a mathematics coach and elementary classroom teacher. Having started her teaching career in a kindergarten classroom, she frequently says that everything she needed to know about teaching she learned in kindergarten. Kim is National Board Certified in Early Adolescence/Mathematics, and she is a recipient of the Presidential Award for Excellence in Mathematics Teaching. Kim is the co-inventor of KP® Ten-Frame Tiles and has authored and co-authored several publications, including the *Math Academy* series for the Actuarial Foundation, *Math Power: Simple Solutions for Mastering Math* for the Rodel Foundation of Arizona, and, most recently, *The Amazing Ten Frame Series* for KP Mathematics. Kim earned her BA in elementary education and mathematics from Grand Canyon University, her MEd degrees in early childhood education and educational leadership from Arizona State University and Northern Arizona University, and her PhD in curriculum and instruction from Arizona State University. She lives in Phoenix, Arizona.

PREFACE

Welcome! This is a math book. And it's all about representing math in ways that make it more relevant, more meaningful, and more accessible to your students. This book intends to help you help your students by using math tools, primarily math manipulatives, in ways that make teaching and learning both profound and productive. Whether you're a classroom teacher, an instructional coach, a paraprofessional, a parent, or a caregiver, this book is for you!

As you engage in this journey of discovering how to make math meaningful for the students with whom you work, you'll be glad to know that this is not the kind of book that typically gets read from cover to cover. So here's a brief look at how it's put together so you can navigate it in a way that supports your work and saves you time.

First, we recommend you skim through the opening chapter, just to see what is in there. It introduces you to some fantastic classroom strategies that will be woven into each chapter of the book. Plus, it provides background on the use of multiple representations, especially manipulatives, as well as some insightful information about using online manipulatives in ways that enhance learning.

Second, you might want to take a peek at the final chapter, given that, along with the opening, it bookends the content and provides tips and answers to many of the family and caregiver questions you're likely to hear from time to time.

And finally, you'll likely spend most of your time perusing the content chapters, with each chapter focused on a different manipulative. Each of those chapters begins with an introduction to the featured manipulative, followed by a set of activities intended to illuminate the range of usefulness for each tool. Keep in mind that this book intends to get you started—it is by no means a comprehensive guide for each manipulative. Rather, its purpose is to get your creative juices flowing.

Each chapter opens with an overview of the manipulative or group of manipulatives discussed:

- Photos and a description of the tools within this category
- A list of mathematical ideas the tools can support
- Key ideas and things to consider
- Information about homemade and virtual options for the tools

At the end of the chapter, there is space for your reflection. How do you currently use these tools? What new ideas have inspired you? In between, each activity generally follows the same structure:

Materials and Organization includes everything you'll need to gather and think about ahead of time. Note that several of the activities feature virtual manipulatives and others physical tools. Please do not feel limited by the selection for that activity. The use of physical and virtual manipulatives is interchangeable throughout.

Mathematical Purpose centers on the math students will encounter through this activity.

Grade-Level Band indicates the grade levels that the activity generally addresses. The darker the color, the more relevant it is to that grade. Once again, do not let yourself feel limited by these indicators—they are just suggestions.

Activity Resources are available for some, but not all, lessons. Most of these are downloadable activity sheets and recording sheets you'll use during the lesson. And some of them include QR codes for you to access a brief demonstration video.

Manipulative Illustrated lets you know what we used for the illustrations in a particular activity. Sometimes the statement is more general, such as Cuisenaire® Rods, and other times it's specific to the company that sells that manipulative or the online app used for that activity.

Steps are provided for each activity, including guiding questions and illustrated examples. You will want to pay particularly close attention to the strategies used to connect concrete representations to other representations, which is explained more under "Featured Connection."

Why This Manipulative? focuses on the specific features of the selected tool and why its unique characteristics make it useful for illustrating the math concept.

Developing Understanding provides insights for you, the teacher, and guides you to think about ways in which you will develop student understanding throughout the activity.

Featured Connection provides further explanation for how to connect the concrete representations to other modes of mathematical representation including visual, symbolic, verbal, and contextual. Once again, we offer suggestions to get you started, with a focus on the six instructional strategies introduced in the opening chapter. (See—you'll be glad you took a look at the opening chapter first!)

So that's it—your short and simple guide for navigating this book. Now it's time to dive in and join in the journey toward making manipulatives meaningful in your classroom!

ACKNOWLEDGMENTS

First and foremost, we thank the teachers and students with whom we have worked over the years. Your teaching, your questions, your engagement, and your risk-taking have helped both of us learn about teaching mathematics with hands-on resources. The activities and ideas here are better because of our work with each of you.

Books are never written in isolation. We are grateful to the team at Corwin for their excellent guidance and expertise. There's a magic in moving from manuscript to book that reminds us of their talents and never ceases to amaze. We also appreciate the input of reviewers and friends who have answered our questions and provided suggestions as we have worked.

~

Kim, thank you for coming on this journey with me. Our collaboration has made this work stronger. I appreciate all I have learned from my colleagues in the mathematics education world—particularly those at ETA hand2mind, at ORIGO Education, and at NCSM. I also thank the community at edWeb.net for their feedback and enthusiasm across many years of webinars around hands-on mathematics instruction. I'm grateful to Bill for his constant love, support, and patience.

—Sara

Sara, you are an inspiration to the math education world and to me. This project brought with it an amazing journey, and I'm so grateful we got to travel this road together. To my friends, colleagues, and mentors who have impacted my heart's work—thank you. Your gracious support, patience, and passion for all things teaching and learning continue to shape me into the educator I am today. To Steve—thank you for believing in me after all these years.

—Kim

PUBLISHER'S ACKNOWLEDGMENTS

Corwin gratefully acknowledges the contributions of the following reviewers:

Lori Breyfogle
Elementary Math Specialist/Interventionist
Fox C-6 School District
Imperial, Missouri

Sarah Buchanan
Elementary Math Resource Teacher
Weyanoke Elementary, Fairfax County Public Schools

Emily Dwivedi
Supervisor of Elementary Mathematics
Baltimore County Public Schools

Jennifer Gibson
Elementary Math Specialist
McLean County Unit 5
Normal, Illinois

Christina Lincoln-Moore
School Administrator
Los Angeles Unified School District, California

Maria Mitchell
Teacher/Purchasing Manager, QEP Books
Plano, Texas

Introduction: We Know Manipulatives Matter, but . . .

The benefits of making mathematics visible for learners permeate math education courses in most pre-service programs. During our math methods classes, so many of us engaged in new ways of teaching and learning math that did not at all resemble the classrooms in which we learned basic fundamentals. However, the journey from college courses to seasoned teacher often includes many twists and turns, and the realities of classroom teaching sometimes get in the way of where we thought we were heading.

Such was the case for this particular group of teachers. During their weekly professional learning community (PLC) discussions, they talked about the importance of teaching elementary and middle school math in ways that made sense to children. These well-seasoned teachers were highly effective in so many ways. They spoke about the value of classroom discourse, context-driven vocabulary development, and the concrete-pictorial-abstract approach for teaching mathematics to young learners.

Regarding the latter, specifically using manipulatives, they also talked about the many things that got in their way. "Time is always the enemy," one teacher said, "and I find it difficult to find the time to let students explore hands-on ideas when I have so much content to cover before state testing."

"That's so true!" replied her teammate. "And sometimes my kids just want to play with the manipulatives instead of using them as tools to help them learn."

This conversation went on for quite some time, with the final agreement being that they would try to find ways to incorporate more hands-on and visual strategies in their upcoming math unit. They all agreed it would be beneficial. However, the realities of their situation got the better of them, again, and little change occurred.

Flash forward to the end of the school year. The entire group was a bit disheartened by their lack of progress with the goal for hands-on, minds-on teaching. As a result, and with buy-in from just about everyone, the instructional coach agreed to inventory the school's math tools over the summer. All teachers brought their manipulatives to the learning lab where the coach was to spend the next three weeks counting and cataloguing all of the tools that were at the school. Everyone dug deep into their cupboards and emptied their shelves of anything that was on the list.

To their surprise, the room was overflowing with tools they didn't even know they had. Some were still in the shrink-wrapped packages in which they'd been delivered five or so years ago. "How did this happen?" one teacher exclaimed, realizing that they had re-purchased class sets of manipulatives that had been hidden away in closets for far too long.

When the teachers returned in the fall, they were greeted by their faculty leadership team's plan. Over the course of the next semester, they were going to spend time during their weekly PLC gatherings diving into the many uses of these tools and how use them effectively. They were determined to make sure that this lesson didn't go to waste. Each grade level would take ownership of how they would use these tools, and cross-grade teams would talk about how they could build on what had happened in previous years. It wasn't always a smooth path, but over the course of the year, the conversations they engaged in and the strategies they investigated transformed not only the students' experiences, but the ways in which the teachers, themselves, thought about mathematics.

This book, in part, resembles the kinds of discoveries these teachers made during that year as they searched for new and innovative as well as tried-and-true ways for using multiple representations to support the learning of and to communicate ideas about mathematics.

WHAT ARE MANIPULATIVES?

Mathematics, especially when presented as symbols, can be very abstract. This abstraction is both the power and the challenge of mathematics. The abstraction means mathematics applies to a great many situations. It also makes it difficult for students, especially those learning new ideas and those still reasoning in concrete ways, to make sense of the math. Understanding mathematics deeply requires that teachers support students to make sense of these abstract symbols as a pathway to grasping what mathematics can do and how it works. This is where mathematical manipulatives come in.

Broadly defined, **manipulatives** are physical objects teachers and students can use to discover, illustrate, and model mathematical concepts. Manipulatives are critical to this sense-making process because they make mathematics tangible. They allow students to see, to touch, and to build their conceptual understanding of math. We know this is important for young learners, and it is equally important for students in the middle grades as concepts get increasingly complex.

Within this book, we focus on manipulatives that are mathematically concrete, meaning they are physical objects that represent mathematical values and concepts in ways that lead to greater understanding. We are sharing activities and ideas for using tools such as counters, base-ten materials, and various fraction models. We are not addressing measurement tools such as rulers or protractors. We are also not including objects such as coins or spinners. We made this decision so we could focus on manipulatives that are most powerful for teaching a broad range of mathematical ideas.

WHY ARE MANIPULATIVES IMPORTANT FOR STUDENTS?

Students benefit from and are motivated by using physical tools and representations like manipulatives for cognitive, social, and language development reasons. This has been supported by a number of developmental theorists. Piaget's (1971) stages of intellectual development, for example, reinforce the idea that the thought, language, and action of children is different from that of adults and that children learn best from concrete activities. Social interaction is also critical to Piaget's discussion of emerging intellect, allowing students to clarify their own understanding and recognize the thoughts of others. Engagement with manipulatives also supports language development as (1) students describe to themselves, to each other, and to teachers the representations they build and (2) students use manipulatives as supports for their verbal explanations.

Building from Piaget, Jerome Bruner (1960) proposes that students develop understanding rather than merely receiving information from adults. Manipulatives support social engagement with learning when students negotiate and work together using these shared materials. Learning readiness, Bruner suggests, comes from a mix of direct experience, visual representations, and work with abstract symbols. He also suggests that children are more driven to learn when they engage in activities that interest them. The active engagement of hands-on learning can be very motivating.

Lev Vygotsky's (1934/2012) concept of the zone of proximal development also brings the idea of social engagement to the center as students accomplish much learning through interacting with adults to bring form and structure to their thinking. Zoltán Pál Dienes is another researcher, specifically in mathematics education, whose work supports developing mathematical understanding through direct experiences. Dienes (1971) proposes a three-stage process beginning with unstructured play around mathematical ideas. Students move from this open-ended exploration to more structured experiences designed to highlight the mathematics and bring forward the third stage of the formal mathematics concept.

In more recent years, much of this research has come together as the CPA (concrete-pictorial-abstract) approach. While you may sometimes see the word *representational* or *semi-concrete* used rather than *pictorial* or the word *symbolic* used instead of *abstract*, the general idea of moving between and among concrete, visual, and abstract representations builds from the theorists whose work we have just discussed. This idea was developed further by Richard Lesh on the **Lesh translation model** in which students connect multiple representations.

Connecting Multiple Representations

The CPA model is often discussed as a linear structure when its real power is in connections, as illustrated by an emphasis on translation between representations. The idea of translating between and among representations (Lesh et al., 1987) is an important instance of deep learning (Hattie et al., 2017). Students build conceptual understanding when they can connect or translate from one representation to another. The strength of using these multiple representations lies not in using them in isolation or as a linear progression. Rather, the power comes from students treating them as interconnected, intertwining representations of mathematical thinking (Karp et al., 2021).

There are five basic representations we use for mathematics, as shown in Figure I.1; each of these can be translated to the other representations as well as within the same category.

Figure I.1 Translation Model

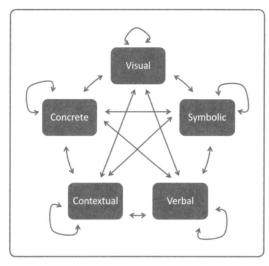

Source: Lesh, Post, & Behr (1987).

Concrete

Concrete representations are those created with physical or tangible objects (see Figure I.2). These might be formal manipulatives, real-world objects, or common real-world objects repurposed with a mathematical focus. Whether primary children are literally taking books off a bookshelf or students in the middle grades are representing an equation with algebra tiles, both are using concrete representations, the heart of this book. Students connect this representation with itself when they create a second representation using a different manipulative or using the same manipulative in a different way.

Figure I.2 Photograph of a Concrete Representation of Unit Fractions

Visual

Visual representations include a wide range of possibilities. Virtual manipulatives are largely visual, although they can be moved in some ways similar to the actions students can take with concrete objects. Visual representations, also called pictorial or semi-concrete, exist on a continuum more than any other category of representation. This spans from more literal sketches to more mathematical charts and diagrams. We use the term *sketch* to represent what a manipulative work surface looks like (see Figure I.3). We use the term *diagram* to represent more formal mathematical visuals such as tables, charts, or graphs. While students certainly might take photographs or screenshots of their work, grabbing these visuals does not prompt the same degree of thinking and active engagement with the mathematics and tools as creating a visual on their own (Wills, 2021). Visuals are connected to themselves when redrawn to be more abstract (e.g., moving from a sketch to a diagram) or to present the ideas differently.

Figure I.3 Visual Representation of Unit Fractions

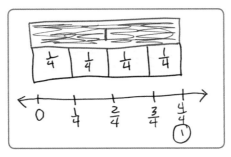

Symbolic

Symbolic representations are the most abstract; they use the formal symbols and notations of mathematics as representations (see Figure I.4). These representations are often efficient and, because they are abstract, can represent the same mathematical idea as it occurs in many different contexts. Symbolic representations can be connected with each other when we create equivalent expressions or show decomposed fractions in different ways.

Figure I.4 Symbolic Representation of Fraction Addition

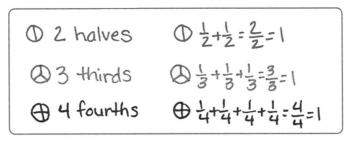

Verbal

Verbal representations are the language we use to communicate our work (see Figure I.5). This language can be oral and/or written. It includes the descriptions we make of manipulatives (e.g., two rods or three red counters and two yellow counters) as well as our ability to read symbolic notation (e.g., knowing that $n \times n$ in the context of area is read "n by n" rather than as a string of three letters, $n \times n$). Verbal representations connect with each other when we move from oral to written or when we refine the language and structure of a verbal representation. This might be accomplished by simply asking students to refine or add onto one another's oral or written explanations.

Figure I.5 Verbal Representation of Fraction Addition

"Four one-fourth-sized pieces is the same amount as one whole."

Contextual

Contextual representations show the application of mathematics in various contexts (see Figure I.6). For example, the abstract expression 2 + 3 can describe a great many real-world contexts, and students must be able to connect these contexts with the other representations of mathematics they see. Contextual representations connect to each other when we take a general idea (e.g., producing something as an example of active **addition**) and apply it in a number of contexts—we bake cookies, the factory manufactures cars, we create artwork, and so on.

Figure I.6 Contextual Representation of Fraction Addition

Valerie cut a loaf of bread into four equal-sized pieces for her family. That means she had four one-fourth-sized pieces. When she put them in a bag, there was still one whole loaf.

Figure I.7 brings together the five representations for a fraction addition problem. These connected representations support learners in making sense of mathematical ideas. They allow students to visualize and represent the work in different ways.

Figure I.7 Multiple Representations of Fraction Addition

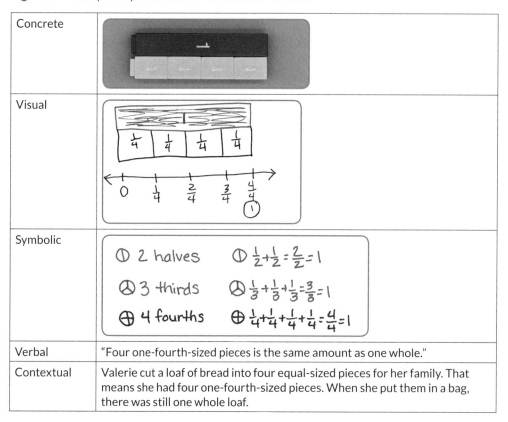

Concrete	
Visual	
Symbolic	
Verbal	"Four one-fourth-sized pieces is the same amount as one whole."
Contextual	Valerie cut a loaf of bread into four equal-sized pieces for her family. That means she had four one-fourth-sized pieces. When she put them in a bag, there was still one whole loaf.

Introducing Manipulatives With Notice and Wonder

Before students can use a new manipulative to represent or support their mathematical thinking, they must first explore and understand the tool (Karp et al., 2021), responding to questions like these:

- *What parts and attributes does the tool have?*
- *How do the parts fit together?*
- *Where do I see mathematics in the tool?*

We suggest that you use a *Notice and Wonder Thinking Routine* (Fetter, 2011) when you introduce a new manipulative to your students. Allow 5–15 minutes for the routine before using the new manipulative for a more formal math lesson.

1. Distribute the manipulatives to students.

2. Allow 2–5 minutes of open exploration guided by the questions "What do you notice?" and "What do you wonder?"

3. Invite students to share their noticings and wonderings with the class, creating a collective list. Facilitate connections when one student's noticing might respond to another student's wondering. If necessary, focus the discussion by asking about the "mathy things" students notice and wonder.

4. Invite students to share what mathematics they see in the manipulative. What kinds of problems could this help solve? How does this relate to math they already know? This discussion could take place in small groups or as a whole class. Gather a class list of mathematical potentials, ideally in a place where students can continue to reference it.

5. Close the discussion by connecting student observations and questions to the mathematics focus for the day's lesson

Strategies for Making Connections

In this book, we share a number of strategies, described in this section, for supporting students to translate between and among representations. Each of these strategies is designed to support students in connecting their thinking from one representation to another representation, with an emphasis on physical representations because of our focus on manipulatives. We incorporate these strategies into the activities of this book. You can use them, of course, with other hands-on activities, and you may decide to emphasize a different connection in an activity by choosing a different strategy. These strategies are listed in an increasingly abstract sequence.

Make a Sketch

In this strategy (see Figure I.8), students sketch a picture or drawing to represent their work with manipulatives (see Figure I.9). This sketch could represent their actions with the manipulatives (e.g., bundling a group of ten straws) or show a relationship they see (e.g., using Cuisenaire® Rods to illustrate a ratio). Students first represent the mathematics using manipulatives and then create a sketch to represent their work. Actions are illustrated by signals like arrows or circling groups of objects to indicate the ways they moved the materials. Relationships can be shown by how the materials are organized in the sketch. Students might even connect one visual to another as they refine their sketch in this strategy. This translation from physical to visual representations supports students continuing to use these thinking strategies even when they do not have access to physical manipulatives.

Figure I.8 Translations Highlighted in the Make a Sketch Strategy

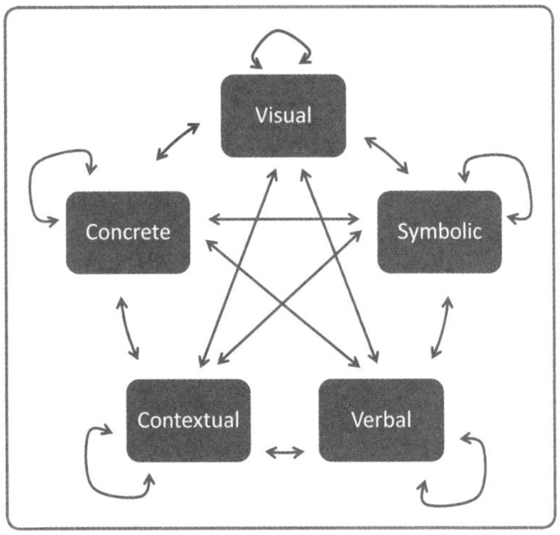

Source: Lesh, Post, & Behr (1987).

Figure I.9 Example of Make a Sketch Strategy

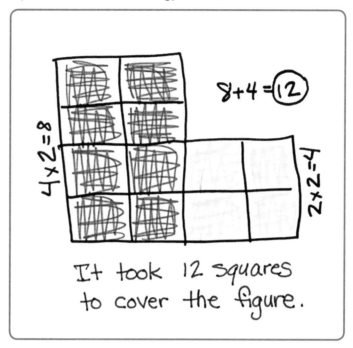

Caption Your Picture

In this strategy (see Figure I.10), students have sketched a picture or drawing to represent their work and compose a caption for the picture (see Figure I.11). Depending on age and language proficiency, the caption can be written or oral. The language of captioning suggests that this is not a long description but that it should address the major mathematical ideas in the picture. This supports students translating from a pictorial representation to a verbal representation. Students might use contextual features in their description. They are also likely to refine their language as they create a caption, connecting the verbal feature to itself.

Figure I.10 Translations Highlighted in the Caption Your Picture Strategy

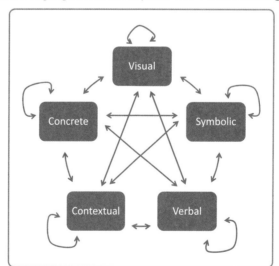

Source: Lesh, Post, & Behr (1987).

Figure I.11 Example of Caption Your Picture

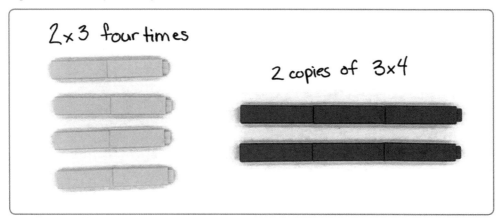

Name Your Model

This strategy (see Figure I.12) supports students in creating an equation or abstract representation for their physical model (see Figure I.13). This "name" is symbolic and is briefer than a caption, encouraging students to use more efficient representations rather than a longer description.

Figure I.12 Translations Highlighted in the Name Your Model Strategy

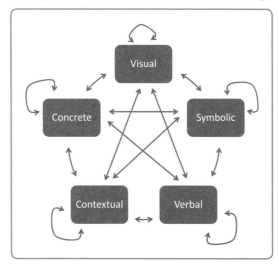

Source: Lesh, Post, & Behr (1987).

Figure I.13 Example of Name Your Model Strategy

Create a Diagram

In this strategy (see Figure I.14), students move from physical representations to formal mathematical images such as charts, diagrams, or tables of values (see Figure I.15).

Figure I.14 Translations Highlighted in the Create a Diagram Strategy

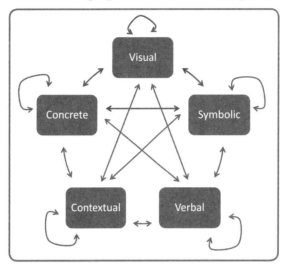

Source: Lesh, Post, & Behr (1987).

Figure I.15 Example of Create a Diagram Strategy

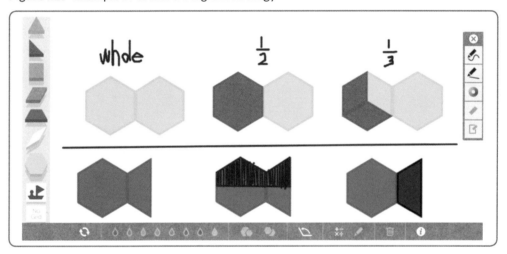

Build the Equation

In this strategy (see Figure I.16), students move from abstract representations to physical representations as they use manipulatives to build a model of a given or derived equation (see Figure I.17).

Figure I.16 Translation Highlighted in the Build the Equation Strategy

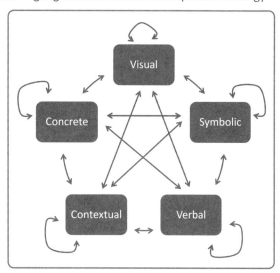

Source: Lesh, Post, & Behr (1987).

Figure I.17 Example of Build the Equation Strategy

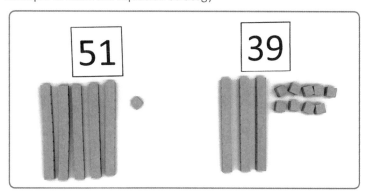

Write a Word Problem

In this strategy (see Figure I.18), students move from a concrete, pictorial, or abstract representation to a contextual representation. Given a **number** sentence, sketch, diagram,

Figure I.18 Translations Highlighted in the Write a Word Problem Strategy

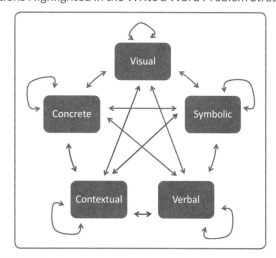

Source: Lesh, Post, & Behr (1987).

or manipulative model, students contextualize the mathematics by identifying a situation or a word problem that corresponds with the given mathematics (see Figure I.19).

Figure I.19 Example of Write a Word Problem Strategy

$$3 + 4 = 7$$

This number sentence could be used to compose a problem like this: Last night, my dog had three puppies, and and last time she had four puppies. How many puppies has she had in all?

How Manipulatives Aid in Access and Equity in Mathematics Learning

Manipulatives are a powerful tool for helping each and every learner reach their full potential in mathematics. Multiple representations of mathematics serve as multiple points of entry to the mathematical ideas. Students who are unclear about the meaning of a mathematical idea might understand more clearly when they build or see a physical model. For example, it is easy to describe **numerator** and denominator as the top and bottom numbers in a fraction. However, that is not their mathematical meaning. By tearing a set of paper fraction strips or exploring various fraction manipulatives, students understand the distinction between unit fractions (the equally sized parts of the whole represented by the denominator) and the count of those unit fractions (represented by the numerator).

Students who cannot yet explain their thinking in words might be able to create a physical model or visual and then describe it. If teacher and student do not share a common language, this physical or visual model serves as a bridge for their thinking.

By translating between representations, students can build their understanding from areas of greater strength or confidence to representations that may be a greater stretch. Abstract mathematical symbols are just that—abstract. For many students, they are visual squiggles on the page, absent of meaning. By helping students connect an abstract representation to concrete objects, visual images, and contexts, that abstract symbol gains meaning. Marshall, Superfine, and Canty (2010) suggest three important instructional principles for developing competence with representation:

- Engaging in explicit dialogue about specific connections between representations
- Discussing connections between representations in both directions
- Selecting representations in a purposeful manner

Furthermore, Karp et al. (2021) share the following principles for successfully using concrete objects to support student learning:

- Consistent use of concrete materials so students are better able to connect them with the concepts they embody
- Avoidance of concrete models that have distracting features, such as using play money for place-value-based operations
- Explicit connection to the relationship between the concrete objects and the math concepts being represented

Implementing these instructional principles using the strategies in this book helps to ensure that each and every student has access to rich mathematics understanding through a variety of representations.

ATTRIBUTES OF MANIPULATIVES

Manipulatives vary greatly in their attributes of color, size, and shape, and it's important to understand why that is, because in some cases, an attribute carries significant meaning that will factor into your choices of what manipulatives to use for what purpose.

Color

For some manipulatives, color is a critical attribute. For example, every pattern-blocks hexagon is yellow. The Cuisenaire® Rod that's 10 units long is always orange (see Figure I.20). Two-color counters typically have a red side and a not-red side (often yellow or white). Square tiles or bear counters are made in a variety of colors, and we use them, at times, without regard to color. Color is a familiar attribute, one of the first children learn, and there is confidence, for teacher and student alike, in saying "take the pink piece" and knowing everyone will have the same item and the right item.

Figure I.20 Cuisenaire® Rods With Consistent Color Sequence

On the other hand, students sometimes ascribe meaning to color where they shouldn't, considering yellowness a defining attribute of a hexagon, for example.

Size and Shape

There is also great variation in size and shape. Some manipulatives come in a larger-scale form designed for use by young children whose fine motor skills are still developing. Fraction tools represent a variety of wholes, varying in both shape and size. They are partitioned in different ways as fractional pieces are created, making it essential to understand how the set is designed to know how each fractional part relates to the whole. We talk about many manipulatives as two-dimensional when, in fact, they are all three-dimensional objects, including paper manipulatives, and we generally ignore the height or thickness of the piece.

Each chapter in this book opens with an overview of the category of manipulatives included. We discuss specific instances of color, size, or shape and how they might support developing mathematics or even, potentially, lead to a misconception, as in the example of yellow hexagons.

Beyond color, size, and shape, there are two attributes worthy of particular attention: whether manipulatives are **pre-grouped or groupable** and whether they are **proportional**.

Pre-grouped vs. Groupable Manipulatives

Think about the rod in a set of base-ten blocks, typically a 1 × 1 × 10 cm shape. This piece is already pre-grouped (see Figure I.21); it represents one group of ten (or a set of ten individual unit cubes), and it cannot be decomposed (deconstructed) into those smaller pieces. The flat (1 × 10 × 10 cm) is also pre-grouped. It represents one group of one hundred (or ten groups of ten or one hundred individual unit cubes) as a single piece. The same is true for the large cube (10 × 10 × 10 cm), representing one group of one **thousand** (or ten groups of one hundred or one hundred groups of ten or one thousand individual unit cubes) as a single piece.

Figure I.21 Pre-grouped Base-Ten Materials

Other manipulatives are groupable; the pieces are not connected in predetermined groups but can be grouped at will. Most counters fall into this category. A single square tile, a single pebble, or a single toy car can be grouped with other (like) counters, but the materials themselves do not provide premade groups.

Manipulatives that connect (linking cubes are a common example) or that can be grouped into holders (such as KP® Ten-Frame Tiles) are an intermediate place for this attribute. The fact that the pieces connect means students can create a group like they would see in a pre-grouped manipulative. There are, for example, some base-ten materials that appear initially as single units and can then be grouped and covered to create a group of ten, a group of one hundred, and so on (see Figure I.22).

Figure I.22 Groupable Base-Ten Materials

There is often an extra button on one end or dimples on some sides that mean the assembled group does not look exactly like a pre-grouped tool. This is fine, but be on the lookout for students who might be confused by this detail.

Proportionality

Proportional manipulatives are in scale with each other. Fraction manipulatives are proportional tools; the whole is 8 times the size (typically length or area) of a one-eighth piece (see Figure I.23). Pattern blocks are also proportional. The pieces are built from the same unit side length and specific **angle** measures in order to fit together nicely. Most counters, on the other hand, are not proportional. There is not a clear scale factor relationship between a single bear counter and a group of ten bear counters as there is between a unit cube and a rod in a set of base-ten blocks.

Figure I.23 Proportional Fraction Towers

While not included in this book, coins are a good example of the problems that can occur when manipulatives are not proportional. For example, there is nothing about the structure of a U.S. coin that indicates its mathematical value: A dime is worth ten cents or one-tenth of a dollar, which has more value than a penny (one cent) or a nickel (five cents), yet it is lighter in weight, thinner in height, and smaller in diameter than the other coins. It still has greater value. For students, this can be very confusing.

Proportional manipulatives are powerful tools for building number sense because they give students a clear sense of the relationship between one quantity and another, building on a common unit. How much more is 1,000 times larger? It's precisely the difference between the unit cube and the large cube in a set of base-ten blocks. Generally defined as a single undivided whole, a unit is the foundation of many key ideas. The unit piece in a base-ten set is the smallest cube. The unit whole is the quantity representing one whole when working with fractions.

Manipulatives can help make these ideas visible for students because the physical and visual patterns and structure are easy to identify.

The opening manipulative description in each chapter will include notes about grouping and proportionality because they are essential attributes for making good instructional decisions about using manipulatives.

Virtual Manipulatives

In today's classrooms, virtual manipulatives have come to have a more prominent place in instruction. Virtual manipulatives extend the powerful tangible resources into a digital age, providing students with the convenience of having manipulable images at their fingertips.

When we consider virtual manipulatives, there are two common benefits and one concern. One benefit is that they provide an endless supply of any given piece. While a physical set of fraction tiles typically contains four one-fourth pieces, students working with virtual tools have an endless supply to use in their modeling. A second benefit is that some virtual manipulatives also provide options for grouping and un-grouping rather than remaining fixed as a grouped or un-grouped tool. In this way, a rod valued as one group of ten can be virtually decomposed into ten single-unit cubes, an action that requires trading when working with physical base-ten blocks. The concern lies in the notion of maintaining proportionality. Because proportionality is so important with many manipulatives, it is important that virtual materials are true to the proportionality of their physical counterparts and that the images cannot be resized. Students can easily lose the proportional understanding of tools if they unintentionally (or deliberately) resize an object.

The concern of virtual manipulatives is that accessing them is an equity challenge. Despite the fact that they can actually increase equity for all learners to access mathematical ideas, that only matters if the students can get their hands on them. This is true of both physical and virtual manipulatives. Schools typically do not have sufficient quantities of physical manipulatives to send a supply home with each student, although die-cut alternatives or common household objects (e.g., dry beans as counters) may suffice. When working with virtual manipulatives, technology can be a limiting feature. While virtual manipulatives may be offered in more rural settings or when students are learning remotely or online, we must ask whether every student has a device and sufficient internet access to use the virtual tools, especially at home. A student accessing the internet through a phone connection with limited data is in a very different place than a student with a personal touchscreen tablet or computer with unlimited high-speed data.

While "virtual manipulatives do not replace the power of physical objects in the hands of learners" (National Council of Supervisors of Mathematics, 2013, p. 1), there are definite advantages to digital tools, particularly when we look at more sophisticated uses of them. Wills (2021) provides several insights into ways to increase success with the use of virtual manipulatives:

- Find a balance between teacher-selected and student-selected virtual manipulatives. Although the teacher-selected option may save time, the student-selected option will likely lead to a more robust learning opportunity.

- Provide opportunities for students to learn how to use the online manipulatives. Just as with physical objects, provide students with opportunities to notice and wonder about the features and to experiment with the functions of a new online tool.

- Take time to teach students how to create and share screenshots of the results of their work as well as screen shares of the actions of their work.

- Beware of apps that "steal" the thinking by using virtual manipulatives that replicate the "freedoms" afforded by their physical counterparts as closely as possible.

- Explore the best options for each situation. Sometimes physical objects and drawing/ sketches are still the best choice to support student explorations and communication due to the ability to show action. Identify common objects students may be able to find at home to use as manipulatives. For example, students may show place value using cereal Os and uncooked spaghetti, LEGO® pieces, paper clips, or beads and string. They may show computation and operations using buttons, beans, beads, or bottle caps. They may build arrays with cheese crackers. They may show fractions with egg cartons, muffin trays, or toys with different attributes.

Despite the benefits and challenges mentioned, the real question is one of purpose. The SAMR Model is a framework designed to assist educators as they describe the level of impact of digital tools, with a focus on the learning goal the tool attempts to achieve (Magiera, 2016).

Most typically, we see teachers using virtual manipulatives to substitute or augment physical tools, keeping many tasks at the Substitution or Augmentation levels. If this is all we do with virtual manipulatives, we fail to gain the real benefits of the digital tools. Instead, teachers should look for opportunities to move to the Modification and Redefinition levels to harness the real power of these tools. Figure I.24 provides examples of what these moves might look like when using virtual manipulatives.

Figure I.24 SAMR for Virtual Manipulatives

SAMR MODEL		Virtual Manipulatives Examples
Transformation	**Redefinition** Technology allows for the creation of new tasks, previously inconceivable	Using screen casting software, student creates a series of math tutorial videos featuring virtual manipulatives as a way to demonstrate mathematical ideas.
Transformation	**Modification** Technology allows for significant task redesign	Student uses collaboration features to discuss and determine the best way(s) to represent a mathematical idea using virtual manipulatives.
Enhancement	**Augmentation** Technology acts as a direct tool substitute, with functional improvement	Student uses virtual manipulatives to represent a mathematical idea in multiple ways, using screenshots to place the representations side by side.
Enhancement	**Substitution** Technology acts as a direct tool substitute with no functional change	Student uses virtual manipulatives to represent a mathematical idea.

CONSIDERATIONS FOR DISTANCE LEARNING

Ideally, instruction will include both concrete and virtual manipulatives. In distance learning situations, a more balanced approach might not be possible. We have chosen to substitute virtual manipulatives for some of the activities in this book so that our representations and discussion include both physical and virtual manipulatives. As a teacher, you should feel free to swap physical and virtual manipulatives where necessary for your teaching situation.

As much as possible, we encourage you to begin instruction with physical manipulatives, incorporating virtual manipulatives where they add to the mathematics (e.g., the endless supply is useful) or where they can Modify or Redefine the task. This will typically include the use of additional software and/or the use of digital communication tools.

If you are using virtual manipulatives as a substitute for physical ones, please consider the following:

- Do students have the technical skills to find and manipulate the online figures?
- Are students able to visualize the objects in their three-dimensional forms (geometric solids, pattern blocks, etc.)?
- Are there ways to enhance the use of virtual tools using online apps such as Nearpod, Pear Deck, or other online presentation tools?
- Might students benefit from using copy and paste, snipping, taking a screenshot, screen sharing, and other online actions to communicate their thinking?
- How might the virtual manipulatives be used for students to communicate and evaluate their thinking?
- How might students use the online platform to collaborate with teachers and other students?

In the activities in this book, we have used publicly available virtual manipulative toolboxes. It is also possible to create shared workspaces in online documents such as Google™ Slides.

 To access the virtual manipulative toolboxes, visit **resources.corwin.com/ MasteringMathManips/K-3**

PREPARING TO USE MANIPULATIVES EFFECTIVELY

Manipulatives are widely viewed as an important part of high-quality mathematics instruction. Yet there are still real obstacles and valid worries to address and overcome in their successful implementation. Some of the most commonly cited concerns appear as follows.

- **Access:** "Students lack access to materials." Either schools must have sufficient quantities of physical manipulatives, or students must have sufficient digital access (devices and connectivity) for manipulatives to be used thoughtfully.
- **Distraction:** "My students just want to play." There is a perception that time is wasted when students play with the materials.

- *Curricular coverage:* "I need to cover the curriculum." There is a perception that time spent in the textbook is more productive in moving learning forward and that manipulatives slow down progress and pacing.

- *Assessment:* "How will I assess my students if they used manipulatives during instruction?" Assessing manipulative-based learning seems challenging.

- *Classroom management:* "Managing all these materials seems overwhelming." It takes time to organize materials and to teach a manipulative lesson, and students may be more likely to misbehave when "toys" are available.

- *Professional preparation:* "I honestly don't even know where to begin." Not all of us yet know enough about teaching with manipulatives to plan effectively.

- *Helping All Learners Develop Deep Understanding:* "I have students in so many different places with their math learning. How do I differentiate with these tools so they meet the needs of *all* my students?"

Each activity in this book provides guidance in how to overcome these obstacles so that the power of learning with manipulatives can be fully realized without sacrificing time, learning progress, or classroom management. For general purposes, explore the following tips to consider how to begin to incorporate manipulatives into instruction.

Access

This can be a problem beyond your control. We encourage you to consider die-cut or homemade alternatives for manipulatives as a way of expanding your collection of physical materials. A great many virtual manipulatives are also available, many at no cost. See the website supporting this book for our list of virtual resources. Devices and bandwidth are still real challenges.

 To access the virtual manipulative toolboxes, visit **resources.corwin.com/ MasteringMathManips/K-3**

Distraction

Toys vs. Tools Discussion

A common objection to using manipulatives in the class centers on the notion that students will play with these tools rather than using them to support learning. Therefore, some teachers opt to withhold opportunities for hands-on learning rather than addressing this issue head-on. One way for you to talk with your students about this issue is to compare and contrast the notion of learning tools vs. toys. Manipulatives, although they may remind students of toys such as building blocks and LEGO® pieces, are intended to support learning rather than to be used in whimsical ways.

A helpful comparison is to compare a LEGO® set with a set of construction tools. While toys provide an open-ended forum for play, learning tools tend to have a more narrow and defined use. When students begin to use manipulatives in ways that are inappropriate, a simple reminder that they are to be used as tools rather than as toys will usually suffice to get students back on track.

Curricular Coverage

Mathematics Lesson Framework

Many teachers find it useful to use a mathematics lesson framework to help shape their lessons. One such framework includes four components:

- Launch
- Develop conceptual understanding
- Practice and application
- Wrap-up

With a lesson framework such as this, one can see that there is room for fitting manipulatives into the structure of the day, sometimes even replacing the content presented in a student textbook. For example, you may launch the lesson by engaging the students in a number routine and then shift into using manipulatives to develop conceptual understanding, perhaps deviating from the textbook's lesson in order to create a hands-on opportunity. Then your students may use those same manipulatives to support their work during the practice and application portion of the lesson.

Going Slow to Go Fast

One must acknowledge that using manipulatives and other hands-on strategies may require additional time compared to a more algorithmic approach to learning. Therefore, a helpful mindset you may adopt is that laying the foundation takes time, and once it is laid, the practice goes much quicker. By taking the time to build conceptual understanding using manipulative tools, your students better understand the mathematics concepts at hand, and the time it takes to connect to visual and symbolic representations often goes relatively quickly. Some call this "going slow to go fast." You may find yourself slowing down a bit in the initial stages, but once understanding is achieved, the later stages often glean faster results.

Assessment

A common adage regarding assessment states, "You should teach the way you"ll test." With many of our state-mandated standardized assessments, our students are expected to exhibit their learning by answering a handful of questions using only paper-and-pencil methods (along with mental math strategies). Unfortunately, this drives many teaching professionals to conclude that every quiz, every check for understanding, every unit test, and every benchmark assessment should use that same structure.

Of course, the paper-and-pencil-only design is sometimes appropriate—it is an efficient way to assess what students do and do not know at one given point in time. But by no means must every assessment take on that same organization.

The following is a list of several ways one might use manipulatives as part of the assessment process.

- Checklist assessments
- Photos and videos
- Sketching actions
- Checks for understanding
- Diagnostic assessments
- Benchmark assessments

Classroom Management

Classroom Setup and Management

- **Tables vs. desks:** Given the choice, tables provide a more cohesive structure to facilitate student interactions while using a variety of tools to demonstrate their math thinking. A group math tool kit may be located in a tub placed in the center of the table. Individual tool kits may be distributed for students to keep in their desks. This brings with it the individual ownership and accessibility to a variety of tools.

- **Long-term storage:** Not all tools are needed for every unit of study. For example, geometric solids and geoboards have a limited time frame in which they lend themselves to representing the learning at hand. Therefore, finding a just-right location for them to be stored is desirable. Students should still have easy access to them throughout the year. Consider placing them on a shelf in the classroom rather than in a closet behind closed doors in order to maintain accessibility for when they may be used creatively.

- **Traffic patterns:** When distributing and storing manipulatives, consider how students will collect and clean up their materials on a daily basis. This includes attending to traffic patterns that facilitate easy pickup and cleanup of mathematics tool kits, table tubs, and so on.

- **Cleaning up with strategic preparation in mind:** Setting up manipulatives for the next time they are to be used can be a huge timesaver for both you and your students. One of the easiest ways for you to prepare the materials ahead of time is to build in such structures when students are cleaning up during a previous lesson. For example, require that students remove all rubber bands from the geoboards, placing them in their corresponding containers. Or ask students to organize their base-ten blocks or algebra tiles in such a way that they are ready to be used the next time students get them out. This also provides an opportunity to take inventory, with students counting the pieces to be sure everything is included before putting their tools away for the day.

Karp et al. (2021) also mention the following practices you may consider:

- Never avoid using representations due to time constraints—using manipulatives during instruction will enhance learning and help in the long run. Remediation and intervention will take much more time for those students who don't get it the first time.

- Take time to teach students how to use the manipulative as well as how to put it away.

- Provide exploration time when new manipulatives are introduced.

- Keep baskets of manipulatives on the table so students can select appropriate tools when they need them. Remember that a major goal is that *students* select appropriate tools strategically for their learning and communication needs.

- Explicitly teach students how to draw visual representations. Provide helpful hints on how to most efficiently create sketches and drawings for base-ten materials, fraction representations, bar models, diagrams, and so on. Also emphasize that this is not art class—students need not draw fingernails and shoe ties on their mathematical sketches. In fact, in most cases, students can simply draw circles or *X*s to represent the objects to which they are referring.

Professional Preparation

Planning: Connecting Activities to the Core Program

The activities in this book stand alone and do not represent a coherent, sequenced unit of study. To get the most from these activities, you will want to be mindful of your core program, thinking about how the activity at hand might lend itself to richer ways of representing the mathematics covered in the curriculum.

For example, Activity 2.5 illustrates the associative property of addition. Consider where this idea best fits and how to integrate these ideas for representation when it is time for this unit of study.

Planning: Providing Opportunities for Students to Select Appropriate Tools

You may notice that in many cases, different representations may be appropriate for the same concept. We encourage you to consider providing options from which students may select rather than dictating which tool to use each day. This affords students the opportunity to "use appropriate tools strategically." Students should become sufficiently familiar with each tool so as to make sound decisions about which tools will support their thinking.

For example, when working on proportional relationships, students might use Cuisenaire® Rods, counters, coordinate pegboards, or a variety of pictorial ways to support and represent their thinking. They should have ample opportunity to choose a tool that works best for them without being limited by what their teacher or other students choose to use.

This requires that they engage in discussions about the advantages and disadvantages of each tool along the way. One way to provide this foundation is to introduce one manipulative at a time at the beginning of the year. Students discuss and explore that single manipulative as well as use it in the learning process. Then it is added to a tool kit for future use. This practice continues with new manipulatives on a regular basis until students have a rich tool kit of appropriate resources.

Free vs. Guided Exploration

When first introducing various manipulatives to students, you will want to consider whether free exploration or guided exploration is most appropriate. Free exploration is more open-ended, facilitating highly creative uses for the materials. This may lead to new ways of using the tools, although it may lead to students going too far with them, such as using linking cubes to create toy weapons.

Guided exploration, on the other hand, typically begins with a question that guides students through their explorations, pointing them toward discoveries that are more math-oriented. Earlier in this chapter, we described a *Notice and Wonder Thinking Routine* (Fetter, 2011) to use when you introduce students to manipulatives. Asking students what they notice and wonder about a new tool provides a foundational expectation that they are looking for mathematical applications for using the new tool. Each chapter opens with suggestions about key ideas for this routine with the specific manipulative discussed.

Helping All Learners Developing Deep Understanding

Universal Design for Learning (Center for Applied Special Technology, 2018; National Council of Teachers of Mathematics, 2020) suggests that students be provided with multiple modes of engagement, of representation, and of action and expression. We must use a variety of strategies to invite students into learning mathematics and to support students while learning mathematics. Because students learn in many different ways, building hands-on learning experiences into core instruction provides all students with access to supportive thinking structures. Manipulatives help students *develop*, *communicate*, *refine*, and *dive deeper* into their thinking. They are a key aspect of providing adequate support to each and every mathematics learner.

First, when students are *developing* their mathematical thinking on a concept, using visual and concrete objects assists them in the learning process. In a sense, the physical models "partner" with the students' thinking, helping them maneuver through mathematical processes and ideas and reinforcing their agency in mathematics. As students' understanding emerges, manipulatives may be especially useful in demonstrating the strengths they bring to the table given the hands-on and visual nature of these tools.

Second, when students use manipulatives to *communicate* their thinking, much thinking has already taken place, and the students may be well on their way to finding the solution. In this case, they are transferring their thinking into the physical world, using the manipulatives as representations of their internal processes. This is especially useful as students develop their language skills, because manipulatives allow learners to communicate their thinking in both verbal and nonverbal ways. It's also important to note that different students may use different manipulatives to communicate their thinking . . . and that's a good thing! Making multiple representations a routine part of classroom instruction also increases access and agency for students. When everyone has a wider range of representations to use in communicating important mathematical ideas, classroom authority is shared among teachers and learners.

Third, students in a variety of settings may find the use of manipulatives helpful in *refining* their thinking and *diving deeper* into foundational mathematical ideas by extending their thinking about a particular concept. Since the pace of developing deep understanding can differ from one student to the next, teachers should resist the temptation to cover more content at the expense of digging deeper. Using multiple representations and translating between and among them focuses students on clarifying their thinking and consciously communicating ideas that they intuit but do not always fully understand.

MANAGING YOUR MANIPULATIVES

Ensuring that all classrooms have the tools needed for student success is a high priority for teachers and leaders alike. That said, how does one know which tools are the "right" tools and on what to spend precious resources? Let's explore guidance on how to select and manage your manipulatives, including taking inventory, prioritizing purchases, and packing and storing manipulatives.

Taking Inventory

Taking an inventory of the tools that teachers and students already have is a necessary first step. And equally important is taking inventory of how those tools have been used and will be used in the future. This is how you'll decide what else you need to buy, borrow, find, or create.

As you take inventory of the math tools that are in your classroom or school, the amount of each manipulative you have at your disposal will be important. Figure I.25 provides a general rule of thumb for how many of each manipulative is ideal for a single student working alone, a small group of students, or a full class. Note that there is no set rule for how many are necessary—we are simply providing a general guideline here. This can serve as a starting point for your thinking about whether you have enough of a given tool or wish to purchase more.

Figure I.25 Suggested Classroom Inventory

Manipulative	Grades K–2	Grades 3–5	Grades 6–8
Algebra Tiles			Per student: 1 set
AngLegs®		1 set per pair of students	1 set per pair of students
Base-Ten Blocks	Per student: 1 flat, 12 rods, and 30 units	Per student: 1 flat, 12 rods, and 30 units, *plus* 10 large cubes for the class	
Color Tiles	Per student: 20 Small group: 100 Whole class: 500	Per student: 100 Small group: 150 Whole class: 1,000	Per student: 100 Small group: 150 Whole class: 1,000
Coordinate Boards			1 per student
Cuisenaire® Rods	1 set per student	1 set per student	1 per student
Fraction Towers Fraction Circles Fraction Tiles/Bars Fraction Squares		1 set per studen	1 per student
Geoboards	1 per student	1 per student	1 per student
Geometric Solids	Per student: 1 set Small group: 1 set Whole class: 1 set per 4 students	Per student: 1 set Small group: 1 set Whole class: 1 set per 4 students	Per student: 1 set Small group: 1 set Whole class: 1 set per 4 students
Linking Cubes	Per student: 20 Small group: 100 Whole class: 500	Per student: 100 Small group: 150 Whole class: 1,000	
Pattern Blocks*	Per student: 1 snack-sized bag Small group: 1 quart-sized bag Whole class: 1 quart-sized bag for every 4 students	Per student: 1 snack-sized bag Small group: 1 quart-sized bag Whole class: 1 quart-sized bag for every 4 students	Per student: 1 snack-sized bag Small group: 1 quart-sized bag Whole class: 1 quart-sized bag for every 4 students
Tangrams**	1 set per student	1 set per student	
Two-Color Counters	Per student: 20 Small group: 100 Whole class: 500	Per student: 20 Small group: 100 Whole class: 500	Per student: 20 Small group: 100 Whole class: 500
Unit Cubes		Per student: 24 Small group: 100 Whole class: 500	Per student: 24 Small group: 100 Whole class: 500

* Note: Try to keep the number of pattern blocks proportional by size: For every one hexagon, students may need two trapezoids, three blue rhombi, and six triangles. Because squares and tan rhombi are less widely used, the number included in each bag is not as important.

** If students are working in groups, it is helpful for each group member to have a different color.

 To download a copy of this resources, visit **resources.corwin.com/ MasteringMathManips/K–3**

Prioritizing Purchases

You may find yourself in the position of having to choose which manipulatives to purchase. When this is the case, you may need to prioritize your purchases. Here are a few guidelines to assist you. Answering these questions may help you in the prioritization process:

- *Major vs. supporting content:* Does this manipulative support major content for your grade level, or is it supporting content?

- *Versatility and frequency:* Does this manipulative have utility across multiple standards and concepts that will be taught throughout the year, or is it limited to a small set of standards and only needed for a couple of weeks?

- *Accessibility:* Do you have access to this manipulative by borrowing from another classroom or checking it out from a resource library?

- *Replaceability:* Are there alternatives for this manipulative?

- *"On-the-cheap" options:* Can you make it yourself? Can you purchase it at a secondhand shop or a teacher outlet? Can you find a lower-cost option? Might you find it at a "retiring teacher garage sale" or an online clearance sale? Can you substitute with everyday objects (e.g., small erasers as counters)?

Storing and Packing Manipulatives

Here is a general rule of thumb: When manipulatives come in sets, find a way to keep them in sets. For example, if your Cuisenaire® blocks come in trays, keep them in the trays and place them in sealable bags. Place sets of fraction tiles (or circles or squares) in sealable quart bags. This will make them easy to **sort**, to use, and to inventory. This also helps you transport the sets as well as to redistribute across classrooms, when necessary.

It's important to communicate these ideas to parents and caregivers. Please see the closing chapter for tips and strategies for supporting them in their journey toward using manipulatives to support their children's learning.

FREQUENTLY ASKED QUESTIONS

And finally, we know that questions come up frequently, especially as you dive into this important work. This section is our attempt to address some of the questions we frequently encounter regarding the use of manipulatives in the classroom.

Management

Q: What do I do if my students are playing with the manipulatives rather than using them as thinking tools?

A: Prevention is always your best tool for this. When introducing manipulatives to your class, clearly outline the expectations, even to the point of rehearsing appropriate use. Some teachers create anchor charts that describe what appropriate use of manipulatives looks like and sounds like. Review these expectations frequently, as needed. Remind students that manipulatives are tools for thinking and learning, not toys.

Q: What if I don't have enough manipulatives for every student to have a full set?

A: The simplest way to handle this is to have students share manipulatives when health and safety conditions allow for this. Ask students to work in pairs, triads, or groups of four. While one student manipulates the tools, others can be representing the same problem(s) on paper, using different representations. Other approaches may include rotating students through stations or small groups, or making additional sets of manipulatives on a paper cutter or die-cut machine. Homemade options are mentioned at the beginning of each chapter in this book.

Q: Is it better for students to work alone or in small groups when working with manipulatives?

A: This depends on your math goal as well as your management style. Giving students independent work time, especially at the beginning of a learning episode, provides them the opportunity to engage in the thinking and discovery opportunities necessary for grappling with the topic at hand. That said, shifting into pairs and/or small groups after a period is also advisable since learning is primarily a social endeavor. Teaching students ways of engaging in meaningful and accountable discourse, a skill useful in all content areas, can help ensure that students maximize the benefits of collaborative work.

Q: My students may feel they are too old for this. What should I do if they see these tools as babyish?

A: Your students will take their cues from you. Manipulative use is completely appropriate from preK through college, and the way in which you, the teacher, introduce these tools for each learning episode can impact students' perceptions. Remind students that manipulatives are tools, not toys, and that they support both thinking and communication. Be sure to integrate the use of manipulatives into your teaching moves, modeling appropriate use and engaging in "think-alouds" to demonstrate how the manipulatives impact thinking and learning. Occasionally engage students in conversations about the many tools they have at their disposal to represent mathematics in various ways—concrete, pictorial, verbal, symbolic, and contextual.

Rationale

Q: Which manipulatives are most important to have on hand?

A: This depends on your math goals. The manipulatives shared in this book certainly do home in on the most prominent and basic tools you should have at your disposal. If you are limited on the number of manipulatives available, here is a list of questions to ask yourself:

- What are my math goals for the year?
- Based on the trajectory of concepts and skills I'll be teaching this year, which tools will have the most utility (e.g., which manipulatives can be used for multiple concepts)?
- Does each manipulative have a completely distinct use? (For example, unit tiles have a clear and distinct purpose in grade levels where area is emphasized; however, they do not have the same level of utility in early grades, where they are simply used as counters.)

Q: How can I help parents access and support the use of manipulatives at home?

A: Accessibility is often an issue when looking for ways to encourage manipulative use at home. Ideally, sending home a "mathematician's tool kit" with various manipulatives would provide students the access they need. This kit may include either commercial manipulatives or alternatives such as those discussed at the beginning of each chapter in this book (e.g., fun foam versions cut on a paper cutter or die-cut machine). You may also send home a list of things that can be gathered and used at home, such as beans and pasta as counters or paper and scissors for making fraction pieces. To encourage famiiy support, you may offer live or virtual mini-workshops for families to give them tips on how to use specific tools to help their children. This has the added benefit of subtly frontloading math content the family members may or may not need to learn for themselves.

Q: What do I do if my principal sees manipulatives-based learning as playing with toys rather than doing math?

A: Communication is key for this one! Be sure that your lesson planning documents include manipulatives in the materials list and that your objectives clearly connect to the use of the manipulatives you intend to use. Include a diagram of the Lesh model for mathematical representations with your lesson plans, and share it with your principal during pre-observation conferences or in conversations about math instruction. Point out the many ways to represent math thinking and how the physical tools play an important role. Perhaps the best preparation for addressing this head-on is to ensure your management is tight (see earlier Q&As) and that when your principals or supervisors walk in, they witness students using the tools productively and with ease. You may also include photos and video evidence (see the following section) in post-observation conferences to further provide evidence of the value manipulatives offer.

Testing and Accountability

Q: How do I collect evidence of student thinking and learning while using manipulatives?

A: Photos and videos provide a fantastic opportunity to demonstrate and archive students' learning using manipulatives. Whether in a face-to-face or virtual setting, while students are working, snap photos of their work and save to online portfolios. Furthermore, brief video clips of students explaining their thinking using manipulatives and other tools can show growth in understanding over time. In addition, ask students to record their use of manipulatives on paper along with reflections on which tools they used and how those tools supported their thinking and learning.

Q: My students can't use manipulatives when taking state tests. Wouldn't letting them use manipulatives in class make them less likely to succeed on these important exams?

A: The goal of manipulatives use is to support student thinking, eventually laying a foundation for internalizing mathematical ideas. If students use manipulatives enough, they will eventually develop a mental image of the tools. And if they can picture the manipulatives in their heads, they can sketch them on paper. And if they are adept at sketching, they can use the scratch paper provided during testing as a tool to support their thinking during test taking. Therefore, using manipulatives to the point of internalization will support and enhance students' thinking during test taking.

Virtual Manipulatives

Q: My school has 1:1 tech devices. Can I replace all the physical manipulatives with virtual manipulatives? My school doesn't have the budget for physical manipulatives. Are virtual manipulatives an adequate alternative?

A: Virtual manipulatives, as mentioned throughout this book, offer some features not inherent in their physical counterparts. These include an endless supply of pieces and a natural way for sharing work with peers and teachers over distance. That said, it's important to realize that students do not cognitively process the same way with two-dimensional figures as they do with three-dimensional objects. Although tech devices do allow students to replicate the manipulations on screen, providing an enhanced two-dimensional experience, the truth is that they still fall into the visual category of representation, not the physical. Ideally, students will have access to both physical and virtual manipulatives, capitalizing on the benefits of both and allowing them to connect representations, a major theme in this book.

LET'S GO!

It's time to dig deep into the closet and dust off the manipulatives! We hope this book inspires you to use these powerful tools regularly to develop deep mathematical understanding. Let's get started.

Notes

Notes

Chapter 1

Two-Color Counters

UNDERSTANDING TWO-COLOR COUNTERS

Two-color counters are typically circular, with a different color on each side. They can easily be flipped over to reveal the alternate color. Commercial two-color counters are typically red and white or red and yellow, one inch in diameter, and constructed from plastic or foam. Because various manufacturers use different colors and materials, keeping the counters separated is relatively simple to do.

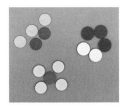

Two-color counters are particularly effective in teaching these topics:

- Counting and **cardinality**
- **Composing** and **decomposing** numbers within 20
- **Comparing** quantities
- Sorting and counting
- Grouping the first ten
- Grouping tens and ones
- Even and odd
- Data collection
- Graphing

Introducing Two-Color Counters to Students

When introducing a new manipulative to students, first give them the chance to explore the limits of the tool. This may include a brief "play" time followed by a class discussion about what would constitute good ways to use the tool for mathematical thinking. You may use the *Notice and Wonder Thinking Routine* (described in the introductory chapter) to guide student observations about the properties of the two-color counters as well as to facilitate discussion about what makes a two-color counter better than a one-color counter for some activities.

Key Ideas With Two-Color Counters

- Two-color counters are best used for numbers within 20. Therefore, they have the greatest utility in Grades K–1 for whole numbers and Grades 6–7 for integers.
- For number sets **greater** than 20, base-ten blocks tend to be the better tool. That said, students may use two-color counters in Grades 1–3 when composing and decomposing two-digit numbers, using one color to represent groups of ten and the other color to represent ungrouped ones.

- In the beginning stages of counting, **one-to-one correspondence** requires the integration of three processes: knowing the counting sequence, assigning exactly one number from the counting sequence to exactly one object, and knowing that the last number stated represents the quantity of the set.

- Young students should also internalize the connection between the quantities, number words, and **numerals**.

- To maximize the benefits of two-color counters, seek out activities that are enhanced by the presence of two colors. This includes concepts such as finding number pairs that **add** up to 10, determining evenness and oddness, and grouping one ten with extra ones.

Things to Consider About Two-Color Counters

Two-color counters offer a great opportunity for students to explore composing and decomposing quantities, beginning addition and subtraction, and, informally, finding **differences** (eventually leading to developing notions of positive and negative integers).

Alternatives to Commercial Two-Color Counters

Although two-color counters may be purchased commercially, they can also be made at home. One simple way is to *paint one side of a set of single-sided counters*, such as poker chips or square tiles. An alternative would be to use lima beans, painting one side of each bean and leaving the other side white.

Another homemade alternative would be to *use spray adhesive to glue together two pieces of fun foam*. Then you may cut squares with a paper cutter to create a class set of two-color tiles.

For many of the activities in this chapter, two-color counters may be substituted with single-color counters. When this is the case, you may use circle counters, square tiles, linking cubes, or any of a variety of countable objects such as buttons, beans, plastic bottle caps, caps from applesauce pouches, and beads. You may also choose from a variety of commercial counters such as bears, dinosaurs, cars, and so on.

Working With Virtual Two-Color Counters

Virtual two-color counters have the same functionality as physical counters. There is an endless supply and no real risk around resizing the counters as long as all the counters resize the same way. A snapping feature is useful when placing two-color counters on **five frames**, **ten frames**, or other organizational structures. Many virtual counters also have added features such as the option to change the colors and shapes (teddy bears, stars, squares, etc.).

ONE-TO-ONE CORRESPONDENCE

Materials

- 10 two-color counters for each student, placed in zip-top bags
- Mixed set of activity sheets for each table
- Recording sheet for each student (optional)
- Stapler and colored paper for book making (optional)

Organization (physical)

- **Getting Started:** Distribute materials to students as they work individually.
- **Winding Down:** At the end of the activity, ask students to count the two-color counters before they put them away. This will reveal progress toward meeting the learning target.

Mathematical Purpose

Students will understand that counting involves assigning exactly one number to exactly one object, using the counting sequence beginning with "one" as they match counters to pictures to help with the count.

Activity 1.1 Resources

One-to-One Correspondence Recording Sheet

 To access resource visit resources.corwin.com/MasteringMathManips/K-3

Manipulative Illustrated

Two-Color Counters (available from multiple sources)

Steps

1. Discuss one-to-one correspondence with the students in small or whole groups. Demonstrate the "see it, touch it, say it" process so students know that as they place one counter on one picture, they should say one number at a time. For example, say something like this: "As we count together, we are going to see each tile, touch it, and say the next counting number." Ask students to count along with you. Support students' thinking by asking guiding questions such as the following:

   - *How did you know what number to say next?*
   - *How did you know when we were done counting?*
   - *How did you know how many there were altogether?*

2. Distribute a stack of mixed activity sheets to each group of students. The activities do not need to be completed in any particular sequence.

3. Ask students to place exactly one counter on each picture. They should count the counters as they place them on the pictures, *or* they can count the counters after placing them on the pictures. Remind students to use the "see it, touch it, say it" process.

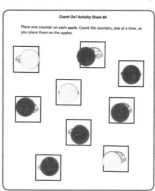

Count On! Activity Sheet #4

Place one counter on each apple. Count the counters, one at a time, as you place them on the apples.

4. *Optional:* Ask students to record the number of objects by drawing *X*s or circles on a recording sheet. Ask students to record the numeral associated with the count. (*Note:* If a student is not ready to record the symbols and numerals, then a quick video of the student counting will suffice as evidence of learning.)

Why This Manipulative?

Simple counters, such as two-color counters, help students associate the counting sequence with the one-to-one nature of counting objects. Being able to see, move, and touch the counters while saying the counting numbers in sequence helps students coordinate the set of skills required to count sets of objects successfully.

Developing Understanding

One-to-one correspondence includes a complex set of skills to be used simultaneously. This work requires that students (1) know the counting sequence, (2) assign exactly one number to exactly one object, (3) understand that each number in the counting sequence is exactly one more than the previous number, and (4) identify the final number said as the number of objects in the set.

Knowing that the act of counting requires assigning exactly one number name to each object comes easier for some students than for others. Provide ample opportunities for students to count objects and pictures throughout the day. This can include something as simple as counting the number of students at the table and then getting that many snacks or papers or books. Once students have mastered one-to-one counting, knowing that the final number in the counting sequence identifies the **total** number in the set, begin connecting the written numeral to the count.

Featured Connection

In this activity, students use the Make a Sketch and Name Your Model strategies to translate between concrete, visual, and symbolic **representations**. As simple as this activity may seem, young learners are still grappling with connecting quantities to verbal number names to numerals. Therefore, asking students to connect all three of these representations is a complex task for them and requires deliberate attention. Some students may have limited skills in numeral writing, yet they can still name the model verbally, which is an abstraction at this developmental stage.

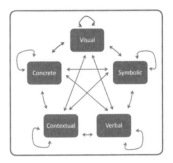

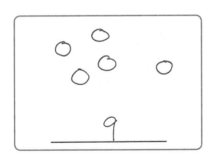

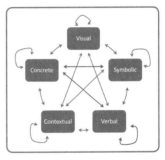

Source: Lesh, Post, & Behr (1987).

Notes

_____

_____

_____

_____

_____

Materials

- 10 or 20 two-color counters per student
- One work mat for each student (colored paper or fun foam)
- Numeral cards for each student (select number set)
- Recording sheet for each student

Organization (physical)

- **Getting Started:** Distribute materials to students as they work individually.
- **Winding Down:** At the end of the activity, ask students to count the two-color counters before they put them away. This will reveal progress toward meeting the learning target.

Mathematical Purpose

Students will understand that the last number stated when counting a set of objects corresponds with the number name and numeral to answer the question, "How many?" In the extension, students will transition to **subitizing** quantities.

Activity 1.2 Resources

Cardinality Numeral Cards and Recording Sheet

 To access resource visit resources.corwin.com/ MasteringMathManips/ K-3

Manipulative Illustrated

Two-Color Counters (available from multiple sources)

Steps

1. Give each student 10 or 20 counters and a set of corresponding "How many?" numeral cards. The numeral cards should be stacked and facedown.

2. Ask students to flip over the top numeral card.

3. Ask students to count out the corresponding number of two-color counters, placing them on the work mat as they count, exhibiting one-to-one correspondence.

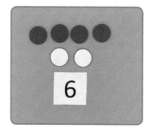

4. Ask students to record the number of objects by drawing *X*s or circles on the recording sheet as well as the numeral associated with the completed count. (*Note:* If a student is not ready to record the symbols and numerals, then a quick video of the student counting will suffice as evidence of learning.)

5. Repeat Steps 1–4 until all sections of the recording sheet are filled out. Support students' thinking by asking guiding questions such as the following:

   - *How many are there altogether?*
   - *How do you know?*
   - *How do you write that number?*

6. *Extension:* As young learners become proficient with counting and cardinality, transition them to a subitizing activity where they become proficient at accurately recognizing a quantity without counting. Simply show the students a group of counters for a short period—long enough for them to see but not long enough for them to count by ones. Then ask them to tell you how many they saw and how they knew it was that many. Most students will rely either on position or on color to talk about the number. For example, when they see a set of five counters, students may say something like, "I know that is five because I see three reds and two yellows," or "I know that is five because I see three across the top and two on the bottom."

7. *Extension:* For students working with teen numbers, ask them to use one color for the group of ten and the other color for the extra ones.

Why This Manipulative?

Simple counters such as two-color counters help students associate the counting sequence with the one-to-one nature of counting objects. Being able to see, move, and touch the counters while saying the counting numbers in sequence helps students coordinate the set of skills required to count sets of objects successfully.

Developing Understanding

Ask students to "see it, touch it, say it" (explained in Activity 1.1) as they count to monitor one-to-one correspondence. As previously mentioned, young learners must work hard to connect quantities with the corresponding number words and numerals. Because this is so challenging, providing a variety of opportunities for them to connect all three is crucial.

As you work through this activity with your students, invite them to count individually or together. Some students may need to review the counting sequence. Some may need support with one-to-one correspondence. Some may need reminders that the final number said when counting names the quantity of the entire set. And still others may need help with numeral writing.

Regardless of the group with whom you are working, you are bound to see a great range in students' abilities to know, understand, and coordinate all of these skills at once. Take care to customize for students as needed. For example, if they are not yet able to write the number to match the quantity, ask them to select the numeral from a card that lists several.

Featured Connection

During this activity, students use the Make a Sketch and Name Your Model strategies, highlighting the connections between the concrete, visual, and symbolic representations. Students work hard to connect the quantities with their number names and numerals.

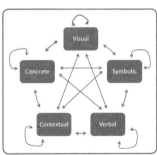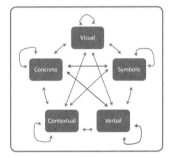

Source: Lesh, Post, & Behr (1987).

By sketching their counters, they are creating a visual of the quantity while engaging in the counting process yet again. And, finally, they have the opportunity to connect to the symbolic representation when they name their sketch with a written numeral.

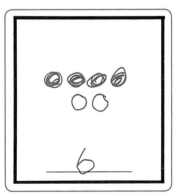

MORE AND LESS

| K | 1 | 2 | 3+ |

Materials

- Several zip-top bags of two-color counters, each with a different quantity of two-color counters, placed in a container
- One work mat for each student (colored paper or fun foam)
- Activity sheet for each student
- Numeral cards for each student (select number set)

Organization (physical)

- **Getting Started:** Students work in pairs. For each round, each student selects one bag of counters to compare with a partner's.

- **Winding Down:** At the end of each round, ask students to count the two-color counters before they put them away. This will reveal progress toward meeting the learning target.

Mathematical Purpose

Students will compare quantities of physical objects to determine which amount is more or less.

Extension: Students can compare quantities with numerals to determine which is more or less.

Activity 1.3 Resources

More and Less Recording Sheet and Numeral Cards

 To access resource visit resources.corwin.com/ MasteringMathManips/ K-3

Steps

1. Students work in pairs. Ask each student to select a bag of counters from the container without looking (each partner has one bag of counters).

2. Ask students to remove the counters from the bags and place them on their work mats. Student A flips the counters to the red side. Student B flips the counters to the yellow side. At this time both students count their counters.

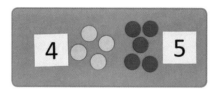

3. Together, the students decide which set is "more" and which is "less." For some students, this may require a one-to-one matching, placing exactly one red counter next to exactly one yellow counter until they see which set has "extras." The set with extra counters has more. Support students' thinking by asking guiding questions such as the following:

   - *How many red counters do you see?*
   - *How many yellow counters do you see?*
   - *How can you tell which color has more and which has less?*
   - *Does it help to match them up in pairs?*
   - *What do you notice when you match them up in pairs?*
   - *What do you know about the color that has extra that can't be matched?*

4. Finally, ask each student to draw the counters and write the corresponding numerals in the correct spaces on the recording sheets.

5. *Extension:* Ask one student to flip a numeral card (included with recording sheets) while the other student selects a bag and counts the counters. Together, the students decide which is more or less by comparing the numeral and the set of objects. This can then be repeated by asking each student to select a numeral card and predict which is more or less and prove it with counters.

Why This Manipulative?

Two-color counters are ideal for this activity because they allow students to compare two sets of objects that are two different colors. This allows them to more easily determine which has more or less by directly matching using one-to-one correspondence. The two colors allow students to distinguish the two distinct sets even when they're moved close together to make matched pairs.

Developing Understanding

Comparing quantities requires that students extend and apply their understanding of one-to-one correspondence and counting out sets of objects. For this activity, they must count out two sets of objects and then either directly or indirectly compare the two sets to determine which has more and which has less.

As you work with students, remain mindful that some may still be working on one-to-one correspondence, the counting sequence, cardinality, and/or numeral writing. This activity provides opportunities for you to guide students at their level, differentiating as needed. For those still struggling with one-to-one correspondence, ask them to "see it, touch it, say it" (described in Activity 1.1) as they count to monitor their progress. Note that the extension options in Step 5 provide chances for some students to move into more symbolic representations as well.

Featured Connection

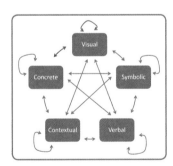

Source: Lesh, Post, & Behr (1987).

In this activity, students use the Make a Sketch and Name Your Model strategies to highlight the connection between the concrete, visual, and symbolic representations. As with Activity 1.2, students benefit from representing the set with a drawing and a numeral after counting out the concrete objects, reinforcing the connection of quantities, verbal symbols, and written symbols. The extensions in this activity (Step 5) also provide accelerated opportunities for students who are ready to work more with symbols and less with concrete objects.

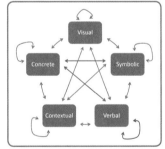

SORTING AND COUNTING

| K | 1 | 2 | 3+ |

Materials

- Several zip-top bags, each containing up to 20 counters, placed in a container (*Note:* Other counters may be used, especially with up to four variables and/ or attributes, so students can sort and count into more than two groups.)

- One work mat for each student (colored paper or fun foam)

- Recording sheet for each student

- Red and yellow crayons, markers, or colored pencils

Organization (physical)

- **Getting Started:** Students work individually. Place a container with several bags in the center of each group for all to use.

- **Winding Down:** At the end of each round, ask students to count the two-color counters before they put them away. This will reveal progress toward meeting the learning target.

Mathematical Purpose

Students will understand that a set can be sorted into smaller sets, and each set can be counted and recorded individually.

Activity 1.4 Resources

Sorting and Counting Recording Sheet

 To access resource visit resources.corwin.com/ MasteringMathManips/ K-3

Steps

1. Students work independently on this activity. Without looking, each student selects a bag of counters from the container.

2. The student removes the counters from the bag and places them on a work mat, leaving the colors faceup as they landed when they were "spilled."

3. The student sorts the counters by color.

4. The student then counts each set and fills out the recording sheet using both sketches and numerals.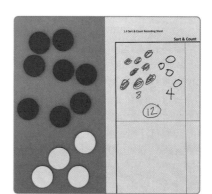

5. To support their thinking, ask students guiding questions as they engage in this activity:

   - *How many red counters did you count?*

   - *How many yellow counters did you count?*

   - *How do you know you drew the correct amount on your recording sheet? Can you count those out loud for me?*

Why This Manipulative?

Two-color counters allow students to begin working with sorting and counting with a limited number of variables. As students remove the counters from the bag, some will be red, and some will be yellow. Students simply sort by color with these counters. To extend student learning, try using other counters that have more attributes so students are able to sort into up to four sets.

Developing Understanding

This activity requires that students first sort the counters by a common attribute, this time color, and then count the number of objects in each set. The multiple steps may seem simple for an adult, but the increased complexity extends cognitive load for the young child. Beginning with the two-color counters helps students focus on only one attribute (color) with two variables (e.g., red and yellow). Once students have experienced this simple sorting, introduce other counters that have more variables as well as more attributes to increase the complexity of the sort, still expecting students to use their counting skills to identify the number of objects in each set.

If students continue to struggle with counting and cardinality, remind them to use the "see it, touch it, say it" process explained in Activity 1.1.

Featured Connection

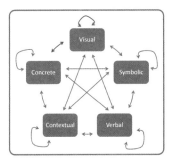

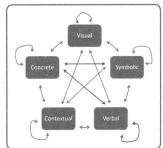

Use the Make a Sketch and Name Your Model strategies with this activity to highlight the connection between the concrete, visual, and symbolic representations. By creating a sketch of the counters, students connect the concrete and visual representations while reinforcing their early number skills (counting sequence, one-to-one correspondence, composing and decomposing, etc.). And by naming the model with numerals, students continue their journey toward understanding mathematics as a symbolic system.

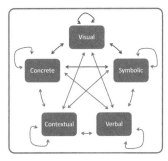

Source: Lesh, Post, & Behr (1987).

In addition, students may engage in the Create a Diagram strategy by translating this work using a number bond representation. This common tool helps students connect their actions of sorting and counting into a visual that is also symbolic.

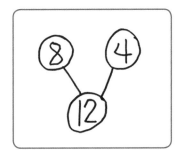

DECOMPOSING NUMBERS INTO PAIRS IN MORE THAN ONE WAY

| K | 1 | 2 | 3+ |

Materials

- Two-color counters, up to 10 for each student, placed in zip-top bags
- Work mat (fun foam or heavy paper), one per pair of students
- Small containers, such as plastic cups, one per pair of students
- Recording sheet for each student
- *Optional:* Stapler, colored paper for book covers

Organization (physical)

- **Getting Started:** Place the bags of two-color counters in the center of each group for all to use.
- **Winding Down:** At the end of the activity, ask students to count the two-color counters as they place them back in the container, one at a time. This ensures all counters are accounted for and returned.

Mathematical Purpose

Students will understand that a whole number can be composed and decomposed into a finite number of unique whole-number pairs.

Activity 1.5 Resources

Decomposing Numbers Into Pairs in More Than One Way Recording Sheet

 online resources — To access resource visit resources.corwin.com/ MasteringMathManips/ K-3

Manipulative Illustrated

Two-Color Counters (available from multiple sources)

Steps

Designate a focus number between 3 and 10. Students place that many two-color counters into the container. Students write the focus number in each section of the recording sheet.

1. Student A shakes the container and "drops" the counters on a work mat.

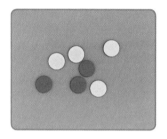

2. Both students record the result by sketching the designated number of circles and coloring them to show the two-number pair. Students then record an expression or an equation to represent the result.

3. Student B places the counters back in the container, shakes it, and "drops" the counters on a work mat.

4. Students continue to play until their recording sheets are filled out. Support students' thinking by asking guiding questions such as the following:

   - *How many counters did you start with?*
   - *How many red counters do you see?*
   - *How many yellow counters do you see?*
   - *How many counters are there in all? Why is that number the same as the start number?*
   - *How can you show that on your recording sheet?*

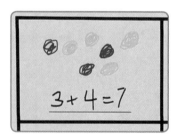

5. *Optional:* Students cut the recording sheet apart on the lines and staple to make a booklet.

6. *Extension:* Repeat this activity with enough counters for two-digit numbers.

Why This Manipulative?

Two-color counters, whether commercial or homemade, provide students with opportunities to compose or decompose any number into two parts. Although they are ideally used with numbers 2–20, they may be used for larger numbers as well.

Developing Understanding

We want students to develop two important understandings from this work. First, students should recognize that a whole number can be composed of or decomposed into smaller numbers. In this activity, the students decompose the designated total into number pairs. This facilitates understanding that a number can be subdivided into smaller numbers, and that there is a finite number of pairs that compose the total.

Second, students should recognize that the total number of counters remains constant after the decomposition has taken place. For example, when 7 is the designated number, the students come to understand that regardless of the number pair that is dropped, seven counters remain.

There are at least two ways to help develop student understanding in this activity:

1. Using systematic counting to find the finite number of pairs for each **sum**.

2. Discussing whether the number pair that includes 0 counts as a decomposition. For example, when decomposing the number 6, students find that there are seven ways to represent 6 using two colors: 0 + 6, 1 + 5, 2 + 4, 3 + 3, 4 + 2, 5 + 1, and 6 + 0. This may lead to a relevant conversation as to whether 2 + 4 and 4 + 2 are the same thing, if the first **addend** is always red and the second addend is always yellow. Another follow-up question may center on whether 0 + 6 and 6 + 0 are really decompositions of 6.

Featured Connection

Use the Make a Sketch and Name Your Model strategies with this activity to highlight the connection between the concrete, visual, and symbolic representations. As students gain practice composing and decomposing into whole-number pairs, they will

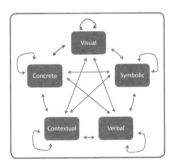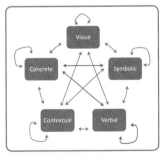

Source: Lesh, Post, & Behr (1987).

naturally transition away from using concrete objects to represent their thinking and begin to rely more on sketches and numbers to represent their thoughts. Students may continue to "see" the two-color counters (or other objects) in their mind's eye as they think about the number pairs that compose and decompose a specified quantity. In the initial stages, they may continue to sketch literal figures that look like the two-color counters. However, over time, they can begin to use alternative representations that gradually become more abstract. For example, they may draw circles, then dots, then tally marks as they move away from the need for concrete objects.

To extend their thinking, students may also use the Create a Diagram strategy by writing their decomposed numbers in a number bond. This simple diagram reinforces the relationship between the parts and the whole and helps students recognize the consistency that exists in this process (e.g., the total number at the end matches the number of counters they started with). This will also help students begin to generalize the notion that there are multiple ways to decompose each given number into pairs.

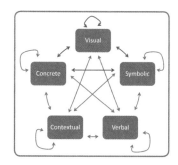

Source: Lesh, Post, & Behr (1987).

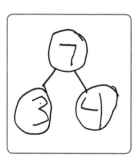

Notes

_____

_____

_____

_____

_____

_____

_____

_____

_____

_____

_____

Notes

Materials

- Virtual counters with ten frame (or buckets of two-color counters and the 1.6 work mat)
- Numeral cards
- Recording sheet for each student (or students may use annotation tools in app and take screenshots)
- Red and yellow crayons, markers, or colored pencils

Organization (virtual)

- **Getting Started:** Ensure students know how to use the virtual counters and ten frames; review annotation tools, taking screenshots, and so on.
- **Winding Down:** Take screenshots to save student work.

Mathematical Purpose

Students will understand that they can count on from any number to find the number pair that totals ten.

Activity 1.6 Resources

Make a Ten Numeral Cards and Recording Sheet

 To access resource visit resources.corwin.com/MasteringMathManips/K-3

Manipulative Illustrated

Two-Color Counters app from Toy Theater: https://toytheater.com/two-color-counter-whiteboard/

Steps

1. Either with the whole class or in a small group, use a virtual ten frame (or the provided ten frame work mat and counters) to demonstrate Steps 2–5. Students will then work individually or in pairs to follow the steps.

2. Ask students to flip over the top numeral card and place that many red counters *on* the ten frame.

3. Ask students to use yellow counters to count up from the red-facing-up number until they get to ten.

4. Ask students to record the number of red and yellow counters on the recording sheet. Students write the number 10 above the ten frame and the number of red and yellow counters below the ten frame. (Students may also use annotation tools if they are available in the app you've chosen.)

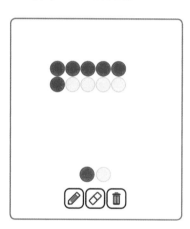

5. Continue Steps 2–5 until the recording sheet is filled out. Support students' thinking by asking guiding questions such as the following:

   - *How many red tiles are on your ten frame?*
   - *How many yellow tiles are on your ten frame?*
   - *How many tiles are there in all?*
   - *How can you know how many there are altogether without counting?*

Why This Manipulative?

Two-color counters, whether commercial or homemade, provide a great context for students to find number pairs that total ten. Since the counters have two colors, those two colors represent the two addends that total ten. Knowing the number pairs that total ten is an important concept for students to internalize. These number pairs occur over and over again throughout the places in our base-ten number system. Knowing these number pairs prepares students for working with multi-digit numbers and operations. Using manipulatives in two colors, especially on a ten frame model, helps students visualize the relationship between number pairs that total ten. The ten frame provides a structure that helps students anchor to 5 and 10 as benchmark numbers. This translates into a mental internalization both positionally (ten frame formation) and relationally (two colors).

Developing Understanding

During this activity, support students' understanding by supporting the "counting on" strategy to make a ten. The Make a Ten strategy plays an integral role throughout the entire base-ten number system, from very large whole numbers to very small decimal fractions. What happens within the first ten is a microcosm of what happens in every place, only the magnitude changes. Therefore, ensure students possess a strong sense of making a ten by reinforcing this notion frequently and deeply.

Featured Connection

In this activity, students use the Make a Sketch and Name Your Model strategies to highlight the connection between the concrete, visual, and symbolic representations. As with Activity 1.5, students begin to internalize the notions of composing and decomposing

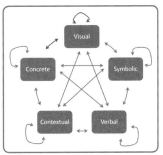 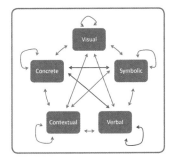

Source: Lesh, Post, & Behr (1987).

ten into whole-number pairs using multiple representations with increasing ease. By transitioning from the concrete/visual representation to sketches and then to symbols, students become increasingly conscious of the connections between these representations, cementing their understanding of the different number pairs that total ten.

As an extension, students may also use the Create a Diagram strategy to begin to connect and generalize their emerging understanding of number pairs that add to ten. One way to make a diagram is to have students record their discoveries with number bonds—one number bond for each possible number pair, with no overlaps. Another diagram that might be useful is a simple table where they might record the first and second addend for each possible number pair. Taken a step further, students may see patterns emerge, such as those pictured here.

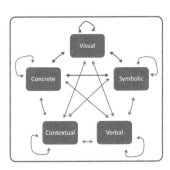

Source: Lesh, Post, & Behr (1987).

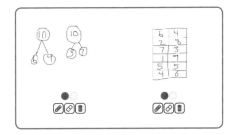

COMMUTATIVE PROPERTY OF ADDITION WITH TWO COLORS

| K | 1 | 2 | 3+ |

Materials

- Virtual two-color counters app (or buckets of two-color counters)
- One work mat per student (heavy paper or fun foam)
- Expression cards for each student
- Recording sheets (multiple sheets per student, or students may use annotation tools in app and take screenshots)

Organization (virtual)

- **Getting Started:** Ensure students know how to use the virtual counters; review annotation tools, taking screenshots, and so on.
- **Winding Down:** Take screenshots to save student work.

Mathematical Purpose

Students will understand that the commutative property allows them to add in any **order** and get the same sum.

Activity 1.7 Resources

Commutative Property of Addition With Two Colors Expression Cards and Recording Sheets

 To access resource visit resources.corwin.com/ MasteringMathManips/ K-3

Manipulative Illustrated

Two-Color Counters app from Toy Theater: https://toytheater.com/ two-color-counter-whiteboard/

Steps

1. Either with the whole class or in a small group, use a virtual ten frame (or the provided ten frame work mat and counters) to demonstrate Steps 2–6. Students will then work individually or in pairs to follow the steps. Ask students to cut apart the cards ahead of time and place them in a pile, facedown.

2. The pair of students flip over one expression card from the pile.

3. Student A represents the expression using red for the first addend and yellow for the second addend.

4. Student B represents the expression using yellow for the first addend and red for the second addend.

5. On the recording sheet, each student sketches Student A's representation on the left and Student B's representation on the right.

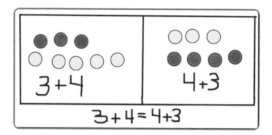

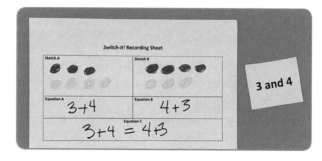

6. Next, each student writes the equation that represents the sketch on the left and then the sketch on the right ($a + b = c$), with the *red* number always going first.

7. Finally, each student writes a new equation that sets the two expressions as equal ($a + b = b + a$).

8. Students repeat Steps 1–6 until time is up.

9. When the recording sheet is filled out, students use the Write a Word Problem strategy to go with one of their equations.

> **Write a Word Problem (sample)**
>
> Sam has 3 dogs and 4 fish. Rafael has 4 dogs and 3 fish. How do you know if they have the same number of pets?

Why This Manipulative?

Two-color counters are ideal for spotlighting the **commutative property** since they distinctly show the two addends as switching roles through the use of either color or position (in this activity, we chose color). Whether commercial or homemade, these counters present a highly effective model for building understanding. The commutative property of addition involves the use of two addends that, when reversed, continue to represent the same amount. Although it seems like such a simple notion, students often struggle with commutativity, especially when applied in a contextual situation.

Developing Understanding

Throughout this activity, bring context into the conversation as much as possible. Talk about situations such as the following:

> 3 cats and 5 dogs is not the same as 5 cats and 3 dogs, even though there are 8 pets altogether.
>
> 2 bananas and 8 oranges is not the same as 8 bananas and 2 oranges, even though there are 10 pieces of fruit altogether.

Invite students to play along, attaching context to the math.

Featured Connection

Use the Write a Word Problem strategy to highlight the connection between the concrete and contextual representations (see "Developing Understanding" for specific examples). Although several connecting representations are included in this activity, using the Write a Word Problem strategy will be the most robust in cementing the thinking necessary to understand the commutative property. As students use concrete/visual representations, convert them to sketches, and record them symbolically, they will be developing an ever-increasing understanding of the abstract nature of the commutative property of addition. However, by

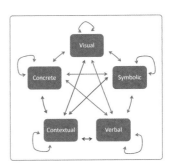

Source: Lesh, Post, & Behr (1987).

adding context, they will also see how this property can be used to explain phenomena in the world around them.

Materials

- 20 two-color counters per pair of students in zip-top bags or small containers

- Work mat (fun foam or heavy paper), one per pair of students

- Teen cards

- Recording sheet for each student

- *Optional:* Portion cup with lid (large enough to hold 10 counters), one per pair of students

- *Optional:* Stapler, colored paper for book covers

Organization (physical)

- **Getting Started:** Students work in pairs. Place the bags of two-color counters in the center of each group for all to use.

- **Winding Down:** Count and put the two-color counters in the containers before collecting, checking to be sure none fell on the floor or got left behind.

Mathematical Purpose

Students will understand that a teen number can be decomposed into one group of **ten** and some extra ones. In the extension, the students will understand that ten ones can be grouped into one ten. This important concept is known as **unitizing**.

Steps

1. Either with the whole class or in a small group, use counters and the provided ten frame work mat to demonstrate Steps 2–6. Students will then work in pairs to follow the steps. Ask students to cut apart the cards ahead of time and place them in a pile, facedown.

2. Student A flips over the top teen card (e.g., 14).

3. Student B represents the designated number using two-color counters, all one color (e.g., 14 yellow counters).

4. Student A counts out ten counters and flips them over to show the other color.

5. Both students record the counters, including the corresponding colors, on their own recording sheets.

6. Both students write a corresponding equation (e.g., 14 = 10 + 4).

7. Students reverse roles and repeat Steps 1–5. Students continue until the recording sheet is filled out. As students go through the process of counting out the set, decomposing the set into one ten and some more ones, and recording the result, ask guiding questions:

   - *Did you have more, less, or the same amount after you flipped over ten of the counters?*

   - *How do you know?*

   - *How does the equation show that you had the same amount before and after you flipped over ten of the counters?*

8. *Extension:* Students may put the ten red counters into one stack, leaving out the extra four yellow counters, to represent "one ten and some extra ones." This is distinct from "ten ones and some extra ones." To support student thinking, ask guiding questions such as the following:

   - *Show me where you have made this part of the number (point to the 1 in the teen number).*

   - *Show me where you have made this part of the number (point to the other digit in the teen number).*

   - *Why did you put the ten counters into a stack instead of leaving them out?*

9. *Optional:* Students cut the recording sheet apart on the lines and staple to make a booklet.

Why This Manipulative?

Two-color counters lend themselves nicely in helping children visualize two sets of objects. In this case, students can focus on the notion that ten ones can be separated into their own group, leaving the rest of the "ones" un-grouped. This process of grouping is critical for building foundational understanding of how the base-ten number system "nests" from one place to the next. Furthermore, because these counters, by definition, have two colors, they may be used to focus on the notion of "unitizing," or forming objects into a single unit. In this case, the use of one color to identify a group of counters as a unit of ten prepares students for thinking of teen numbers (and beyond) as a group of ten and some extra ones.

Developing Student Understanding

Building numbers to ten and building numbers with tens are two of the most important structures addressed in the early years. As you work with students in this activity, ask guiding questions to help them understand the importance of ten when creating numbers. In most state standards frameworks, kindergarteners are asked to think of teen numbers as "ten ones and some more ones" while first graders are asked to think about teen numbers as "one group of ten and some more ones." This activity centers on the former, but the extension can be used to help students understand the latter. This understanding is pivotal in laying a foundation for all the place-value understanding that takes place throughout Grades K–5. Do not hesitate to review this concept, even in Grades 2–5, as a precursor for place-value work.

Featured Connection

In this activity, students use the Make a Sketch and Name Your Model strategies to highlight the connection between the concrete and pictorial representations. In this case, students are using the two-color counters to show ten ones and some more ones and, in the extension, one group of tens and some more ones. Cementing this foundational place-value understanding plays a critical role in future work with numbers and operations in base ten, both whole numbers and decimals. Therefore, asking students to translate from concrete to visual to abstract is worthy of repetition to ensure students internalize and generalize these ideas.

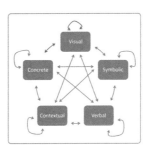

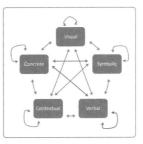

Source: Lesh, Post, & Behr (1987).

Activity 1.8 Resources

- Teen Cards
- *Number Pairs* Recording Sheet
- *Ten Ones and Some More Ones and One Group of Ten and Some More Ones* Activity Video

 online resources

To access resources visit resources.corwin.com/MasteringMathManips/K-3

Manipulative Illustrated

Two-Color Counters (available from multiple sources)

Materials

- Virtual two-color counters and ten frames (or a bucket of about 60 two-color counters for each pair of students)

- 2 six-sided number cubes (die) for each pair of students

- Activity sheets, three for each student

- Recording sheet for each student

Organization (virtual)

- **Getting Started:** Ensure students know how to use the virtual counters and ten frames; review annotation tools, taking screenshots, and so on.

- **Winding Down:** Take screenshots to save student work.

Mathematical Purpose

Students will understand the concept of even- and oddness for numbers through 20 and beyond.

Activity 1.9 Resources

- *Even and Odd* Activity Sheet

- *Even and Odd* Recording Sheet

 To access resource visit resources.corwin.com/ MasteringMathManips/ K-3

Manipulative Illustrated

Two-Color Counters app from Toy Theater: https://toytheater.com/ two-color-counter-whiteboard/

Steps

1. Either with the whole class or in a small group, use virtual counters and ten frame work mats to demonstrate Steps 2–7. Students will then work in pairs to follow the steps.

2. Student A rolls one number cube.

3. Student B places that number of counters on the activity sheet, yellow-side-up. Counters should be placed in pairs (top-bottom, then top-bottom, then top-bottom, etc.) so students can see if they are evenly matched or if there is an extra (odd) counter left over.

4. Students A and B work together to decide if the number is even or odd.

5. Student B rolls the die.

6. Student A places that number of counters on the activity sheet, yellow-side-up.

7. Each time a ten frame is filled, the students flip the counters so that each full ten frame is filled with red counters.

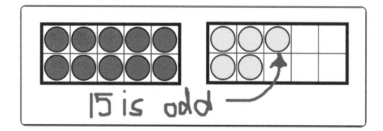

8. Repeat Steps 1–7 until all activity sheet cells are full. To support students' thinking, ask guiding questions such as the following:

   » *How do you know when a number is even or odd?*

   » *Why is it okay to just look at the ones place to determine if a number is even or odd?*

9. *Class discussion:* Discuss what students noticed when a number was even or odd. To support students' thinking, ask guiding questions such as the following:

   - *Did you need to use the filled ten frames to help determine evenness or oddness?*

   - *Why not?*

   - *Do you think this would be true if we had more groups of ten?*

10. *Extension:* Students may continue this activity using two-digit numbers in order to explore that last question about having additional groups of ten. Continue asking similar guiding questions to facilitate generalizations.

   a. Student A rolls two number cubes to form a two-digit number.

   b. Student B writes the number next to a ten frame on the recording sheet. Then Student B colors in the cells on the ten frame to represent the ones place. Counters should be placed in pairs (top-bottom, then top-bottom, then top-bottom, etc.) so students can see if they are evenly matched or if there is an extra (odd) counter left over.

   c. Students A and B work together to decide if the number is even or odd. They write "even" or "odd" next to the colored-in ten frame.

   d. Students reverse roles and repeat Steps 1–4 until the recording sheet is filled out.

Why This Manipulative?

Using two-color counters to help students focus on tens and ones helps them focus on the tens and ones separately. This is a necessary stage for helping students realize that the tens are always even and, therefore, do not need to be "consulted" when determining evenness or oddness. Using a ten frame provides a structure that allows students to develop the notion that all counters must have matched pairs for a number to be considered even.

Developing Understanding

When working with the number property of even or odd, two major ideas emerge. The first is to understand that an even number is defined as any integer that is divisible by two with no remainder. Younger students often describe this property as being able to "put objects into two even groups."

The second idea, which is a generalization of the first, is to understand that every multiple of ten is even, so one only need to look at the ones place to determine if the entire number is even. Teachers often jump to this second idea too quickly, simply telling students to just look at the ones place without first helping them understand that every multiple of ten is even, making the "look at the ones place" rule a possibility.

During this activity, help students begin to generalize that they only need to "consult" with the ones place to determine whether a number is even or odd. Ask guiding questions to facilitate thinking:

- *Does every counter have a matched pair?*

- *How can you tell if there's an odd number of counters?*

- *If there are more than ten, do you need to look at all the counters on both ten frames?*

- *What's a simpler way to tell if a number is even or odd?*

Featured Connection

Although this activity is very dependent on student use of the concrete/visual representations, connecting their work to multiple self-made representations will be useful as they begin making generalizations. Therefore, students should use the Make a Sketch strategy to highlight the connection between the concrete and visual representations.

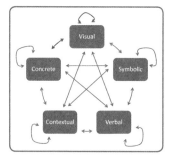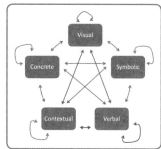

Source: Lesh, Post, & Behr (1987).

After several sketches have been generated, students can begin to make generalizations about using the ones place to determine even- and oddness. At that point, students should use the Caption Your Picture strategy to connect the visual and verbal generalizations that emerge, labeling the total number and whether it is even or odd.

Notes

_____

_____

_____

_____

_____

_____

_____

_____

_____

_____

_____

Notes

_____

_____

_____

_____

_____

_____

_____

_____

_____

_____

_____

_____

_____

_____

_____

_____

_____

_____

_____

_____

_____

Materials

- Two-color counters in containers for small groups
- Work mats (fun foam or heavy paper) for each student
- Blank paper for recording sketches and word problems

Organization (physical)

- **Getting Started:** Distribute a container of two-color counters to each group of students.
- **Winding Down:** Count and put the two-color counters in the containers before collecting them, checking to be sure none fell on the floor or got left behind.

Mathematical Purpose

Students interpret multiplication problems using the "equal groups" interpretation and compose corresponding word problems.

Manipulative Illustrated

Two-Color Counters (available from multiple sources)

Steps

1. Post 4×5 and $5 + 5 + 5 + 5$ for all to see.

4×5 $5 + 5 + 5 + 5$

Depending on your grade level and math goal, you may want to choose just one of these expressions rather than both. Ask students to talk with a partner about the relationship between these two expressions. To support students' thinking, ask questions such as the following:

- *What is multiplication?*
- *What does 4×5 look like?*
- *What does $5 + 5 + 5 + 5$ look like?*
- *How are these expressions related to one another?*

2. Ask students to work in pairs, using the two-color counters to represent each expression using the Build the Equation strategy. Help students arrive at the conclusion that both of these can be used to describe combining equal groups. Encourage students to use location and color to demonstrate their units of five, noting that there are several ways to show this.

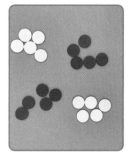

Also, if students represent five groups of four rather than four groups of five for the multiplication expression, note that that is a fair interpretation, but for today's purposes, we are interpreting this as four groups of five.

3. Once students have completed the task, ask them to use the Sketch Your Model and Write a Word Problem strategies to record and expand their work on blank paper. Once again, if students draw a problem that represents five groups of four and writes a corresponding word problem, accept it as correct.

Write a Word Problem (sample)
Shayla had 4 boxes of healthy snacks for her soccer friends. There were 5 treats in each box. How many treats did she have in all?

4. Repeat with other multiplication and/or repeated addition problems.

5. *Alternative:* Younger students may use only repeated addition problem expressions to engage in this same activity.

Why This Manipulative?

Two-color counters, by their very nature, lend themselves to unitizing as students can use either color or location to create units of a particular number (units of three, units of four, units of five, etc.). Although this activity focuses on using two-color counters as the primary manipulative, note that unit squares and linking cubes can also be used for a similar purpose. In fact, Activity 2.6 in this book provides a version of this activity using linking cubes.

Developing Understanding

As students develop their understanding of repeated addition and/or multiplication as an "equal groups" situation, they often need much support in understanding the unique roles of the two **factors**. One factor plays the role of multiplier while the other plays the role of multiplicand, or the quantity that is being multiplied (Morrow-Leong et al., 2020). For young learners, this is a big jump since up until this point, they have generally worked with addition, where both addends play similar and equivalent roles. Using a variety of representations will support students as they learn to make this distinction.

As you support students in their emerging understanding of multiplication, take care to be as accurate as possible. As is typical in the United States, we often tell young learners that the first factor is the multiplier and the second factor is the multiplicand. Although this can be very helpful in the formative stages, as it provides a common way to look at the numbers, it may lead to confusion in later years where this distinction is no longer necessary. In most situations, context is the key. When context is provided, the role of each of the factors falls into place naturally. Be mindful that your students compose word problems that match the pictures they sketch.

Featured Connection

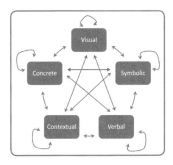 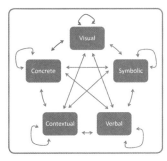 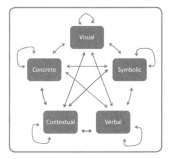

Source: Lesh, Post, & Behr (1987).

In this activity, students use the Build the Equation strategy to translate the symbolic expressions to concrete representations with the two-color counters. This provides evidence that students are beginning to make the distinction between the roles of the factors, as mentioned earlier. Then students use the Make a Sketch strategy to create a visual representation, quickly moving into the Write a Word Problem strategy to connect with contextual representations. Take care that the students' sketches match their word problems, regardless of which role they assign the factors.

Materials

- Two-color counters in containers for small groups
- Work mats (fun foam or heavy paper) for each student
- Blank paper for recording sketches and word problems

Organization (physical)

- **Getting Started:** Distribute a container of two-color counters to each group of students.
- **Winding Down:** Count and put the two-color counters in the containers before collecting them, checking to be sure none fell on the floor or got left behind.

Mathematical Purpose

Students interpret multiplication problems using arrays to represent and compose corresponding word problems.

Manipulative Illustrated

Two-Color Counters (available from multiple sources)

Steps

1. Review the idea of arrays with students, reminding them that when they make an array, they should have equal rows and equal columns. This may be a good place to connect to the area model that is represented well with unit squares (see Activities 4.3 and 4.4 in this book) to compare area models with arrays.

2. Post the task 3 × 6 where all students can see it.

   > 3 × 6

   Ask students to work individually or with a partner to create an array with two-color counters. To support students' thinking, ask guiding questions such as the following:

   - *What is the role of each of these factors?*
   - *What is the role of the 3 in this array?*
   - *What is the role of the 6 in this array?*

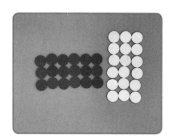

3. Once students have completed the task, ask them to use the Sketch Your Model and Write a Word Problem strategies to record and expand their work on blank paper. Support students in composing word problems that correspond to the arrays that they sketched. Encourage them to compose word problems that lend themselves to an array model (e.g., cookies on cookie sheets, band members in a parade, rows of desks), though this is not completely necessary.

   > **Write a Word Problem (sample)**
   >
   > Felicia drew a map of her classroom. There were 3 rows of desks. There were 6 desks in each row. How many desks did she draw altogether?

4. Repeat with other multiplication problems.

5. *Alternative:* Younger students may use repeated addition problem expressions to engage in this same activity.

Why This Manipulative?

Because two-color counters are uniform in size, they work well for students working with the array model for representing multiplication. The counters can easily be put into equal rows and columns with little confusion. Connections to other manipulatives may support student understanding of the array/area models for multiplication, such as unit squares (see Activities 4.3 and 4.4 in this book) and **geoboards** (see Activity 8.7 in this book).

Developing Understanding

Although the array and area models are often used interchangeably when talking about multiplication, you may want to be careful about how you talk about this idea with students. By definition, area is measured in square units, so the use of non-square counters does not quite fit the attributes of area. When using non-square units such as in this activity, you may want to refer to the arrangements of equal rows and columns as "arrays," making an ever-so-slight distinction. Using non-square counters is perfectly acceptable, and it might be helpful for the future study of area to keep these ideas distinct. See earlier discussion for connections to the area model using unit squares and geoboards.

Featured Connection

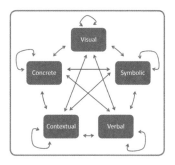 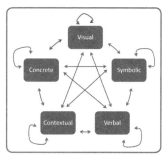 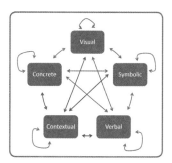

Source: Lesh, Post, & Behr (1987).

In this activity, students use the Build the Equation strategy to translate the symbolic expressions to concrete representations with the two-color counters. This provides evidence that students are beginning to make the distinction between the roles of the factors, as mentioned earlier. Then students use the Make a Sketch strategy to create a visual representation, quickly moving into the Write a Word Problem strategy to connect with contextual representations. Although this process is very similar to what was done in Activity 1.10, providing opportunities for students to make a distinction between "equal groups" representations and "array/area" representations is worth the effort.

Notes

_____

_____

_____

_____

DISTRIBUTIVE PROPERTY OF MULTIPLICATION OVER ADDITION WITH TWO-COLOR COUNTERS

K	1	2	3+

Materials

- Two-color counters in containers for small groups
- Work mats (fun foam or heavy paper) for each student
- Blank paper for recording sketches and word problems

Organization (physical)

- **Getting Started:** Distribute a container of two-color counters to each group of students.
- **Winding Down:** Count and put the two-color counters in the containers before collecting them, checking to be sure none fell on the floor or got left behind.

Mathematical Purpose

Students represent the distributive property of multiplication over addition using arrays and captions.

Manipulative Illustrated

Two-Color Counters (available from multiple sources)

Steps

1. Post the problem 4 × 6 for all to see.

4 × 6

   Ask students to describe what they already know about 4 × 6 to a partner. To support students' thinking, ask guiding questions such as the following:

   - *What might the 4 mean in 4 × 6?*
   - *What might the 6 mean in 4 × 6?*
   - *How might you figure out the product?*
   - *What is another way to figure out the product?*

2. Talk with students about how they might use multiplication facts they know quickly to help them figure out facts they don't know quickly. To demonstrate, ask students to use the Build the Equation strategy as they each build a 4 × 6 array using two-color counters. (If needed, review the notion of an array from Activity 1.11.)

   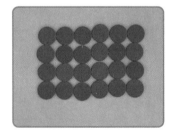

3. Next, ask students how they might "split" their array to help them see smaller facts that they might already know. Students might arrive at a variety of combinations including the ones pictured as follows. Ask students to show these simpler problems by flipping over the two-color counters in one group so they can distinctly see the entire array split into two parts.

   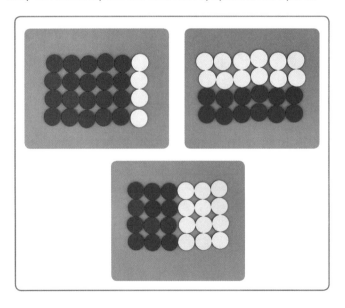

4. Ask students to use the Make a Sketch strategy to record a visual representation of their array. Then they should use the Caption Your Picture strategy to label each part of the array that they created.

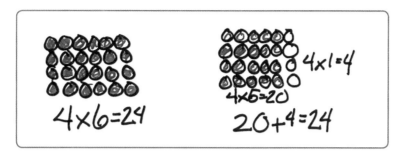

5. Ask students to work in small groups to share their arrays. Encourage them to notice that although all of their arrays represent 4 × 6, there are many ways to split it into parts that are easier to multiply and then add together.

6. Repeat this activity with other multiplication facts that lend themselves to the utility of the distributive property. Problems that are useful, but not exclusively, include 4 × 6, 4 × 7, 4 × 8, 4 × 9, 6 × 7, 6 × 8, 6 × 9, 7 × 8, 7 × 9, and 8 × 9.

Why This Manipulative?

Two-color counters are especially useful for representing this concept because of both their uniformity in size and the nature of the two colors. First, students are able to build arrays easily, as in Activity 1.11, because the counters are all exactly the same size and shape. Second, the two colors allow students to flip over the counters in one of the two groups once they have decided where to "split" the array to show the distributive property.

If you would like to connect to another manipulative using a similar focus, check out Activity 4.6 in this book where students use unit squares to show an area representation (no gaps or overlaps).

Developing Understanding

As with the previous two lessons, you will want to reinforce two notions important to the distributive property. First, each of the factors has a distinct role. When creating an array, one factor indicates the number of rows (or columns) while the other indicates the number that will be in each row (or column). Second, multiplication facts can be subdivided into parts to make the multiplication problem easier. By using two colors to indicate the two smaller problems, students can more easily see that they can multiply each of the smaller areas and then add them together.

Although you don't want to do this too soon, it may be useful to eventually point out that when using the distributive property to help with mental math, one of the factors remains the same for both of the new facts. Which one remains constant depends on which way you divide the array.

Featured Connection

In this activity, students use the Build the Equation strategy to translate the symbolic expression to concrete representations with the two-color counters. By building the array and then changing the colors to show the distributive property, they have the opportunity to gain understanding.

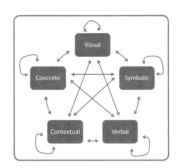

Next, students use the Make a Sketch strategy to create a visual representation, quickly moving into the Caption Your Picture strategy to connect with contextual representations. This process provides students with the opportunity to record their actions and further build their understanding of how the distributive property assists with solving difficult multiplication facts.

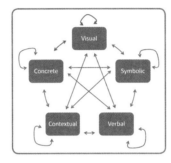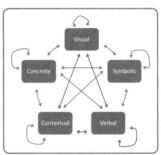

Source: Lesh, Post, & Behr (1987).

Notes

_____

_____

_____

_____

_____

_____

_____

_____

_____

_____

Notes

DATA COLLECTION AND GRAPHING

| K | 1 | 2 | 3+ |

Materials

- Two-color counters app (or a bucket of two-color counters)
- Markers, stickers, or small rubber stamps for pictographs
- Data set cards for scales with multiples (picture graphs or bar graphs)
- Recording sheet for each student (or use annotation and screenshot tools if available in the app)

Organization (virtual)

- **Getting Started:** Ensure students know how to use the virtual two-color counters; review annotation tools, taking screenshots, and so on.
- **Winding Down:** Take screenshots to save student work.

Mathematical Purpose

Students will understand that survey data can be represented with objects and with graphs.

Steps

1. Either with the whole class or in a small group, use virtual counters and ten frame work mats to demonstrate Steps 2–7. Students will then work in pairs to follow the steps.

2. Students select a data set card.

3. Students work together to represent the data with the two-color counters app.

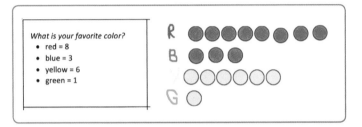

4. Students use the counters and ten frame app to individually record the data on a graph. If the app lacks annotation tools, then the students should use the provided recording sheet.

   - *Write the categories along the bottom or left-hand side (in the example shown, the colors are recorded on the left-hand side).*
   - *Write the scale along the bottom or left-hand side, when appropriate.*
   - *Write the title at the top.*
   - *If using the app, take a screenshot to save work. If using the recording sheet, students will need to use markers, stickers, or small rubber stamps to represent the counters with pictures on the recording sheet. The data cards are cut out and placed in a pile, facedown.*

5. Students compare their graphs to check for accuracy.

6. To support students' thinking, ask questions about the data such as the following:

   - *How many counters do you have in each category?*
   - *Do the counters match the numbers?*
   - *When you wrote your scale, did you focus on the spaces or the lines (remember that the lines are key to understanding quantities on bar graphs)?*
   - *How many people participated in this survey?*
   - *How many people liked _____ more than _____?*
   - *How many more people preferred _____ over _____?*

7. To further their thinking, ask students to generate their own questions about the data.

Why This Manipulative?

For the purpose of graphing, any simple counters will work, including two-color counters. It is not necessary to distinguish the data categories with the different colors indicated by two-color counters. That said, two-color counters are as good as any other counter for representing data sets, and they are easily available in many classrooms. When representing data sets with physical objects, students count out and organize sets for specified quantities. They use the counters to represent other objects. They organize the sets into rows using one-to-one correspondence to compare the quantities between and among sets. Finally, they transfer the quantities to a diagram (graph). They connect quantities and numerals by writing and using the scale.

Developing Understanding

During this activity, directly support students as they combine several different skills into one activity, concepts such as counting, sorting, and representing quantities. Ask guiding questions to help them make connections.

Featured Connection

Because of the nature of collecting, representing, and interpreting data, this activity is uniquely suited to using the Create a Diagram strategy to highlight the connection between the concrete and visual representations. Although students create a bar graph with counters, creating a visual allows them to add labels, comments, and other annotations.

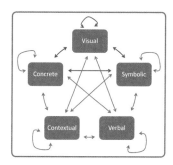

Source: Lesh, Post, & Behr (1987).

Activity 1.13 Resources

- *Graph It!* Data Set Cards
- *Graph It!* Recording Sheet
- *Data Collection and Graphing* Activity Video

 To access resources visit resources.corwin.com/ MasteringMathManips/ K-3

Manipulative Illustrated

Two-Color Counters app from Toy Theater: https://toytheater.com/ two-color-counter-whiteboard/

CLOSING REFLECTION: TWO-COLOR COUNTERS

How do I use two-color counters in my classroom now? What concepts do I use them to teach?

_____

_____

_____

_____

_____

_____

_____

_____

_____

_____

_____

What new ways have I found to use two-color counters to better support student understanding?

_____

_____

_____

_____

_____

_____

_____

_____

_____

_____

_____

What are my goals to make two-color counters a more regular part of my instruction?

_____

_____

_____

_____

_____

_____

_____

_____

_____

_____

CHAPTER 2
Linking Cubes

INTRODUCTION

Understanding Linking Cubes

Linking cubes have been a staple in primary classrooms for decades. Because linking cubes are made by many manufacturers, and because there is not a standard color scheme, dimension, or connecting style, different types of linking cubes tend to lack the quality of being interchangeable. They are available in many forms, from connecting options on only one **face** to connecting options on all faces. In the classroom, it's important to keep them separated by type.

Linking cubes are particularly effective in teaching these topics:

- Number concepts
- Base-ten **place value**
- Properties of operations
- Arithmetic operations
- Number patterns
- Graphing
- Measurement

Introducing Linking Cubes to Students

Encourage learners to explore linking cubes using the *Notice and Wonder Thinking Routine* (described in the introductory chapter) before starting to teach with them. Students may notice that there are many colors from which to select. They may notice ways in which the cubes connect. They may wonder how the linking cubes might be put together to create various structures.

Depending on the type of linking cubes available, students may build towers (vertical stacks), create trains or number tracks (horizontal rows), or put them together in a variety of formations. The term *number tracks* is often referenced when linked cubes are used to create a concrete representation of a **number line**. See the accompanying photo for examples. Students may be intrigued by the countability of the cubes, comparing which structures have more or fewer than others when using the cubes to create various structures.

Key Ideas With Linking Cubes

- Depending on the linking cube brand, cubes may be used to create only trains and towers, or they may be used to create other structures.

- Linking cubes provide opportunities for unitizing, creating equal groups such as tens for place value or different-sized factors for multiplication.

- Linking cubes offer many opportunities for students to explore number concepts such as place value, even and odd, and properties of operations.

- The linear structure of trains and towers made with linking cubes makes them good tools for connecting representations such as **bar models** and number lines.

- In addition, this linear characteristic also makes linking cubes useful when working with linear measurement, including perimeter.

- Because linking cubes are groupable manipulatives, they often provide young learners with a better learning opportunity for early place value than base-ten blocks.

Things to Consider About Linking Cubes

- Linking cubes present a wide variety of learning opportunities for students and can be used to explore concepts across domains, including algebraic thinking, number and operations, fractions, measurement, and geometry.

- Linking cubes are useful for helping students unitize, either for place value purposes (units of ten) or for multiplication purposes (units that show equal groups, such as units of three).

- Students can group linking cubes into unit trains, supporting the concepts of place value, multiplication, fractions, and measurement, to name a few.

- Take care to keep different brands of linking cubes separated as they will not fit together well, and this will likely detract from concepts that require consistent units.

Alternatives to Commercial Linking Cubes

Linking cubes are difficult to re-create in different forms. Unit cubes can be used for some purposes, but they do not link, thus limiting their ability to promote unitizing. Some items that may be linked together for limited purposes, such as **nonstandard** measurement, include paper clips, plastic links, and LEGO® pieces. Paper squares may be used to replicate linking cubes by gluing them to an activity sheet or blank sheet of paper, but this is not much different from using unit tiles.

As students use various linking materials to explore mathematical concepts, uniformity of the unit size must be maintained. If you are using paper clips, be sure they all have the same dimensions. The same holds true for paper squares, plastic links, LEGO® pieces, or any tool being used.

Working With Virtual Linking Cubes

Virtual linking cubes hold the advantage of offering an endless supply. If you are using virtual manipulatives, a snapping feature is useful when making towers or trains so cubes are well aligned and unit towers or trains can be constructed. Linking cubes must be of a consistent size to be useful in making unit towers or trains. Teachers should be careful that students do not unintentionally resize the pieces and change the uniformity among them.

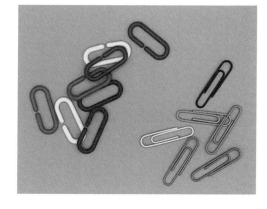

LINKING CUBES AS COUNTERS

Materials

- Linking cubes placed in containers for small groups of students
- Work mats for each student (heavy paper or fun foam)
- Blank paper or whiteboards for labeling linking cube trains

Organization (physical)

- **Getting Started:** Place the containers of linking cubes in the center of each group for all to use.
- **Winding Down:** Ask students to tidy up their workspace, making sure all cubes are put back in the container and work mats are stacked on top.

Mathematical Purpose

Students will apply their counting skills to represent different contexts using linking cubes to show their thinking.

Manipulative Illustrated

Linking Cubes (available from multiple sources)

Steps

1. Present students with the following scenario:

> Sydney has 5 books. Her mom gave her 4 more for her birthday.

To support students' thinking, ask guiding questions such as the following:

- *What is this story about?*
- *What quantities and math relationships are in the story?*
- *What do you think the math questions will ask?*

2. Ask students to pretend the linking cubes are books and to act out the story:

> Sydney has 5 books. Her mom gave her 4 more for her birthday. How many books does she have now?

To support students' thinking, ask guiding questions such as these:

- *What does the 5 represent?*
- *What does the 4 represent?*
- *How do the linking cubes show each part of the math story?*

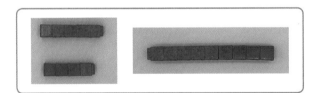

3. Ask students to retell the story with a partner, acting out the actions with stacks of five and four linking cubes.

4. Next, ask students to use the Make a Sketch and Name Your Model strategies to record their work. Simply put, students should sketch their linked cubes, adding labels to each part, and then write a corresponding number sentence.

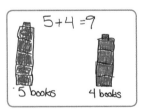

5. Repeat this process with two or three scenarios per day for several days.

6. *Extension:* Students may solve two-digit addition problems by snapping together groups of ten to have several tens and ones. You may choose to modify the context problems to use larger numbers.

Why This Manipulative?

Linking cubes function well as counters and can serve the same purpose. However, they have the added benefit of connecting and disconnecting to show action beyond what can be done with discrete counters. The action of connecting and disconnecting the linking cubes can be helpful in the problem-solving process as it helps students concretely see and feel the actions such as joining and separating. Furthermore, linking cubes lend themselves nicely to making connections to number lines and bar models due to their linear nature.

Developing Understanding

In this activity, linking cubes are used as simple counters that can be linked together rather than remaining separate. While working with students, lean into this attribute to help students act out scenarios such as those presented here. This makes a great warm-up or small-group activity, giving students many opportunities to develop their problem-solving skills over time.

Featured Connection

In this activity, students use the Make a Sketch strategy to connect the concrete representations made with the linking cubes with a sketched visual representation. Once the sketch is on paper, students can add labels, connecting back to the original context problem. Finally, students use

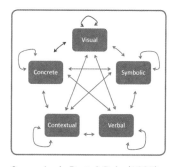 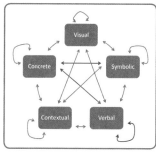

Source: Lesh, Post, & Behr (1987).

the Name Your Model strategy to write the corresponding number sentence. By connecting the concrete, visual, and symbolic representations to one another and then referencing back to the original context problem, students increase the likelihood of understanding how the symbols of mathematics can describe real-life contexts.

Notes

_____

_____

_____

_____

_____

COMPARING QUANTITIES (MORE AND LESS)

| K | 1 | 2 | 3+ |

Materials

- Linking cubes placed in containers for small groups of students

- Work mats for each student (heavy paper or fun foam)

- Blank paper or whiteboards and markers

- Number cards (choose 1–9, 11–19, or both), one set per student

Organization (physical)

- **Getting Started:** Place the containers of linking cubes in the center of each group for all to use.

- **Winding Down:** Ask students to tidy up their workspace, making sure all cubes are put back in the container and work mats are stacked on top.

Mathematical Purpose

Students determine quantities that are "greater than" and "less than" using linking cubes. Furthermore, they compare length models of quantities, building foundational measurement concepts.

Activity 2.2 Resources

Comparing Quantities Number Cards

 To access resource visit resources.corwin.com/MasteringMathManips/K-3

Manipulative Illustrated

Linking Cubes (available from multiple sources)

Steps

1. Students will work in pairs for this activity. Ask each student to cut apart a set of number cards and place them in a pile, facedown.

2. Have each student flip over the top card and build a tower with that number of linking cubes. Color is not a defining attribute in this situation, though some students may find it easier to use one color for each tower. Note that most young learners will find it easier to compare vertical towers than horizontal trains, so the word *towers* will be used throughout this activity in reference to both.

3. Ask students to directly compare their two towers, determining which has more and which has less. Ask guiding questions to support their understanding:

   » *Which tower has more?*

   » *Which has fewer?*

   » *How do you know?*

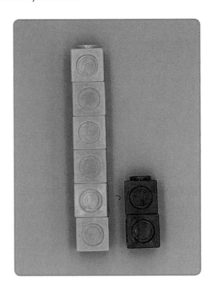

4. Ask students to use the Name Your Model strategy to record the two numbers, circling the one that is greater.

5. Repeat with other numbers, continuing to ask guiding questions.

6. After a couple of rounds, ask students to use the Write a Word Problem strategy to add context to the situation. You may need to provide examples, such as "Tina has 6 apples, and Antonio has 2 apples. Who has more?" Encourage students to contextualize the situation, as well, pretending that the cubes represent different objects.

7. *Extension:* Students may compare larger numbers by snapping together groups of ten to have several tens and ones or by placing the rods and units from base-ten blocks in rows (see Chapter 5 for discussion on base-ten blocks).

Why This Manipulative?

Linking cubes are uniquely suited for comparing quantities, more so than discrete counters, because of their linking quality. Students can directly compare the lengths of two towers to determine which represents the greater or lesser amount. Furthermore, directly comparing the towers leads to an easier way to visualize "how many more" and "how many less" by simply snapping off the "extra" cubes to show the difference between the two quantities.

Developing Understanding

In this activity, lean into the characteristics of length as you help students grapple with the concepts of more and less. Emphasize the importance of lining up the towers at a common start point to compare length to help students understand that this is a critical step for comparing lengths. Note that this is the same process students will use when they are learning measurement concepts.

To extend students' thinking, once they have determined the quantity that is greater or lesser, you might nudge them to focus on the question "How many more?" or "How many less?" by simply snapping off the extra cubes in the longer tower. Help students identify these extra cubes as the difference between the two quantities.

Featured Connection

In this activity, students use the Name Your Model strategy to highlight the connection between the physical and symbolic/verbal representations. They first build and compare linking cube towers to determine which is greater and which is less, and then they connect

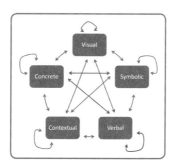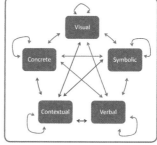

Source: Lesh, Post, & Behr (1987).

those concrete representations to the symbolic representation by writing the numbers to represent each stack and circling the one that is greater.

Eventually, students use the Write a Word Problem strategy to make a connection from the visual and symbolic representations to the contextual representation. Although you may need to provide examples for the students, asking them to create context will deepen their understanding of number comparisons by making the symbolic representation relevant to real-life situations.

Materials

- Virtual linking cubes (or physical linking cubes and work mats)
- Blank paper for recording thinking if not using an annotation tool

Organization (virtual)

- **Getting Started:** Ensure students know how to use the virtual linking cubes. Review annotation tools, taking screenshots, and so on.
- **Winding Down:** Take screenshots to save student work.

Mathematical Purpose

Students will connect physical and visual representations as they use linking cubes and number lines to represent addition problems.

Manipulative Illustrated

Unifix® Cubes app from Didax: www.didax.com/apps/unifix

Steps

1. Write the **expression** 3 + 4 for all to see.

   > 3 + 4

   Ask students to describe what it means with a partner. Encourage them to use linking cubes to help them in their explanations.

2. Introduce the notion of a number line, comparing and contrasting it to a "number track" made from linking cubes. Specifically, point out that the tick marks on the number line correspond to the grooves between each linking cube and represent the distance between the tick marks, not just the tick marks themselves.

3. Ask students to use virtual annotation tools (blank paper or whiteboards for physical linking cubes) to record a number line that corresponds to the number track they created in Step 1.

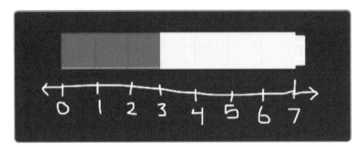

4. Repeat this process once or twice on the first day and then a few times per week for four weeks.

5. *Extension:* Students may use a similar process for solving subtraction, multiplication, and division problems. In addition, students may solve two-digit addition problems by snapping together groups of ten to have several tens and ones *or* by using the rods and units from base-ten blocks. This method may also be used to support students with skip counting, repeated addition, or multiplication by creating linking cube trains of a designated unit.

Why This Manipulative?

Because of the ability for linking cubes to fit together into trains, towers, or tracks, they have a linear attribute that resembles that of a number line. This provides an opportunity for making concrete connections to number line diagrams. Furthermore, the attribute of snapping provides a concrete and visual way to show the actions of joining and separating that are prevalent in context problems in the primary grades. Whether adding and subtracting single units or working with joining or separating equal groups, the action of physically snapping the cubes together and apart to indicate joining and separating is a worthy feature.

Developing Understanding

Working with number lines proves to be quite difficult for many young learners. Seeing quantity as linear as indicated by the distance between the number line tick marks often eludes understanding. Therefore, using a tool like linking cubes can help fill in this gap. Often referred to as number tracks, linked cubes can be substituted for number lines, allowing the students to count the number of cubes that run the length of the number track.

When helping students make the connection between linked cubes, or "number tracks," and number lines, explicitly point out that each space on the number line represents one cube. The tick marks, usually enumerated, show the end points of each cube. As seen in the photo to the left, the tick marks align with the spaces between each cube. Once again, it's important to point this out to young learners as they often think of the tick mark itself, rather than the space between tick marks, as the object of the count. Repeat similar activities frequently, helping students make these connections.

Featured Connection

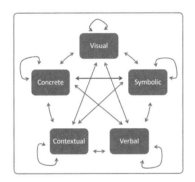 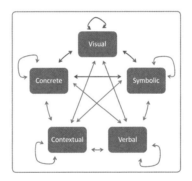 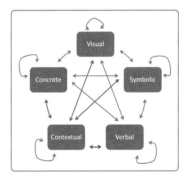

Source: Lesh, Post, & Behr (1987).

This activity begins with the Build the Equation strategy as students connect symbolic to concrete representations by building the given equation with linking cubes. The next connection is made by using the Create a Diagram strategy as students create, examine, and discuss the relationships between the linked cubes, or "number tracks," and number lines. This connection is deeply critical in helping students understand how a number line works, as described earlier. Finally, it is optional for students to Write a Word Problem to show how the symbolic, concrete, and visual representations connect to a contextual situation. Because this activity is intended to be repeated multiple times, you may choose to scaffold these strategies over time rather than doing them all at once.

REPRESENTING COMPARE PROBLEMS WITH A BAR MODEL

K   1   2   3+

Materials

- Virtual linking cubes (or physical linking cubes and work mats)
- Blank paper for recording thinking if not using an annotation tool

Organization (virtual)

- **Getting Started:** Ensure students know how to use the virtual linking cubes. Review annotation tools, taking screenshots, and so on.
- **Winding Down:** Take screenshots to save student work.

Mathematical Purpose

Students will connect physical and visual representations as they use linking cubes and number lines to represent addition problems.

Manipulative Illustrated

Unifix® Cubes app from Didax: www.didax.com/apps/unifix

Steps

1. Support students in using the Build an Equation strategy to make a stack of eight linking cubes and a stack of three linking cubes. Ask them to find the difference between the two. To guide students' thinking, ask guiding questions such as the following:

   - *How many cubes are on this track [point to the 8 number track]?*
   - *How many cubes are on this track [point to the 3 number track]?*
   - *How I can I easily compare these to find out how many more cubes are on the longer track?*
   - *When I line them up on one end, what is the difference between these two number tracks? How many more cubes are on this one? How many fewer are on that one?*

2. Ask the students to use the Write a Word Problem strategy to connect this problem to context. If needed, provide examples such as the following:

   » Kris has 8 cats and 3 dogs. How many more cats does she have than dogs?
   » Sofia has 8 crackers, and her sister has 3 crackers. How many fewer does her sister have?
   » Angel has 8 red toy cars and 3 black toy cars. How many more red cars does he have?

3. Introduce the notion of a bar model, comparing and contrasting it to a number track made from linking cubes. Ask students to use the Create a Diagram strategy to create the bar model using the app's annotation tool, or they may create it on paper. Help them see that in order to find the difference, they will create a third section with a question mark (?) to show where the difference is found in a bar model. This is the area that indicates how many more or how many fewer each bar has than the other.

4. Use different numbers, contexts, and problem types to repeat this process once or twice on the first day and then a few times per week for four weeks.

5. *Extension:* Students may use a similar process for solving word problems for any operation or situation type. Although the linking cubes are best suited for problems with smaller numbers, the bar models can be used to represent problems with any number set.

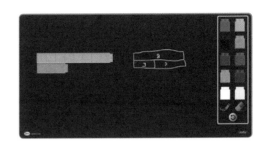

Why This Manipulative?

Linking cubes, along with Cuisenaire® Rods, provide an ideal way for students to create "bars" that resemble those made with bar models (and bar graphs; see Activity 2.9 in this chapter). The linked cubes clearly represent the quantities from the word problems, and students can then generate a bar model and add the labels, numbers, and so on to represent the given problem or situation. When students use linked cubes as bars in the beginning, the bars will remain proportional to one another.

Developing Understanding

When using linking cubes to help students understand and create bar models, begin by using small numbers, regardless of the grade level with which you are working. Help students "see" that each bar represents a part of the word problem, whether it's representing an addend, a minuend, a subtrahend, a factor, a sum, a difference, a product, or a **quotient**—you name it. Help students understand that bar models offer them a way to see the relationships between all the numbers in a problem or context, and it's up to them to figure out which value indicates the total and which values indicate the parts.

Over time, as students transfer their thinking from the concrete cubes to the visual/symbolic diagrams, you will also want to support them in discovering that the bars in a bar model need not remain proportional in order to represent their assigned quantities.

Featured Connections

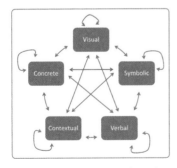 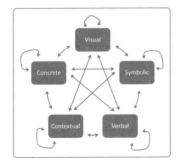 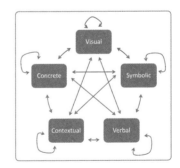

Source: Lesh, Post, & Behr (1987).

As with the number line work in Activity 2.3, connecting the concrete, visual, symbolic, and context representations as described in this activity may take time. Begin by asking students to **Build the Equation** by representing the given equation, in or out of context, with the linking cubes. Once students have built the concrete model, ask them to Write a Word Problem if context was not already provided. And finally, move into having them Create a Diagram to connect the visual and symbolic representations typically used with bar models. This progression will assist students in gradually gaining mastery over the use of bar models as problem-solving tools for any number set and operation.

ASSOCIATIVE PROPERTY OF ADDITION WITH THREE TOWERS

K   1   2   3+

Materials

- Linking cubes placed in containers for small groups of students
- Work mats for each student (heavy paper or fun foam)

Organization (physical)

- **Getting Started:** Place the containers of linking cubes in the center of each group for all to use.
- **Winding Down:** Ask students to tidy up their workspace, making sure all cubes are put back in the container and work mats are stacked on top.

Mathematical Purpose

Students explore the **associative property of addition** as they add three one-digit numbers together, noting that one can add in any order and the sum remains the same.

Manipulative Illustrated

Linking Cubes (available from multiple sources)

Steps

1. Ask students to work with a partner to build three linking cube trains with the lengths of five, three, and seven units.

2. Ask students to snap two of the trains together and then count the total. Spotlight different students' work to highlight the different pairs that could have been combined. As students share out, record their thinking for all to see 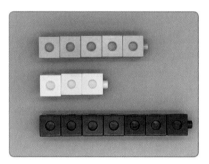 so that students may compare and contrast the strategies. To support students' thinking, ask guiding questions:

   - *Which two towers did you combine first?*
   - *How many did they add up to?*
   - *How many cubes do you have in all?*
   - *What if you started by putting together two other towers?*
   - *Would the total still be the same?*

3. Repeat with other numbers. After a couple of rounds, use the Write a Word Problem strategy to add context to the activity. Example:

Write a Word Problem (sample)

"Ana is going on a trip and needs pet sitters. She has 5 dogs, 3 cats, and 7 fish. Last time she sent the dogs and cats to her mom's house and the fish to her uncle's house. This time she is sending the dogs to her mom's house and the cats and fish to her uncle's house. Is the total number of pets the same either way? Show your thinking with linking cubes."

Ask students to pretend that the cubes are pets and to try adding them in different orders. Continue asking guiding questions such as the following:

- *What happens when you combine in different orders?*
- *Do you still get the same total?*

4. Finally, select one number trio and ask students to use the Make a Sketch strategy to combine the concrete, visual, and symbolic representations. Then use the Caption Your Picture strategy to add the verbal representation. Students may label this picture as the "Add in Any Order" picture or something along those lines.

5. Revisit this activity frequently as a warm-up or as a sponge activity.

6. *Extension:* Students may solve two-digit addition problems by snapping together groups of ten to have several tens and ones.

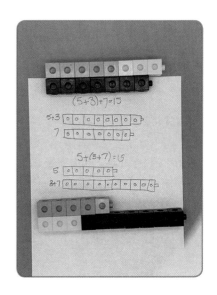

Why This Manipulative?

Linking cubes provide a great avenue for conveying the associative property because they snap together and maintain their individual quantities. Furthermore, the use of color to distinguish each quantity helps students visualize the distinct quantities as they are being combined in different orders. Focusing on the properties of operations in the early years provides a critical foundation for future work with operations and in algebra. Most immediately, understanding the associative property supports students with mental math strategies (e.g., knowing one can make a ten by adding 3 + 7 can be very helpful).

Developing Understanding

In the beginning, encourage students to experiment with first adding different pairs of numbers, then adding the third number. Ask students to compare their work with that of their group-mates so they can see that there are different start places when adding three numbers. This process will be even more meaningful when connected to mental math strategies, as mentioned earlier.

Adding context to this activity will help students gain an appreciation for using math to describe real-life situations, further increasing their understanding of the usefulness of the associative property. Ask students to add context to this activity to further their perceptions of the usefulness for the properties of operations.

Featured Connection

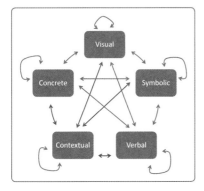 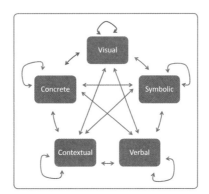 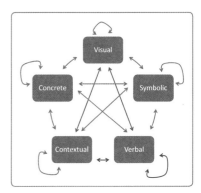

Source: Lesh, Post, & Behr (1987).

In this activity, students connect all five modes of representation. First they use the Write a Word Problem strategy to verbally connect the concrete work they are doing with the cubes to context. Next, they Make a Sketch to connect the concrete and visual representations, which is especially useful for looking at multiple problems they complete over time. Finally, as they Caption the Picture, they create a generalization that will hold true in a variety of situations since adding three (or more) numbers in any order supports their work with mental math, solving multistep arithmetic problems, and solving word problems. Whenever possible, ask students to record their work using these steps to increase the likelihood that they will internalize the notion that you can add in any order.

"GROUPS OF" MULTIPLICATION

| K | 1 | 2 | 3+ |

Materials

- Linking cubes placed in containers for small groups of students
- Work mats for each student (heavy paper or fun foam)
- Blank paper for students to record their work

Organization (physical)

- **Getting Started:** Place the containers of linking cubes in the center of each group for all to use.
- **Winding Down:** Ask students to tidy up their workspace, making sure all cubes are put back in the container and work mats are stacked on top.

Mathematical Purpose

Students add three one-digit numbers together, noting that one can add in any order and the sum remains the same.

Manipulative Illustrated

Linking Cubes (available from multiple sources)

Steps

1. Ask students to work individually or with a partner, using linking cubes to build as many single-color units of three as they can.

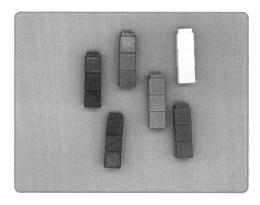

2. Provide a contextual situation for working with units of three. Example:

> T-shirts come in packs of three. How many T-shirts are in one pack? Two packs? Three packs? ... Ten packs?

3. Ask students to pretend the units of three are packs of T-shirts and to figure out how many T-shirts are in one through ten packs. They should record their work as they go. To support students' thinking, ask guiding questions such as the following:

   - *How many T-shirts are in one pack? Two packs? Three packs? ... Ten packs?*
   - *What do you notice?*
   - *Do you see any patterns?*
   - *What might be a good way to capture what you're noticing?*

4. Ask students to Make a Sketch of their linked cubes, showing multiples of three for each pack of T-shirts. Then students should Name Your Model by writing a repeated addition or multiplication sentence to show how many T-shirts are found in different numbers of packs.

5. Repeat this activity several times in short bursts. Use a different unit and context each time. This activity is especially well suited as a warm-up or sponge activity. Eventually, ask students to engage in the Write a Word Problem strategy so that they, themselves, are connecting to context.

Why This Manipulative?

Linking cubes provide a great way to develop the concept of unitizing since they have the quality of snapping together. In this case, students can use them to help distinguish between the functions of each factor. Unlike addition, where each addend has a similar function, in multiplication each factor's role is unique. One factor identifies the unit size, and the other factor is the multiplier, indicating the number of times the unit is being increased or reduced. This distinction provides a foundation for future work with operations and with algebra.

Developing Understanding

In this activity, be sure to emphasize the different roles each factor plays. Allow students to create units, combine units, and compose stories to playfully explore the concepts of multiplication. Wait a few rounds before introducing the symbolic notation in order to avoid the common misconception that factors play similar roles in the same way that addends have similar roles. This distinction is critical for future success. Also, be careful about the way you introduce repeated addition. Repeated addition is *not* the same as multiplication; rather, it is one way to interpret multiplication. If students overgeneralize multiplication as repeated addition, this will cause confusion in future studies.

Featured Connection

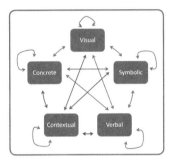 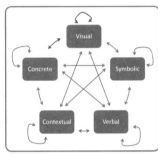 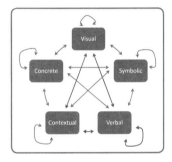

Source: Lesh, Post, & Behr (1987).

Although this activity engages students in using multiple representations such as Make a Sketch and Name Your Model, the primary emphasis centers on the Write a Word Problem strategy where students are to connect their concrete, visual, symbolic, and verbal representations to contextual situations. You provide the context at first, but eventually, students should engage in creating the context for this work. This process will help students grapple with the different roles of the two factors, with one being a multiplier and the other being the multiplicand, or quantity for each set. Students will make great progress in understanding these distinct roles when they generate the context themselves.

Notes

_____

_____

_____

_____

Materials

- Virtual Linking Cubes app (or physical linking cubes in containers and work mats)

Organization (virtual)

- **Getting Started:** Ensure students know how to use the virtual linking cubes. Review annotation tools, taking screenshots, and so on.
- **Winding Down:** Take screenshots to save student work.

Mathematical Purpose

Students explore the commutative property of multiplication while using linking cubes to further understand the unique role of each factor.

Activity 2.7 Resources

- *Commutative Property of Multiplication (3 × 9 vs. 9 × 3)* Activity Video

 To access resource visit resources.corwin.com/ MasteringMathManips/ K-3

Manipulative Illustrated

Unifix® Cubes app from Didax: www.didax.com/apps/unifix

Steps

1. Post these two expressions: 3 × 9 and 9 × 3.

3 × 9   9 × 3

   Ask students what they notice and wonder about these two expressions. Listen to see if anyone possesses an emerging understanding of commutativity.

2. Ask students to represent 3 × 9 or 9 × 3 with linking cubes. Specifically look for students or pairs who interpret this differently.

3. Select two examples to be shared out—one that demonstrates three units of nine and another that demonstrates nine units of three. Ask students to compare and contrast these two models. Note that both have the same total but they behave differently.

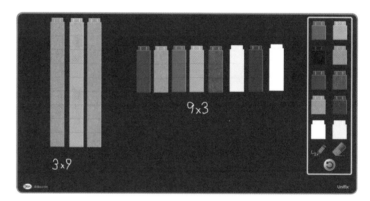

4. Repeat with at least two more examples, this time asking each pair of students to demonstrate both expressions.

5. With the final example, ask students to use the Write a Word Problem strategy to compose context problems that illustrate the distinction, either verbally or in writing. For example:

3 × 9 shows three bags of cookies with nine cookies each. 9 × 3 shows nine bags of cookies with three cookies each.

6. Repeat this activity several times over the course of a few days. Students' understanding of the roles of the factors and the notion of commutativity will evolve over time.

Why This Manipulative?

Because of their ability to snap together, linking cubes provide an excellent means for unitizing. This is especially important when exploring the commutative property of multiplication since the changing role of the factors is central in helping students develop conceptual understanding. For example, although 3 × 9 and 9 × 3 result in the same product (27), they do not behave the same since one is centered on units of three while the other uses units of nine.

Developing Understanding

As with Activity 2.6, be sure to distinguish the roles of the factors. One factor tells the unit size while the other reveals the number of units. Although the order of the factors in a number sentence does not necessarily indicate which factor is the multiplier and which is the multiplicand, students must realize that the roles switch with the commutative property. In U.S. classrooms, we generally consider the first factor as the multiplier and the second as the multiplicand. For this activity, you will find it helpful to make this distinction so that all students are referencing the same numbers when they talk about their findings.

As with the previous activity in this chapter, asking students to attend to context will make a huge impact on their understanding. When working with symbolic symbols, students may not internalize the need to know that although the product is the same either way, the two expressions do not represent the same situation. Context makes a huge difference in understanding what's going on with the factors.

Featured Connection

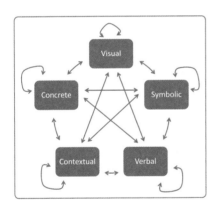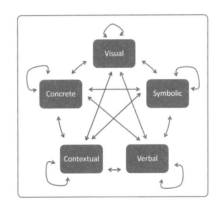

Source: Lesh, Post, & Behr (1987).

In this activity, students first engage in the Build the Equation strategy to connect from symbolic to concrete representations. This is the first step to building understanding of what the symbols are "saying" when looking at commutative pairs. To further build understanding, students use the Create a Word Problem strategy to highlight the connection between physical, verbal, and contextual representations. After creating a concrete representation of the commutative property, creating a word problem helps students verbalize a context in which the order of the factors matters. In doing so, students must make a distinction between the roles of the factors, an important idea in multiplication.

Materials

- Virtual linking cubes (or physical linking cubes in containers and work mats)

Organization (virtual)

- **Getting Started:** Ensure students know how to use the virtual linking cubes. Review annotation tools, taking screenshots, and so on.
- **Winding Down:** Take screenshots to save student work.

Mathematical Purpose

Students explore the measurement interpretation of division as they use linking cubes to make units from a given quotient (start number).

Manipulative Illustrated

Unifix® Cubes app from Didax:
www.didax.com/apps/unifix

Steps

1. Post the problem 15 ÷ 5 for students to view.

   | 15 ÷ 5 |

   Ask students to talk to a partner about what this means. When back together, ask probing questions to detect students' thinking such as the following:

   - *What does this symbol [point to the division sign] mean?*
   - *What does it mean to divide something up?*
   - *What does the 15 tell us?*
   - *What does the 5 tell us?*

2. Ask students to use the Build the Equation strategy using linking cubes to illustrate 15 ÷ 5. As students work, look for students who make three groups of five and for others who make five groups of three. Select two students, one for each of these interpretations, to share out when the whole group comes back together.

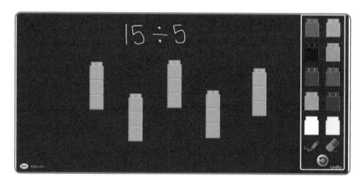

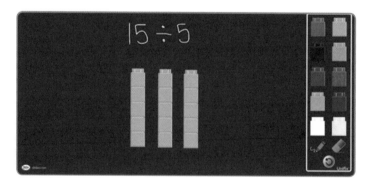

3. When students are finished, ask your selected two students to share their thinking. Then ask the class to discuss what they notice and what they wonder. To support students' thinking, ask guiding questions such as the following:

   » *Which of you had the same interpretation as [Student A]?*

   » *Which of you had the same interpretation as [Student B]?*

   » *Which of these is correct?*

   » *How do you know?*

   » *Can you give me a situation where [Student A]'s interpretation would make sense?*

   » *Can you give me a situation where [Student B]'s interpretation would make sense?*

   The goal of this conversation is to help students realize there are two different interpretations for this division problem. One interpretation is to make the number of groups as indicated by the divisor, often called "fair share" division. The other interpretation is to make groups the size indicated by the divisor, often called "measurement" division. Both are completely acceptable.

4. Give the students another problem, say 12 ÷ 4. Ask them to work in pairs to show both interpretations. Together, they should use the Write a Word Problem strategy to come up with a context that would show how both are correct (see the accompanying photo for an example).

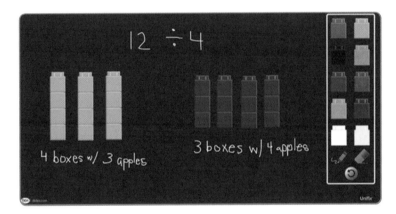

Why This Manipulative?

Linking cubes lend themselves to unitizing, which is an important feature for making the distinction between partitive (fair share) and quotative (measurement) division. Students can use the linking cubes to create and/or pull out equal groups, as indicated by the divisor. When using linking cubes, students can simply snap together cubes to create same-sized units until all the cubes are used up. If there are any extra cubes that can't make a full unit, those are the remainders.

Developing Understanding

This activity is especially powerful in helping students make the distinction between the two interpretations for division, partitive (fair share) and quotative (measurement). While facilitating the opening problem, you will want to help students understand that both of these interpretations are completely acceptable and useful for different situations. You may need to provide several guided opportunities for students to make the distinction between "making fair shares" (putting the cubes into the number of groups indicated by the divisor) and "making units" (putting the cubes into equal-sized units as indicated by the divisor). Repeat this as many times and as frequently as necessary.

By adding context to the problems, you will increase the likelihood that students will eventually grasp the distinction. Examples you may use include the following (all examples for 15 ÷ 5):

- 5 bags with 3 cookies each vs. 3 bags with 5 cookies each
- 5 boxes with 3 markers each vs. 3 boxes with 5 markers each
- 5 tables with 3 students each vs. 3 tables with 5 students each
- 5 fishbowls with 3 fish each vs. 3 fishbowls with 5 fish each
- 5 pumpkins weighing 3 pounds each vs. 3 pumpkins weighing 5 pounds each

Featured Connection

In this activity, students first use the Build the Equation strategy to connect the symbolic equation to a concrete representation. This powerful strategy assists students in arriving to the conclusion that there are two ways to interpret the given division problem. After

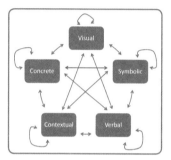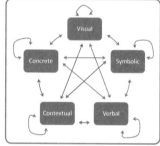

Source: Lesh, Post, & Behr (1987).

students have discovered the two-interpretations structure for division, they use the Write a Word Problem strategy to connect their existing concrete and symbolic representations to the contextual and verbal representations. By adding context to the existing problem, students are able to grapple with the notion that there are two different ways that the dividend can "behave" for a given division problem.

Notes

_____

_____

_____

_____

_____

_____

_____

Notes

Materials

- Virtual linking cubes (or physical linking cubes in containers and work mats)

Organization (virtual)

- **Getting Started:** Ensure students know how to use the virtual linking cubes. Review annotation tools, taking screenshots, and so on.
- **Winding Down:** Take screenshots to save student work.

Mathematical Purpose

Students use linking cubes to represent various scaled units in bar graphs.

Manipulative Illustrated

Unifix® Cubes app from Didax: www.didax.com/apps/unifix

Steps

1. Ask a question of the class that will provide **data** for two to four categories, preferably between zero and eight data points per category. Questions that might be asked include the following:

   » What color are your eyes?

   » What color is your hair?

   » What ice cream flavor do you like best: vanilla, strawberry, or chocolate?

   » Which superhero do you like best: Batman, Spider-Man, Superman, or Wonder Woman?

   » What kind of shoes are you wearing: lace-up, Velcro®, slip-on, or no shoes?

2. Once the data are collected and tallied, ask students to use the Create a Diagram strategy to represent the data using linking cubes. Each category of data should have its own tower (see the accompanying photo for an example). Students should also include a title and the categories on their graphs.

3. Students may benefit from creating several class graphs prior to working in pairs or individually.

4. *Extension:* Each linking cube may represent a multiple, in which case the scale would need to be included.

5. *Extension:* Ask students to use the Write a Word Problem strategy to ask questions based on the data in this graph.

Why This Manipulative?

Linking cubes can be snapped together to represent specific quantities, and in the case of bar graphs, each tower has the appearance of a bar. This can be especially useful when comparing the data in two categories. Students often struggle with "how many more" and "how many fewer" questions. When comparing two quantities, students can simply snap off the "extra" cubes to examine how many extras there are to help them determine the **more/fewer** relationships between data points.

Developing Understanding

Data analysis in the primary grades allows students to investigate and apply numerous mathematical concepts. Some of these include counting, skip counting, comparing, solving word problems, comparing quantities, determining "how many more" and "how many less," and so on. Using concrete objects such as linking cubes to create concrete representations of data is especially useful when connecting to these number concepts.

Here are some tips for creating graphs with linking cubes:

- When students represent data with linking cubes, be sure they line up the cubes correctly so they have a common start point, either at the bottom (for vertical bar graphs) or on the left-hand side (for horizontal bar graphs).

- Students can collect the data using the cubes by simply asking each student to add one cube to the tower that corresponds with their "vote."

- Linking cubes are unmarked. Therefore, each data point becomes anonymous, an important idea for young children to grasp. The unit of observation is the entire group, not the individuals within that group.

Featured Connection

Because students are actually creating graphs, this activity uses the Create a Diagram strategy, highlighting the connections between the concrete, visual, and symbolic representations. Students take the data set and create a visual representation of the data

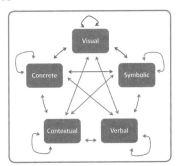 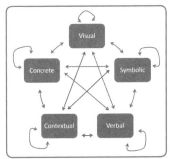

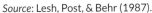

Source: Lesh, Post, & Behr (1987).

using the linking cubes. To take this strategy a step further, students may Make a Sketch of the graph on blank paper or graph paper. This will further enhance their understanding of creating graphs.

And finally, to extend student learning, you might ask students to use the Write a Word Problem strategy to connect verbal and contextual representations to this complex work. Primary students should both answer and ask questions about data, and this activity provides a perfect avenue for that.

Materials

- Linking cubes placed in containers for small groups of students

- Work mats for each student (heavy paper or fun foam)

- A list of classroom objects to measure (pencils, books, tables, papers, etc.)

- Recording sheet for each student (list classroom objects before printing copies)

Organization (physical)

- **Getting Started:** Place the containers of linking cubes in the center of each group for all to use.

- **Winding Down:** Ask students to tidy up their workspace, making sure all cubes are put back in the container and work mats are stacked on top.

Mathematical Purpose

Students explore concepts of linear measurement as they use linking cubes as nonstandard rulers.

Activity 2.10 Resources

Measuring Trains Recording Sheet

 To access resource visit resources.corwin.com/ MasteringMathManips/ K-3

Manipulative Illustrated

Linking Cubes (available from multiple sources)

Steps

1. Talk with students about what it means to measure something. Generate many different measurable attributes such as length, weight, capacity/liquid volume, height, distance, and so on. Student examples may be more concrete like "how far I drive to school," "how heavy my dog is," or "how tall my dad is."

2. Next, put out a variety of classroom materials that can be measured using units of length such as a piece of paper, a pencil, a glue stick, and a book. Then pull out a container of linking cubes and ask students how they might use the linking cubes to measure the lengths (or heights or widths) of those objects. To support students' thinking, ask guiding questions such as the following:

   - *How might you use the linking cubes to measure this **side** [point to one side] of the paper?*

   - *Would it be easier to keep them separate or stacked?*

   - *How would you "match up" the cube train and the **edge** of the paper?*

   - *How many cubes long is that side of the paper?*

3. Once students seem acquainted with the measuring process, ask them to work individually or in pairs, using the linking cube trains to measure the lengths of the objects listed. (*Optional:* You may have students list their own objects.)

4. After students have completed the task, ask them to compare their measurements with one another to check for accuracy. When they have different measurements, they should re-measure with a train and then agree on the length.

Why This Manipulative?

Linking cubes provide an especially useful way for students to engage in nonstandard measurement using a tool that resembles a ruler. Although using linking cube trains to measure lengths may not completely translate to ruler use, they make a great transition. In addition, students should be reminded that measurement units may be iterated with no gaps and no overlaps, a built-in feature when using linking cube trains.

Developing Understanding

During the introduction of this activity, be sure to emphasize common measurement tool techniques such as the following:

- Make sure all of the cubes are linked tightly so there are no gaps between them.
- Line up the end of the linking cube train with the edge of the object being measured.
- Match up the length of the object being measured with the linking cube train.
- Accurately count the number of units that match the length of the object.

Note that linking cubes have the added feature of providing students with countable objects rather than simple tick marks on the ruler. When using rulers, young students tend to view the tick marks themselves, rather than the spaces between the tick marks, as the units. Using linking cube trains helps to avoid this misconception during the early stages of developing measurement understanding. Depending on the grade level and age with which you are working, you may want to use this experience to transfer understanding to the use of a ruler.

Finally, many students independently discover that they can use linking cube trains to measure the perimeter of objects such as books and tables. Encourage this discovery and talk about how they are putting together multiple linear measurements to find the distance around the object.

Featured Connection

This activity lends itself to the Create a Diagram strategy as students are translating their measurements with concrete objects to symbols that are recorded on the measurement chart.

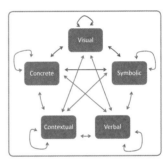

Source: Lesh, Post, & Behr (1987).

Notes

_____

_____

_____

_____

_____

_____

_____

CLOSING REFLECTION: LINKING CUBES

How do I use linking cubes in my classroom now? What concepts do I use them to teach?

_____

_____

_____

_____

_____

_____

_____

_____

_____

_____

_____

What new ways have I found to use linking cubes to better support students' understanding?

_____

_____

_____

_____

_____

_____

_____

_____

_____

_____

_____

_____

What are my goals to make linking cubes a more regular part of my instruction?

_____

_____

_____

_____

_____

_____

_____

_____

_____

_____

_____

Chapter 3
Cuisenaire® Rods

INTRODUCTION

Understanding Cuisenaire Rods

Cuisenaire Rods have been a part of mathematics teaching for almost 100 years. They are proportional manipulatives made from a series of rods of increasing length. The white unit cube (1 cm per side) is the smallest piece. The pieces increase in length by 1-cm increments through the tenth (orange) rod, which is 10 cm long with a 1-cm² cross section. The color sequence for Cuisenaire Rods is fixed. The rods are available in traditional wood or plastic, with end connectors, and in a jumbo size (based on a 2-cm cube) for young learners.

Cuisenaire Rods are particularly effective in teaching these topics:

- Composing and decomposing
- Properties of operations
- Basic addition, **subtraction**, **multiplication**, and **division**
- Fractions
- Problem solving with **tape diagrams**

Introducing Cuisenaire Rods to Students

Encourage learners to explore the rods using the *Notice and Wonder Thinking Routine* (described in the introductory chapter) before starting to teach with them. Students may notice that same-size rods are also the same color. They may build staircases, highlighting the constant difference in length. They may create trains where they explore combinations of rods with the same total length. Encourage students to wonder about the relationships between different-colored rods. These can be additive relationships:

What two-rod combinations are the same length as yellow (5) or orange (10)?

Or they can be multiplicative relationships:

> How many copies of red (2) does it take to make orange (10)?

These can be good informal assessments of your students' number sense and relational thinking.

Key Ideas With Cuisenaire Rods

- Cuisenaire Rods can be used as length models or as quantities.
- The linear structure of Cuisenaire Rods makes them a good tool for connecting physical representations to linear visual representations, including bar models and number lines.

In addition to the examples included here, Cuisenaire Rods can be used when working with measurement for two- and three-dimensional figures. The white cubes are 1 cm³, ideal for measuring volume, and the single-centimeter side lengths are reasonable for building and counting/calculating perimeter, area, **surface** area, and volume at these grade levels and in future grades.

Things to Consider About Cuisenaire Rods

- Cuisenaire Rods are a very flexible manipulative. Because the rods are unlabeled (other than by color), they can take on many values and show a wide range of relationships.
- Cuisenaire Rods are useful for helping students unitize. As students become confident that the yellow rod is always 5 white rods long, they can see the yellow rod as the quantity 5, rather than 5 copies of a quantity of 1.
- Be cautious about rigidly labeling the white unit cube as always having a value of 1 as this can make it difficult to view the pieces flexibly later. As students learn about the rods, consider asking them the value of various colored rods if the white unit cube has a value of 2 or $\frac{1}{2}$ or another age-appropriate quantity. This is why the rods are not labeled with a number value.

Alternatives to Commercial Cuisenaire Rods

Cuisenaire Rods are built from a 1-cm unit cube. This means centimeter grid paper provides a useful alternative if rods are not available. Students can use the same 10 colors (white, red, light green, purple, yellow, dark green, black, brown, blue, and orange) to color strips of the same length (1 cm to 10 cm in order). Students can then cut apart and manipulate the strips. Students who have more experience with the rods might simply sketch the relationships without first working with a physical rod.

For base-ten mathematics, commercial alternatives to Cuisenaire Rods include the Mortensen® Math Blocks and the Math-U-See® Blocks. Both of these sets of rods incorporate quantities drawn in for each size rod and include a "flat," similar to base-ten blocks, most frequently used to represent 100.

Working With Virtual Cuisenaire Rods

Virtual Cuisenaire Rods have the advantage of an endless supply. A snapping feature is useful when making trains so rods are well aligned and lengths can be compared. As with many manipulatives, Cuisenaire Rods are proportional. Teachers should be careful that students do not resize the pieces and change the proportional relationships between the various pieces unintentionally.

Materials

- One set of Cuisenaire Rods per pair of students

- Paper for recording results (inch or centimeter grid paper allows for easy sketches for older students)

Organization (physical)

- **Getting Started:** Distribute one set of rods (in a bag or tray) per pair of students.

- **Winding Down:** Return the rods to their bag or tray, counting or attending to all slots being filled.

Mathematical Purpose

Students find number pairs that add to a given total.

Manipulative Illustrated

Cuisenaire Rods (available from multiple sources)

Steps

1. Ask students to pull out all of the dark green Cuisenaire Rods.

2. Ask students to use two smaller Cuisenaire Rods to form a two-car train (number pair) that is the same length as one dark green Cuisenaire Rod. To facilitate students' thinking, ask guiding questions such as the following:

   - *Is your train the same as or different than mine?*

   - *Do you see other trains that match yours?*

   - *How did you make sure your two-car train is the same length as one dark green rod? [For example, "I made sure they were pushed together and that they started and ended at the same place as the dark green train."]*

3. Ask students to repeat this process until they have found as many two-car trains as possible that are the same length as one dark green Cuisenaire Rod.

4. As students work, use guiding questions like these to help them explain their thinking:

   - *As you put together two-car trains, how can you tell they are the same length as one dark green rod?*

   - *Is there more than one way you can use two rods to total the dark green rod?*

   - *When you look at all the two-car trains that are the same length as one dark green rod, do you see any patterns?*

   - *How might you use patterns to help you check to be sure you have all the possible two-car trains?*

5. Repeat this activity with other rods (e.g., start with orange or blue).

6. When students are ready, ask them to use the Make a Sketch strategy to record their discoveries with pictures, numbers, and words. Ask them to use the Caption Your Picture strategy to assign numerical values to each rod to assist in their recordings.

7. *Extension:* Students may create a table to indicate the different number pairs that total the dark green rod (or any color selected).

Why This Manipulative?

Cuisenaire Rods are useful for building notions of composing and decomposing quantities for several reasons. First, they echo the shape of linking cubes and lend themselves to linear representations, eventually connecting to number lines. Second, the size increments between pieces are clear, so there is a straightforward structure to the work. Third, the rods are useful for working with **part-part-whole** thinking with whole numbers and will eventually be used for understanding the part-whole relationships with fractions.

Developing Understanding

It is important for students to compare quantities using a variety of tools. Young students often use counters that represent distinct single units such as two-color counters, linking cubes, and square tiles. Activities like this one help students transfer their thinking about counting, composing, and decomposing with whole numbers to tools that are not distinct single units. With Cuisenaire Rods, they begin to see the attribute of length as a countable, additive attribute.

For students to be successful with this number pairs activity, prior exposure to Cuisenaire Rods will be helpful. Since students will be using the Cuisenaire Rods to make a direct connection between length and quantity, be sure they understand that the smallest rod has a value of 1, the next-sized rod has a value of 2, and so on. Some primary teachers find it helpful to create a chart to help students see the corresponding lengths, which are color-coded, and their relative values when the smallest rod has a value of 1.

Please note that although young learners will not be using these units flexibly, the rods will eventually carry different values, depending on the context. For example, the smallest rod may have a value of 2, 5, 100, $\frac{1}{2}$, $\frac{1}{4}$, and so on. When the unit is redefined for a set of Cuisenaire Rods, students must then determine the relative values for each rod in the set.

The way you, as the teacher, talk about the rods is important. Take care to not inadvertently indicate that the smallest rod will *always* carry a value of 1. Leading with color, then talking about the value today, is an effective strategy for teachers.

Featured Connection

Use the Make a Sketch strategy to help students see the connection between the concrete objects (Cuisenaire Rods) and visual representations (sketches). Use the Caption Your Picture strategy to help students see the connection between the Cuisenaire Rods and the expressions that represent each of the addend pairs to compose six. Students can use blank paper if proportionality is not important. If proportional rods are desirable, either inch or centimeter grid paper can be provided to students to color in the

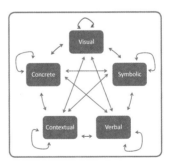 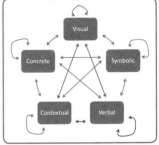

Source: Lesh, Post, & Behr (1987).

quantity represented by each rod, indicating the relationship between each two-car train and the whole. Students may also assign symbolic notation to each rod, further indicating that the larger quantity is composed of the combination of the two smaller quantities.

CREATING BAR MODELS FOR ADDITION

| K | 1 | 2 | 3+ |

Materials

- One set of Cuisenaire Rods per pair of students

- Paper for recording results (inch or centimeter grid paper allows for easy sketches for older students)

- Activity sheet for each student

Organization (physical)

- **Getting Started:** Distribute one set of rods (in a bag or tray) per pair of students.

- **Winding Down:** Return the rods to their bag or tray, counting or attending to all slots being filled.

Mathematical Purpose

Students use Cuisenaire Rods to represent "join" situations with the missing quantity in different places.

Activity 3.2 Resources

- *Creating Bar Models for Addition* Activity Sheet

- *Creating Bar Models for Addition* Activity Video

online resources ↖ To access resources visit resources.corwin.com/ MasteringMathManips/ K-3

Manipulative Illustrated

Cuisenaire Rods (available from multiple sources)

Steps

1. Distribute the rods and problem page to the class. Read the first problem together and discuss the situation.

> Maria had 6 balloons. Juan had 3. How many balloons did they have in all?

Prior to working on a solution, ask students questions about the situation, such as these:

- *What is this story about?*

- *What are the quantities and relationships between those quantities?*

- *What is the question asking you to do?*

2. Ask students to use the rods to represent the first problem situation. Share the different approaches students used and discuss the ways each representation helps them understand the problem situation. Encourage students to show each quantity on a separate line when they draw their pictures. To prompt students' thinking, ask guiding questions such as the following:

- *How is each quantity represented?*

- *Which rod represents Maria's balloons?*

- *Which rod represents Juan's balloons?*

- *Which rod represents the total number of balloons?*

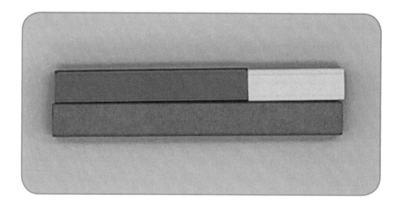

3. Ask students to use the Make a Sketch and Name Your Model strategies to represent the first problem on the recording sheet. Students should include sketches of the bars, label each bar, and record a corresponding equation.

4. Allow students time to complete the rest of the problems on the page. They may need support with reading the problems. Continue asking the guiding questions listed earlier, as warranted, focusing particularly on how each quantity is represented with the rods.

5. Bring students together to discuss the last two problems at the bottom of the page.
   - *What do you notice and wonder about these three situations?*
   - *What do you notice about where the missing number appears in each situation?*

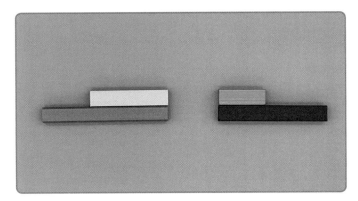

6. *Extension:* To explore similar word problems for larger number sets, consider using the Thinking Blocks web page at www.mathplayground.com/thinkingblocks.html.

Why This Manipulative?

Cuisenaire Rods are useful for highlighting the constant difference between quantities. The fact that there is a different-colored rod for each value means that students easily distinguish between the quantities in the problem situation, representing each with the corresponding rod. This lays the foundation for future work with other problem situation types involving whole numbers. Specifically, when students work with "join" problem types, the Cuisenaire Rods will help them see how quantities are joined to create a larger total. Note that eventually students will use Cuisenaire Rods to represent alternative values that are not necessarily connected to the actual value specified by the rod, so continue to name the rods by their colors, assigning values as needed in each activity.

Although Cuisenaire Rods best exemplify the notion of a bar model, especially when the bars no longer need to be proportional, young learners may find it helpful to use linking cubes or unit squares to explore beginning bar model concepts when still working with units of one. See Activity 2.4 in this book for an example of using linking cubes as bar models.

Developing Understanding

Developing a strong understanding of numerical relationships builds a critical foundation for number and operations in base ten as well as algebraic reasoning. Concrete experiences, such as described in this activity, facilitate student understanding in two ways. First, students understand that there is a constant difference between quantities. Second, students see that rods can be joined together to represent larger quantities, which lays the foundation for both composing and decomposing quantities in problem situations.

Note that in this activity the missing number changes positions each time. You may want to slow this process down by providing a few problems with the missing number in the same position each time to provide students with opportunities to detect patterns for when the missing number is in the "result" position or in one of the addend positions.

Featured Connection

Use the Make a Sketch and Name Your Model strategies to connect concrete, visual, and abstract representations inherent in solving word problems using bar models. The Cuisenaire Rods lend themselves to bar modeling, and this lesson is ideal for the beginning stages of "combine" situation types. By adding names to the model (e.g., expressions or equations), students focus on the constant difference feature of the Cuisenaire Rods. As you work with students on seeing the connections between concrete, pictorial, and abstract representations, focus on the relative sizes of the Cuisenaire Rods and the quantitative values each represents.

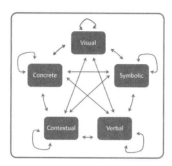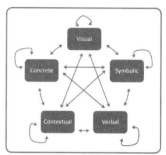

Source: Lesh, Post, & Behr (1987).

As an extension, you may want to ask students to use the Create a Diagram strategy to connect the work they are doing with the manipulatives to a word problem structure. For example, students might create a simple diagram that displays the structure of their equations when the missing number is in different positions.

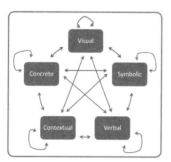

Source: Lesh, Post, & Behr (1987).

Note that bar models are exceptionally useful for "part-part-whole" situation types, where the addition is not necessarily active, as with "join" situation types. For active situations, we recommend using visual representations such as number lines or number tracks where the act of combining is more explicitly recorded.

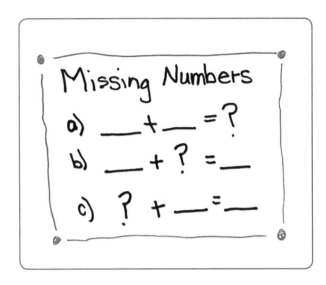

Missing Numbers

a) __ + __ = ?

b) __ + ? = __

c) ? + __ = __

Notes

CREATING BAR MODELS FOR SUBTRACTION

| K | 1 | 2 | 3+ |

Materials

- Virtual Cuisenaire Rods (or physical Cuisenaire Rods and work mats)
- Recording sheet for each student

Organization (virtual)

- **Getting Started:** Ensure students know how to use the virtual Cuisenaire Rods. Review annotation tools, taking screenshots, and so on.
- **Winding Down:** Take screenshots to save student work.

Mathematical Purpose

Students use Cuisenaire Rods to represent "separate" situations with the missing quantity in different places.

Activity 3.3 Resources

Creating Bar Models for Subtraction Recording Sheet

 To access resource visit resources.corwin.com/ MasteringMathManips/ K-3

Manipulative Illustrated

Math Bars app from Math Playground: www.mathplayground.com/ mathbars.html

Steps

1. Distribute the recording sheet to students. Read the first problem together and discuss the situation.

> Raul counted 7 soccer balls in the playground basket. When he looked later, there were only 2. How many were taken?

Prior to working on a solution, ask students questions about the situation, such as these:

- *What is this story about?*
- *What are the quantities and relationships between those quantities?*
- *What is the question asking you to do?*

2. Ask students to use the rods to represent the first problem situation. Share the different approaches students used and discuss the ways each representation helps them understand the problem situation. Encourage students to show each quantity on a separate line when they draw their pictures. To prompt students' thinking, ask guiding questions such as the following:

- *How is each quantity represented?*
- *Which rod represents the number of soccer balls at first?*
- *Which rod represents the number of soccer balls that were left?*
- *Which rod represents the total number of soccer balls that were taken?*

3. Ask students to use the Make a Sketch and Name Your Model strategies to represent the first problem on the recording sheet. Students should include sketches of the bars, label each bar, and record a corresponding equation.

4. Allow students time to complete the rest of the problems on the page. They may need support with reading the problems. Continue asking the guiding questions listed earlier, as warranted, focusing particularly on how each quantity is represented with the rods.

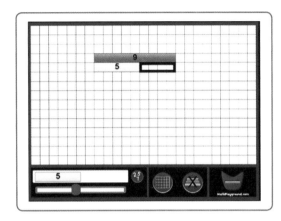

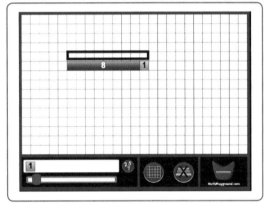

5. Bring students together to discuss the last two problems at the bottom of the page.
   - *What do you notice and wonder about these three situations?*
   - *What do you notice about where the missing number appears in each situation?*

6. *Extension:* To explore similar word problems for larger number sets, consider using the Thinking Blocks web page at www.mathplayground.com/thinkingblocks.html.

Why This Manipulative?

Cuisenaire Rods are useful for highlighting the constant difference between quantities. The fact that there is a different-colored rod for each value means that students easily distinguish between the quantities in the problem situation, representing each with the corresponding rod. This lays the foundation for future work with other problem situation types involving whole numbers. Specifically, when students work with "separate" problem types, the Cuisenaire Rods will help them see that quantities can be separated to represent parts of larger quantities. Note that eventually students will use Cuisenaire Rods to represent alternative values, so continue to name the rods by their colors, assigning values as needed in each activity.

Note that the Math Playground app used in the examples does not have a notation device in the "free" version. Therefore, you may want to ask students to take a screenshot and then add the "missing number bar" using annotation tools on their computers, as was illustrated previously.

Although Cuisenaire Rods best exemplify the notion of a bar model, especially when the bars no longer need to be proportional, young learners may find it helpful to use linking cubes or unit squares to explore initial subtraction concepts when still working with units of one. Activity 2.4 in this book provides an example of using linking cubes as bar models, a transition lesson to this one.

Developing Understanding

Developing a strong understanding of numerical relationships builds a critical foundation for number and operations in base ten as well as algebraic reasoning. Concrete experiences, such as described in this activity, facilitate student understanding in two ways. First, students understand that there is a constant difference between quantities. Second, students see that rods can be joined together to represent larger quantities, which lays the foundation for both composing and decomposing quantities in problem situations.

The problems presented in this activity have the missing number in different places each time. Students may need additional support in working with one type of problem at a time prior to working with sets of problems where the missing number is in different places, as they appear here.

Featured Connection

In this activity, students use the Make a Sketch and Name Your Model strategies to connect concrete, visual, and abstract representations inherent in solving word problems using bar models. The Cuisenaire Rods lend themselves to bar modeling, and this lesson is

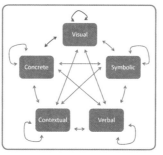

Source: Lesh, Post, & Behr (1987).

ideal for the beginning stages of "combine" situation types. By adding names to the model (e.g., expressions or equations), students focus on the constant difference feature of the Cuisenaire Rods. As you work with students on seeing the connections between concrete, pictorial, and abstract representations, focus on the relative sizes of the Cuisenaire Rods and the quantitative value each represents.

As an extension, you may want to ask students to use the Create a Diagram strategy to connect the work they are doing with the manipulatives to a word problem structure. For example, students might create a simple diagram that displays the structure of their equations when the missing number is in different positions.

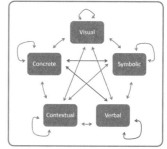

Source: Lesh, Post, & Behr (1987).

Notes

Materials

- Cuisenaire Rods, one set per pair of students
- Paper for recording results (centimeter grid paper allows for easy sketches)

Organization (physical)

- **Getting Started:** Distribute one set of rods (in a bag or tray) per pair of students.
- **Winding Down:** Return the rods to their bag or tray.

Mathematical Purpose

In this activity, students explore factors and multiples by creating single-color trains of rods. Students extend the exploration to common factors and multiples by comparing trains.

Manipulative Illustrated

Cuisenaire Rods (available from multiple sources)

Steps

1. Distribute Cuisenaire Rods and ask students to represent 12 by creating a train of rods in a single color. Share the variety of trains created and discuss them using questions such as these:

   - *How do you know each train represents 12?*
   - *What addition sentence could you write for each train?*
   - *What multiplication sentence could you write for each train?*
   - *How can you describe your trains using the words factor and product?*
   - *What do you notice about the factor pairs for each train?*

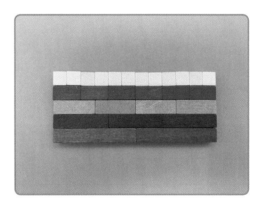

2. Ask students to create all the possible trains for other values. To limit the number of possibilities for each, choose values such as 8, 10, 15, or 16. Continue to ask guiding questions such as the ones listed in Step 1.

3. Once students have completed this task, discuss the trains students created using similar questions as in Step 1 to highlight their understanding of the multiplication, including the terms *factor* and *product*.

Why This Manipulative?

The proportional nature of Cuisenaire Rods, combined with the fact that each rod represents a different factor, makes it easy to represent equal groups situations using the rods. The single-color trains represent repeated addition or **equal groups multiplication situations**. As long as trains are the same length, they have the same product. Activity 3.5 also uses the rods to represent equal groups situations, with an emphasis on problem solving rather than factors and multiples.

Developing Understanding

In this application, students are representing multiplication using length models. As students build different trains to represent the same total, be sure to guide them in understanding the different roles of each factor. One factor tells how many rods were used while the other tells the value of each rod. This is an important transition from working with addends, where, generally speaking, both numbers have the same function.

By asking students to create multiple trains for the same quantity, you invite them to explore the notion that there are many ways to create a product using different factors. As time permits, you may want to have students detect patterns that emerge, such as what happens when the number of rods increases (e.g., the value of each rod decreases).

Featured Connection

Students use the Caption Your Picture strategy when they write a multiplication sentence for each train and explain how the trains are related. Depending on the specifics of the lesson, these captions are excellent opportunities for using vocabulary about properties of operations.

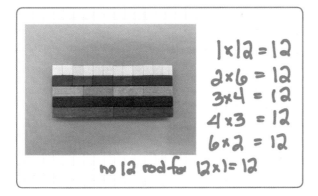
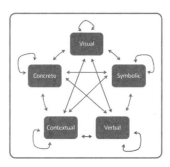
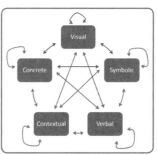

Source: Lesh, Post, & Behr (1987).

For the extension included in the "Developing Understanding" section, students may Create a Diagram to detect and display patterns that emerge, such as when one factor increases, the other decreases.

Notes

_____

_____

_____

CREATING BAR MODELS FOR EQUAL GROUPS MULTIPLICATION AND DIVISION

Materials

- Cuisenaire Rods app
- Paper for recording results (centimeter grid paper allows for easy sketches)
- Activity sheet (one for each student)

Organization (virtual)

- **Getting Started:** Ensure students can access and use the virtual tool; review annotation tools, process for taking screenshots, and other important supports.
- **Winding Down:** Use screenshots to save student work.

Mathematical Purpose

Students will use bar models to represent the equal groups interpretation for multiplication.

Activity 3.5 Resources

Creating Bar Models for Equal Groups Multiplication and Division Problems Activity Sheet

To access resource visit resources.corwin.com/ MasteringMathManips/ K-3

Manipulative Illustrated

Virtual Number Bars (Mathigon):
https://mathigon.org/polypad

Steps

> Juan received 4 book awards from the library. Each award included a $3 gift card to spend at the school book sale. How much money does Juan have to spend at the book sale?

1. Distribute the rods and problem page to the class. Read the first problem together and discuss the situation. Prior to working on a solution, ask students questions about the situation, such as these:

   - *What is this story about?*
   - *What are the quantities and relationships between those quantities?*
   - *What is the question asking you to do?*
   - *How might you use the rods to represent the problem? If the rods don't make sense for you, what other tool might you use? Build that model first, then try again with the rods.*

2. Ask students to work with a partner to create a representation of the problem with Cuisenaire Rods. Continue to ask guiding questions if needed.

3. Ask students to share their thinking and representations, and listen for their understanding of these important elements:

   - *How many groups are there? Where are these groups in your representation?*
   - *How large is each group? Where can we see this in your representation?*
   - *What is the total amount? Where does this appear in your representation?*

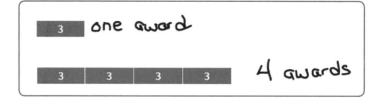

4. Use the Make a Sketch and Name Your Model strategies to support students while they sketch and label a bar model for their solution.

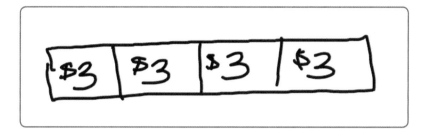

5. Repeat this cycle with the other two problems on the handout. Problems 2 and 3 are also equal groups situations, but typically described as division situations because students are figuring out the number of groups or the size of each group.

Why This Manipulative?

Visually, Cuisenaire Rods look like bar models. With smaller quantities, such as those in these problems, students can choose bars whose length represents the value in the problem. In this case, you see the light green rods (three units in length) used to represent each award. Because the rods are not marked with their length, this representation could be used for any problem with four equal groups, regardless of group size.

Developing Understanding

In equal groups situations, the two factors in the multiplication problem do different jobs. One tells the number of groups while the other tells the size of the group. The product is the total quantity or value. In the first problem, each group is an award of $3. In the second problem, each group is the flowers for one friend, and students are figuring out how many flowers each friend will receive. In the third problem, each group is four songs played for one friend, and students are figuring out how many friends can hear four songs without repetition. This range of contexts supports students to understand the wide range of situations where equal groups thinking can support their work.

You may notice that each of these problems has the "missing number" in different positions of the written equation. You may find it necessary to offer multiple opportunities for students to work with each configuration multiple times as they begin to grapple with figuring out where the missing number should be positioned. For example, your students may need additional practice and support with the multiplication version of equal groups (Problem 1) before moving on to the division variations (Problems 2 and 3). You can use this same structure to solve additional equal groups situations, remembering that the rods can have any value students choose. The examples in this activity will serve to get you started.

Featured Connection

This activity uses the Make a Sketch and Name Your Model strategies to support students while they draw and label a bar model for their solution. The images that follow show the solutions to Problems 2 and 3 on the handout. The bar model is easy to draw when beginning with Cuisenaire

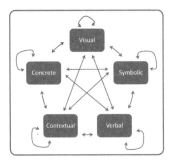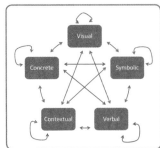

Source: Lesh, Post, & Behr (1987).

Rods because the figure already looks like a bar model. By naming the model, students connect the concrete and visual representations with the equation. Notice that the two division situations have been written both as missing-factor multiplication and as more traditional division equations. Units are included to help students see the role of each factor in the situation.

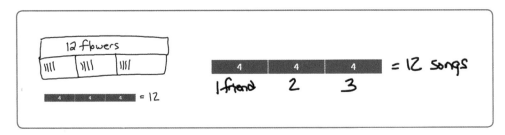

Notes

_____

_____

_____

_____

_____

_____

_____

_____

_____

_____

_____

Notes

COMMUTATIVE PROPERTY OF MULTIPLICATION (2 × 3 VS. 3 × 2)

Materials

- Cuisenaire Rods app
- Paper for recording results (inch or centimeter grid paper allows for easy sketches for older students)

Organization (virtual)

- **Getting Started:** Ensure students know how to use the virtual Cuisenaire Rods; review annotation tools, take screenshots, and so on.
- **Winding Down:** Take screenshots to save student work.

Mathematical Purpose

Students explore the connections between factors when they change positions and functions.

Manipulative Illustrated

Math Bars app from Math Playground: www.mathplayground.com/mathbars.html

Steps

1. Write the expression 2 × 3 for all students to see.

   > 2 × 3 and 3 × 2

   Ask students to use virtual manipulatives to represent the expression 2 × 3 using Cuisenaire Rods. Then ask students to represent 3 × 2. As students do this, use the *Notice and Wonder Thinking Routine* (from the introductory chapter) to prompt students' thinking. If needed, use guiding questions such as the following:

   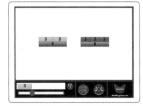

   - *How did you represent 2 × 3?*
   - *How did you represent 3 × 2?*
   - *Can you represent it a different way?*
   - *What is the same about using two rods of 3 and three rods of 2?*
   - *What is different about using two rods of 3 and three rods of 2?*

2. Next, ask students to use the Write a Word Problem strategy to connect their representations to contextual situations. Possible contexts might include number of cookies in bags, number of spiders in jars, or number of children at tables. The goal is for students to understand, for example, that three cookies in each of two bags has the same number of cookies as two cookies in each of three bags. However, although the total number of cookies is the same, the way this context plays out is not the same. In other words, the product is the same, but the factors behave differently in those two scenarios.

   Word Problem (sample)

   Jamir has 3 fishbowls with 2 fish in each bowl. Fynn has 2 fishbowls with 3 fish in each bowl. Do they have the same number of fish? How do you know?

   ---

3. Allow students time to explore other commutative pairs such 2 × 4, 2 × 5, and 3 × 3. As students work, use guiding questions like these to help them explain their thinking:

   - *How do you know the values of each rod?*
   - *Can you predict which large rod is going to match up with the trains before you're finished?*
   - *What is different about 3 × 3 compared to the other expressions you worked with?*

4. For each commutative pair in Step 3, ask students to assign a context and sketch a picture to show each context. They may use the same context as in Step 2, if they choose.

5. Provide blank paper for students to record their work. Encourage students to use the gridlines to help them record the commutative pairs.

6. Repeat the activity with different expressions, noting that when the product is greater than 10, there will no longer be a single rod to which students can compare the trains.

Why This Manipulative?

Cuisenaire Rods lend themselves to a linear representation of quantity, thus providing a unique approach to comparing combined quantities such as 2 × 3 and 3 × 2. Furthermore, the consistent use of color to represent each value between 1 and 10 provides consistent opportunities for students to view the switch in factor roles (e.g., three reds or two light greens will each *always* be the same length as one dark green).

Developing Understanding

With the commutative property, the important conversation centers on the behavior of each factor. Unlike the addends in addition, which each play a similar role, the factors in multiplication each have different functions. During this activity, the use of guiding questions will help students understand that one factor indicates the number of groups or iterations (multiplier) while the other indicates the size of each group. This lays an important foundation for understanding more complex arithmetic. This principle is uniquely highlighted when working with the commutative property. Although, in the United States, the first number is typically considered the multiplier, this is not universally consistent. Emphasize the changing roles of the factors over the order in which they appear in the expression.

Featured Connection

In this activity, students engage in two connections strategies: Build a Model and Create a Word Problem. Initially, students are given a pair of expressions for which they are asked to use Cuisenaire Rods to demonstrate the commutative property. This affords students the

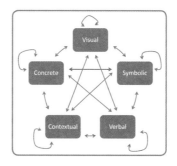 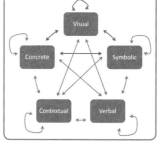

Source: Lesh, Post, & Behr (1987).

opportunity to translate from the abstract to the concrete. Then they are asked to compose a contextual situation in which the pair of expressions can be explained. By contextualizing the abstract commutative property, students translate from a physical representation to a verbal representation, helping them to see that with the commutative property the products for each equation are the same but the factors do not behave in the same way.

ASSOCIATIVE PROPERTY OF MULTIPLICATION WITH 2 × 3 × 4

Materials

- One set of Cuisenaire Rods per pair of students
- Paper for recording results (inch or centimeter grid paper allows for easy sketches for older students)
- Activity sheet (one for each student)

Organization (physical)

- **Getting Started:** Distribute one set of rods (in a bag or tray) per pair of students; this activity requires that students organize the rods by same colors, so having the students sort the rods ahead of time may be helpful.
- **Winding Down:** Return the rods to their bag or tray, counting or attending to all slots being filled.

Mathematical Purpose

Students use Cuisenaire Rods to compare the grouping structures inherent within the associative property of multiplication.

Steps

1. Ask students to use Cuisenaire Rods to represent 2 × 3 × 4.

   > 2 × 3 × 4

   Encourage them to explore different ways to do this. Use guiding questions to help students think about what this means:

   - *How might you break this problem into smaller chunks?*
   - *Once you've found the product of two factors, what might you do next?*
   - *Did everyone in the class do this the same way?*

2. Choose one student's representation that shows (2 × 3) × 4. Ask students to describe what they notice and wonder. Choose another student's representation that shows 2 × (3 × 4). Again ask students to describe what they notice and wonder.

3. Have students work individually or with partners to show the associative property with other numbers. Focus on smaller numbers that will work easily with the Cuisenaire Rods. This might include three-factor problems in any order such as 2 × 4 × 5; 3 × 4 × 5; 2 × 2 × 3; 2 × 2 × 4; 3 × 3 × 4; and so on.

4. *Extension:* Use a modified version of the Write a Word Problem strategy to share a couple of story situations where 2 × 3 × 4 could play out.

   a. I have 2 boxes of cookies. Each box has 3 sleeves of cookies. Each sleeve has 4 cookies. What does 2 × 3 tell me? What does 3 × 4 tell me? What does 2 × 3 × 4 tell me?

b. I have 2 crates of oranges. Each crate has 3 bags. Each bag has 4 oranges. What does 2 × 3 tell me? What does 3 × 4 tell me? What does 2 × 3 × 4 tell me?

c. I have 2 cars. Each car has 3 passengers. Each passenger won 4 raffle prizes. What does 2 × 3 tell me? What does 3 × 4 tell me? What does 2 × 3 × 4 tell me?

5. Ask students to work with a partner to complete the *Associative Property of Multiplication With 2 × 3 × 4* activity sheet.

Why This Manipulative?

Cuisenaire Rods are uniquely suitable to demonstrate multiplication principles because they are designed to represent units of different sizes. In this activity, Cuisenaire Rods may be used to show either linear thinking or array thinking. Students may choose to represent the first expression with an array and then duplicate it multiple times, as indicated by the third factor. Or students may choose to create the first expression linearly and then duplicate that multiple times, as indicated by the third factor. Either way, the rods will help students see the difference between the two starting points.

Developing Understanding

Developing understanding of the associative property of multiplication is critical in the early grades. It builds a deeper understanding of the behavior of the factors beyond the work with the commutative property since the role of the multiplier shifts from one stage to the next.

This is best understood when represented with physical models such as Cuisenaire Rods. When students first represent 2 × 3 × 4 with the rods, they will likely represent "two rods of 3, four times." Be on the lookout for students who may take the other representation of "three rods of 4, two times." Ask many guiding questions, leading the students to understand that although the product remains constant, no matter the order in which the factors are multiplied, the factors do not behave the same way in each situation. Adding context, as seen in the example, helps tremendously in helping students understand the distinction.

Activity 3.7 Resources

- *Associative Property of Multiplication With 2 × 3 × 4 Activity Sheet*

 To access resource visit resources.corwin.com/ MasteringMathManips/ K-3

Manipulative Illustrated

Connecting Cuisenaire Rods from hand2mind

Featured Connection

This activity spotlights the connecting strategies: Build the Equation and Write a Word Problem. Use Build the Equation to connect the abstract expression to a physical model, in this case, Cuisenaire Rods. This connection drives students to grapple with the notion of associativity and how it "looks" in two variants.

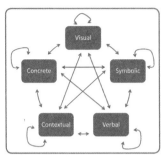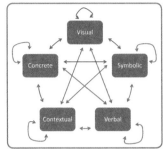

Source: Lesh, Post, & Behr (1987).

Use the Write a Word Problem strategy to connect the concrete representation to a contextual situation. The Cuisenaire Rods lend themselves to understanding what's happening mathematically, and the contextual situation helps students gain a greater appreciation of the behavior of the associative property. (*Note*: This activity may also be achieved using linking cubes.)

Notes

_____

_____

_____

_____

_____

_____

_____

_____

_____

_____

_____

Notes

Materials

- Cuisenaire Rods, one set per pair of students
- Paper for recording results (centimeter grid paper allows for easy sketches)

Organization (physical)

- **Getting Started:** Distribute one set of rods (in a bag or tray) per pair of students.
- **Winding Down:** Return the rods to their bag or tray.

Mathematical Purpose

In this activity, students identify fractional values greater and less than one for a variety of fractional relationships. Students learn to extend their fractional reasoning beyond the explicit relationships in fraction manipulatives.

Activity 3.8 Resources

- *Reasoning About Fractions* Activity Video

online resources ↗

To access resource visit resources.corwin.com/ MasteringMathManips/ K-3

Manipulative Illustrated

Cuisenaire Rods (available from multiple sources)

Steps

1. Ask students to use the Cuisenaire Rods to model one-half. Encourage them to explore and justify that they have found all the possible ways to represent $\frac{1}{2}$ using the rods. Encourage discussion using questions such as these:

   - *Which rod represents the whole, and which rod represents the half in this model? [Point to one to select.]*
   - *How do you know that the half is half of the whole?*
   - *Why does the [pick a color] rod represent half in this model and a whole in that one?*
   - *Can you use any color rod to represent the whole in this task? Why or why not?*

2. Choose one rod to represent the whole. For example, if the purple rod is $\frac{1}{2}$ of the brown rod, the brown rod is the whole. If brown represents 1 whole, what is the fractional value of each other rod? Students have already determined that purple is $\frac{1}{2}$ and will work to find the fractional value of each of the other rods.

3. As students work, use guiding questions like these to help them explain their thinking:

   - *How do you know this rod has this value?*
   - *Can you predict which rods will be worth more than one and which will be worth less than one?*
   - *Do you see a pattern in the naming of the rods?*

4. Repeat the activity with different rods as the whole. Extend the range of the activity by including combination rods (e.g., orange plus another rod). Extending beyond orange would be orange + white, orange + red, orange + light green, orange + purple, and orange + yellow. The first two extensions are shown in the accompanying image.

   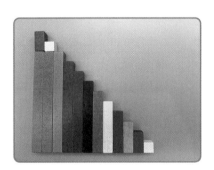

Why This Manipulative?

Cuisenaire Rods are useful for extending fraction thinking beyond formal fraction tools for several reasons. First, they echo the shape of fraction tiles or towers and lend themselves to a number line representation. Second, the size increments between pieces are clear so there is a straightforward structure to the work. Third, the rods will be useful for ratio and proportion thinking, another possible use of fraction notation. By connecting the rods with part-whole fractions, students begin to see the rods as a tool for representing relationships between quantities.

Developing Understanding

It is important for students to see fractions with a variety of tools. Typical fraction manipulatives (like those in Chapter 7) are important for understanding fractions. Activities like this one help students transfer their thinking about fractions to a tool not specifically designed for fractions. They expand thinking to another whole and develop the idea that the fractional value of each piece changes depending on the defined whole. You can follow this same activity structure with pattern blocks and/or tangrams to have a wider range of shapes for the wholes and parts.

Featured Connection

Use the Make a Sketch strategy with centimeter grid paper to create number line representations of each set of fractional relationships. Students use the length of each rod to indicate a position from 0 on the number line and label each point with its assigned fractional value. If students keep a constant denominator (e.g., record $\frac{2}{4}$ for red rather than $\frac{1}{2}$ when the whole is purple), it will be easy to see the pattern of counting by a unit fraction.

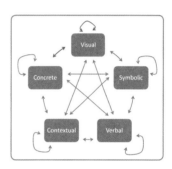

Source: Lesh, Post, & Behr (1987).

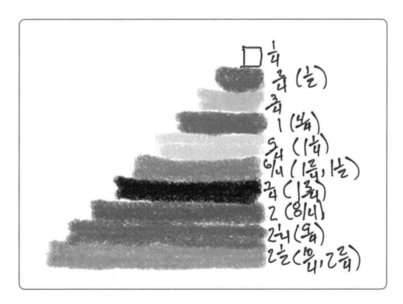

Materials

- One set of Cuisenaire Rods per pair of students

- Paper for recording results (inch or centimeter grid paper allows for easy sketches for older students)

Organization (physical)

- **Getting Started:** Distribute one set of rods (in a bag or tray) per pair of students.

- **Winding Down:** Return the rods to their bag or tray.

Mathematical Purpose

Students use Cuisenaire Rods to represent fractions. More specifically, students come to understand that a **fraction** can be renamed as a sum of **unit fractions**.

Manipulative Illustrated

Cuisenaire Rods (available from multiple sources)

Steps

1. Pose the following problem to students:

> Christina has a brownie bar that she is sharing with her baby brother. Her mom suggested she keep $\frac{3}{4}$ for herself and give $\frac{1}{4}$ to her brother. Show Christina's share of the brownie bar with Cuisenaire Rods.

2. Ask students to identify rods that will best help them represent the whole brownie bar, the part that Christina will keep, and the part that her baby brother will get. Ask guiding questions to help students explain their reasoning:

   - *Which rod would best be used to represent the whole brownie bar if you're going to cut it into fourths?*

   - *Which rods will best show three one-fourths?*

   - *Which single rod might show Christina's portion?*

   - *What do you notice about three one-fourths and one bar that shows three-fourths?*

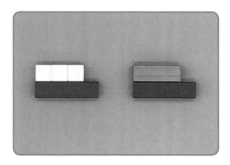

3. Discuss how Christina's piece of the brownie bar might be represented with three white rods *or* with one light green rod. Ask guiding questions to help students see that in both cases Christina is getting $\frac{3}{4}$ of the brownie bar.

   - *What do you notice about the representation of Christina's share of the brownie bar when there are three white rods that are one-fourth-sized?*

   - *What do you notice about the representation of Christina's share of the brownie bar where there is one green rod that is three-fourths-sized?*

   - *With each of these representations, does Christina get the same amount?*

   - *Why do you think that?*

4. Repeat the activity with different fractions, always indicating that Christina is getting a fraction of the brownie bar. Use guiding questions such as these to help students determine the best bar to use as the "whole," based on the denominator of the portions Christina and her baby brother will be getting.

5. Provide blank paper for students to record their thinking with pictures, numbers, and words.

Why This Manipulative?

Cuisenaire Rods lend themselves to number line thinking, both with whole numbers and with fractions. Activities like this help students explore equivalent fractions as fractions that have the same length but are configured in different ways. This particular look at equivalence focuses on how any fraction can be renamed as a sum of unit fractions. This lays an important foundation for working with equivalent fractions and fraction operations.

Developing Understanding

It is important for students to see fractions with a variety of tools. The area model is used most often during classroom instruction, so providing linear models helps students visualize fractions flexibly. Activities like this one help students transfer their thinking about fractions to a tool not specifically designed for fractions. And the connection to number lines will help them connect beginning fraction understanding to more complex concepts in later grades.

Featured Connection

Use the Create a Diagram strategy to connect the concrete to the visual and abstract representations, encouraging students to use either sketches or number lines to represent the brownie bar. Cuisenaire Rods lend themselves to number line representations, so this is a good time to make that connection. Students can simply draw a number line, mark it into fourths, and then draw a line segment that is three-fourths of the unit. Then they can draw a second number line, mark it into fourths, and draw four one-fourth unit segments.

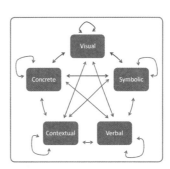

Source: Lesh, Post, & Behr (1987).

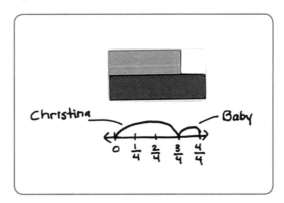

CLOSING REFLECTION: CUISENAIRE RODS

How do I use Cuisenaire Rods in my classroom now? What concepts do I use them to teach?

_____

_____

_____

_____

_____

_____

_____

_____

_____

_____

_____

What new ways have I found to use Cuisenaire Rods to better support student understanding?

_____

_____

_____

_____

_____

_____

_____

_____

_____

_____

_____

_____

What are my goals to make Cuisenaire Rods a more regular part of my instruction?

_____

_____

_____

_____

_____

_____

_____

_____

_____

_____

_____

Chapter 4

Unit Squares

INTRODUCTION

Understanding Unit Squares

This chapter includes activities that use unit squares (typically small squares). Unit squares are used in the early primary grades in many of the same ways as counters. They are small square units, often 1 inch per side, and this gives them the added advantage of representing area easily. As students move into multiplication concepts, the unit squares facilitate the use of an array model, also useful when developing the concepts of area and perimeter. Unit squares are available in a variety of colors and materials, including wood, hard plastic, and foam.

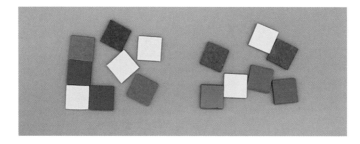

Unit squares and counters are particularly effective for teaching these topics:

- Counting and cardinality (when used as counters)
- Beginning base-ten groupings (when used as counters)
- Area
- **Perimeter**
- Multiplication facts
- **Distributive property of multiplication over addition**

Introducing Unit Squares to Students

Use the *Notice and Wonder Thinking Routine* (described in the introductory chapter) to introduce unit squares to your students. Students may notice the square shape, the congruent sides, the **right angles**, the number of colors, or the fact that the shapes tessellate. Students may wonder how tall a tower they can build or how to use the squares to create letters or other familiar shapes.

Key Ideas With Unit Squares

- Unit squares are typically made in a variety of colors. Color can be useful for highlighting aspects of a pattern or bringing emphasis to one part of a representation. At other times, students will need to work without regard to color. It is important to discuss this with students so they understand how to decide when color is important.

- Unit squares may be used as counters in the early primary grades.

- Unit squares, usually presented as 1-inch squares, provide great opportunities for students to explore area, including attributes such as the additive nature of area and the relationship between area and perimeter. Specifically, unit squares may be used to help students understand that area refers to the number of square units that cover a figure or surface, while perimeter refers to the linear distance around the outside of the figure or surface.

- Unit squares are especially useful in supporting students as they develop an understanding of the multiplication facts using an area model. Students may use unit squares to explore the relationship between factors and products as well as the composing and decomposing concepts embedded in the property.

- When working with data representations, students will often use digital tools for creating charts or graphs and identifying descriptive statistics. Deliberate practice with hands-on tools and small data sets provides insight into what happens "behind the curtain" of digital tools.

Things to Consider About Unit Squares

- In the United States, most unit squares are squares, 1 inch on each side. If you mix squares from multiple sources, be sure they have the same side length.

- You can use unit squares to iterate length. It is important to help students recognize that they are using only one side of the tile to represent length. The rest of the tile functions as a "handle" in this context. Younger students find difficulty in distinguishing between the length of one side and the area of the entire tile.

- Unit squares also present a great opportunity for students to explore multiplication using an array or area model.

- Unit squares can help students establish a benchmark understanding of a single square inch of area.

Alternatives to Commercial Unit Squares

Small bathroom tiles from the hardware store or Habitat for Humanity ReStores make great sturdy substitutes for unit squares. Just be sure all your squares really are the same size. Furthermore, ceramic squares may be painted on one side, creating a unique array of opportunities similar to those used for two-color counters.

It is also easy to cut unit squares from a die-cut machine. Fun foam is an especially useful medium for this purpose. Unit squares may also be created by cutting apart 1-inch grid paper.

Working With Virtual Unit Squares

Virtual unit squares have the same functionality as physical unit squares. There is an endless supply and no real risk around resizing the squares as long as all the squares resize the same way.

Materials

- Unit squares placed in containers for small groups
- Work mats (colored paper or fun foam)
- Recording sheet for each student
- *Optional:* Precut paper squares and glue

Organization (physical)

- **Getting Started:** Distribute a container of unit squares to each group of students.
- **Winding Down:** Count and put the unit squares in the containers before collecting, checking to be sure none fell on the floor or got left behind.

Mathematical Purpose

This activity builds understanding of counting and cardinality as students count out a specified number of unit squares and arrange them in a formation of their choice. For the teen numbers, the activity can be extended to include groups of ten unit squares and extra unit squares.

Steps

1. Ask students to count out five unit squares and to build a figure with them. To support students' thinking, ask guiding questions such as the following:

   - *How many squares are in your figure? How do you know?*
   - *How do you see the number 5? [For example: "Three reds and two yellows" or "One on top and four on the bottom."]*

2. Ask students to work in pairs to describe one another's figures, and prompt them with questions such as the following:

   - *How many squares are in your partner's figure?*
   - *How do you know?*
   - *How do you see the number 5?*

3. Repeat this process and ask the same questions for other numbers such as 7, 11, and 14. If desired, focus on one ten and some more ones for teen numbers. Students can use either color or position to make distinctions between groups of the unit squares.

4. Distribute the recording sheets and ask students to use the Make a Sketch strategy to connect the concrete and visual representations. You may want to simply focus on the first two pages of the recording sheet for one-digit numbers or the last two pages for teen numbers. To support students' thinking, continue asking the guiding questions included earlier:

- *How many squares are in your figure? How do you know?*

- *How do you see the number ____?*

As an extension, students can use the Caption Your Picture strategy to connect the visual representation to contextual and verbal representations. Note that this may also be completed using a virtual app, such as the Didax Color Tiles app, as pictured.

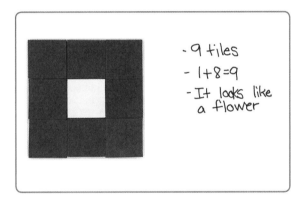

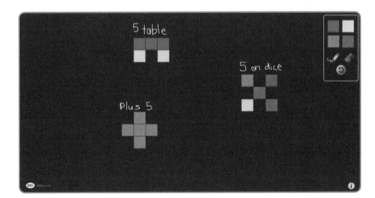

5. *Optional:* Provide precut colored paper squares and glue for students to reproduce their configurations rather than sketching.

6. *Extension:* This activity may also be used to represent number pairs that total a given number. For example, for the given number 8, students can show the nine ways to use tiles to make 8: $0 + 8$, $1 + 7$, $2 + 6$, $3 + 5$, $4 + 4$, $5 + 3$, $6 + 2$, $7 + 1$, and $8 + 0$. Students may use color or position to make the distinction between the two numbers in each pair.

Activity 4.1 Resources

Unit Squares as Counters Recording Sheet

 To access resource visit resources.corwin.com/ MasteringMathManips/ K-3

Manipulatives Illustrated

- Unit Squares (available from multiple sources)

- Color Tiles app from Didax: www.didax.com/apps/color-tiles/

Why This Manipulative?

Unit squares, used as counters, provide opportunities for young learners to create figures with the properties of area and perimeter. Of course, these topics are not generally formally introduced until second or third grade. Exploring them in the early years provides students with the opportunity to develop the spatial, geometric, and number skills, laying a foundation for when they are formally introduced.

Additionally, unit squares typically come in four colors, affording students the opportunity to use both color and position to make distinctions between quantities within a single configuration. This may support additional skills such as subitizing and composing or decomposing quantities.

Developing Understanding

This activity supports students as they develop their understanding of counting and cardinality as well as of beginning place-value concepts. It provides additional opportunities for students to use one-to-one correspondence, label the quantity of the set as the last number counted, and identify the notion of inclusion (each counting number is one more than the amount identified by the previous counting number).

For the last two activities, students may further develop their beginning notions of place value by creating figures that include ten ones and some more ones (or one group of ten and some more ones).

Featured Connection

In this activity, students use the Make a Sketch strategy to connect the concrete and visual representations. By first creating the figures with unit squares, students have freedom to move the squares around, reminding them that the quantity remains consistent even when the figure is altered. Then, when students make sketches, they create a lasting model of the objects they used. Remind them that their sketches need not look exactly like the concrete objects. For example, they can use circles or *X*s to represent each square rather than literally drawing squares.

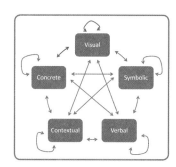

You may also ask students to use the Caption Your Picture strategy to add a title to their figures. They might name their pictures after real-life objects they resemble, but be sure the captions include a mathematical element such as the number of unit squares. For example, students may caption their figures as "Five Friends," "My 5 Table," or "A Fish With 5." Or they may simply have a caption that says, "Five."

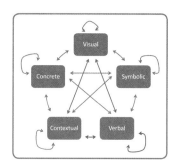

Source: Lesh, Post, & Behr (1987).

Notes

REPEATED ADDITION WITH UNIT SQUARES

| K | 1 | 2 | 3+ |

Materials

- Virtual unit squares app (or physical unit squares and work mats)
- Blank paper to record work

Organization (virtual)

- **Getting Started:** Ensure students know how to use the virtual unit squares. Review annotation tools, taking screenshots, and so on.
- **Winding Down:** Take screenshots to save student work.

Mathematical Purpose

Students use repeated addition to describe a situation related to the area model for multiplication.

Manipulative Illustrated

Color Tiles app from Didax: www.didax.com/apps/color-tiles/

Steps

> Shiloa was planting a garden with her mom. They used string to divide the rectangle-shaped garden into 3 rows with 4 squares in each row. How many sections did they have for different plants?

1. Ask students to read the problem together. To support their thinking, ask guiding questions such as the following:
   - *What is this story about? Have you ever planted a garden? What do you think they'll plant?*
   - *What are the quantities and math relationships in this story?*
   - *What is the math question asking? What might a good answer sound like?*

2. Ask students to use their virtual unit squares to represent the garden, pretending that the squares are the sections Shiloa and her mom measured out.

3. Ask students to Make a Sketch of their work to Caption Your Picture with labels and numbers. They can do this using the annotation tools in the virtual app or on blank paper. They should include a repeated addition equation as one of the captions.

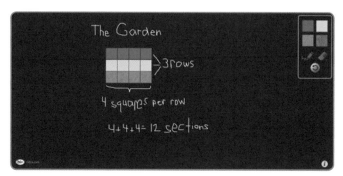

4. Ask students to repeat this process, making arrays with dimensions such as 3×3, 2×6, and 5×4. Repeat as many times as will benefit your students.

5. *Extension:* Ask students to use the Write a Word Problem strategy to add context to at least one of the rectangles they created with unit squares.

> **Write a Word Problem (sample)**
>
> Cami has a box of square candies. There are 3 rows with 3 candies in each row. How many candies does she have in all?

Why This Manipulative?

Many state standards frameworks emphasize the connection between repeated addition and the equal groups interpretation of multiplication. This is often presented specifically as using an area model to reinforce this notion. Therefore, unit squares present an ideal format since their uniform size and square-shaped pieces resemble the square units used in area models.

Unit squares are superior to linking cubes, which are not recommended for this activity, because the linking cubes have extra knobs that detract from the notion of square units. Furthermore, the cubic shape of the linking cubes does not lend itself to the notion of area as does the flat shape of the unit squares.

Another excellent tool for exploring repeated addition using an area model is the geoboard. And if you venture into using arrays alongside area, then two-color counters also offer a great way for exploring these principles (see Activity 1.11 in this book).

Developing Understanding

Repeated addition is often used as a stepping-stone toward beginning multiplication and division concepts. Although it is important for children to eventually realize that the equal groups interpretation is but one of many for multiplication, it is a solid starting place for young learners. Whether you use this activity as part of your sequence for teaching addition, multiplication, or geometric measurement, your students will benefit tremendously from first building the model with unit squares, then sketching the model by **partitioning** a **rectangle**, and finally labeling the parts and writing the repeated addition equation that corresponds with the model.

Featured Connection

In this activity, students use the Make a Sketch and Caption Your Picture strategies to connect their concrete representations to visual, symbolic, and verbal representations. After creating their concrete representations of the area models, re-creating them as sketches helps them internalize the notion of same-sized rows and columns, and the captions help them connect repeated addition to the pictures they created.

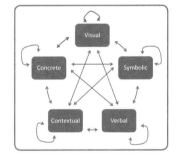

By asking the students to use a modified version of the Write a Word Problem strategy in the extension, you give them the opportunity to connect their thinking to context, helping them realize that repeated addition does have meaning in the world around us.

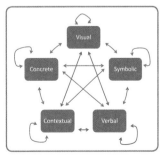
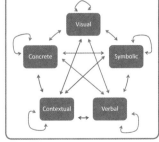

Source: Lesh, Post, & Behr (1987).

ITERATING UNIT SQUARES TO FIND AREA

| K | 1 | 2 | 3+ |

Materials

- Unit squares placed in containers for small groups
- Work mats (colored paper or fun foam)
- Recording sheet for each student

Organization (physical)

- **Getting Started:** Distribute a container of unit squares to each group of students.
- **Winding Down:** Count and put the unit squares in the containers before collecting, checking to be sure none fell on the floor or got left behind.

Mathematical Purpose

Building from the perspective of the attributes of area, students iterate square units to cover a figure and then count how many squares cover the area. In Part B, students decompose the figure into rectangles, developing the notion that area is additive.

Activity 4.3 Resources

Iterating Squares to Find Area Recording Sheet

 To access resource visit resources.corwin.com/ MasteringMathManips/ K-3

Manipulative Illustrated

Unit Squares (available from multiple sources)

Steps

1. Distribute the recording sheet, Part A. Ask students to look at the figure and estimate how many unit squares will completely cover the figure with no gaps and no overlaps. Encourage them to share their estimates with their partners.

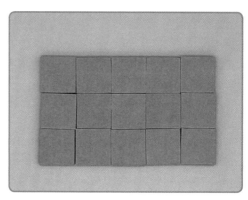

2. Ask students to fill out the figure using unit squares. Emphasize the rule that there must be no gaps and no overlaps. Ask questions like these:

   - *How many squares did it take?*
   - *Did you get the same total as your partner?*
   - *Did you use the same colors?*
   - *Did you get the same number, even if you used different colors?*
   - *Did the colors you chose change the total?*
   - *If color doesn't matter, what do you notice about the attributes of area?*
   - *What does area tell us?*
   - Optional: *Is there a systematic way to count the number of squares on the rectangle? Might addition or multiplication help?*

3. Once students have successfully covered the rectangle, ask them to use the Make a Sketch and Caption Your Picture strategies to connect the concrete representation to visual and symbolic representations.

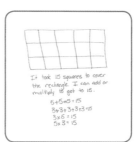

4. Continue with similar opportunities, or go to Part B to explore partitioning of **rectilinear figures**.

Why This Manipulative?

The idea that unit squares are the basic measurement unit for area is strongly reinforced by the use of a literal square, as introduced in this activity. Because unit squares are uniform, they can cover a rectangular surface with no gaps and no overlaps. When using virtual unit squares, the pieces generally snap into place, reinforcing the idea that there should be no gaps or overlaps when covering a surface with unit squares.

Geoboards also provide a sound opportunity for students to explore the idea of area by partitioning shapes into square units. Other manipulatives such as linking cubes are occasionally used to reinforce the idea of area, as well. However, linking cubes have extra buttons or notches on them that distract from the idea of area. Plus, because linking cubes are cubic rather than square, students may be distracted by the added attribute of height.

Developing Understanding

This activity conceptually develops the notion that area is the amount of space that covers a figure or surface and that the basic unit of area is a square. Eventually, students will generalize the idea of concrete squares to the units of square inches, square feet, square meters, square miles, and so on. This stage is critical since the notion of literal squares can sometimes be overlooked once students get to the stage of simply using multiplication of the length and width to determine the area of a figure or surface.

One way to understand the concept of area is to recognize that it literally describes the number of squares that cover a figure or surface with no gaps and no overlaps. This activity helps teachers point out this attribute by asking students to iterate squares. The iterations performed in this activity can be used to build understanding of both repeated addition and multiplication, as will be addressed in other activities in this chapter.

Featured Connection

In this activity, students use the Make a Sketch strategy, along with the Caption Your Picture strategy, to connect the concrete representations from the unit squares to visual, verbal, and symbolic representations. Using the concrete unit squares, students compose the larger rectangle using square units. When making their sketches, they partition the rectangle into square units. By moving in both directions, building from pieces to whole and then partitioning the whole into pieces, students build a deeper understanding of

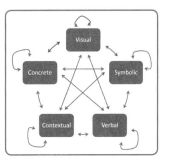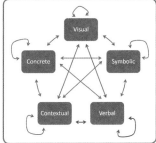

Source: Lesh, Post, & Behr (1987).

the basic foundations of area. Finally, by describing their process for figuring out the total without counting, students are verbalizing their strategies in ways that may eventually lead to generalization.

Materials

- Virtual unit squares app (or physical unit squares and work mats)
- Recording sheet for each student

Organization (virtual)

- **Getting Started:** Ensure students know how to use the virtual unit squares. Review annotation tools, taking screenshots, and so on.
- **Winding Down:** Take screenshots to save student work.

Mathematical Purpose

Students explore the connections between area and multiplication. Unit squares are used to create arrays that represent problem situations, and students can use counting and repeated addition to verify their multiplication work.

Activity 4.4 Resources

Connecting Iterated Squares and Multiplication as Ways to Find Area Recording Sheet

 online resources To access resource visit resources.corwin.com/ MasteringMathManips/ K-3

Manipulative Illustrated

Color Tiles app from Didax:
www.didax.com/apps/color-tiles/

Steps

> Gabriel was helping his mom make brownies. They cut the brownies into 4 rows with 6 brownies in each row. How many brownies did they have when they were finished?

1. Read the first problem situation on the recording sheet together. Ask each student (or pair of students) to use unit squares to show what the pan of brownies would look like after being cut.

2. As students work through the activity, support their learning by asking guiding questions about the relationship between the rows and columns:

   - *How many brownies are in each row?*
   - *How many rows are there?*
   - *How many brownies are there altogether?*
   - *How might we show that as repeated addition?*
   - *How might we show that as multiplication?*
   - *What is similar about the array, the repeated addition equation, and the multiplication equation?*

   Note that the rows and columns may be interchanged, depending on the orientation of the drawing. The factors may be interchanged, but the important thing is to note the "behaviors" of the factor—one describes how many rows there are, and the other describes how many brownies are in each row.

3. Ask students to use the Make a Sketch and Caption Your Picture strategies to connect the concrete representation to the visual, verbal, and symbolic representations (as seen).

4. Once students understand the task, ask them to represent the situations in the next two problem situations. Continue asking questions to ensure students are understanding the two different roles of the factors. Continuously ask the students questions about the factors:

- *What does the _____ represent in the array?*
- *What does the _____ represent in the array?*
- *How is the array like multiplication?*
- *How is the repeated addition equation similar to multiplication?*

Why This Manipulative?

Unit squares create area models easily and are available in sufficient quantities for making both small and large arrays. Students are frequently introduced to the array model when learning multiplication, using multiplication equations (and repeated addition equations) to represent the rows and columns of the arrays.

This is a situation where virtual manipulatives can be particularly helpful as students can use as many unit squares as needed, and they will "snap" together to represent the situations. Students can also use the virtual screen to record their addition and multiplication equations. And, if available, they can use the text feature to type their descriptions for how the factors in the multiplication equation relate to the array and to the repeated addition equation.

It's important to note that other manipulatives such as color counters are used to help students make use of the array model for multiplication. This is completely satisfactory. Just take care to make the distinction that square units can be used to represent the "area model of multiplication," while counters of other shapes are simply using "equal groups" or "equal rows" to model multiplication as an array. Only square units truly demonstrate the area model.

Developing Understanding

There are several connections that must be made during this activity. Use guiding questions to help students make the following connections:

- Unit squares can be used to make an array that has no gaps and no overlaps. That array can also be called an area model since, by definition, area is the number of square units that cover a figure or surface with no gaps and no overlaps.*

- When unit squares are put together into a rectangular array, multiplication can be used to represent the model.

- Repeated addition can also be used to describe a rectangular area model, representing the equal number of rows or the equal number of columns.

---

* *Important vocabulary distinction:* When using unit squares to create rectangles, the figure can be labeled both as an array and as an area model. Arrays are composed of any of a number of objects that are arranged into equal rows and columns (see Figure 4.4.1). An array composed of unit squares that are pushed together with no gaps and no overlaps also represents area; thus, the figure can be correctly labeled as either an array or an area model. That said, area models are not always arrays. Figure 4.4.1 illustrates the comparison and distinction between arrays and area models.

- It's important to note that repeated addition and multiplication are *not* the same thing. Repeated addition is but *one* way to describe multiplication when working only with whole numbers. Ask students to describe the connections between the repeated addition equations and the multiplication equations.

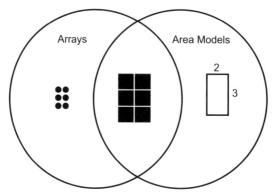

Figure 4.4.1 Connecting Arrays and Area Models

Featured Connection

Students can use the Make a Sketch strategy, along with the Caption Your Picture strategy, to connect the concrete representations they build to visual, verbal, and symbolic notations. This activity lends itself to sketching on grid paper and then describing the sketch

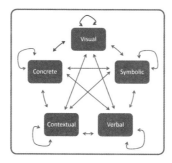 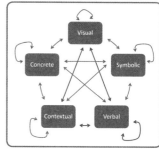

Source: Lesh, Post, & Behr (1987).

either verbally or with words and numbers. Connecting these many representations will serve to help students understand the relationship between area and multiplication (or repeated addition).

Notes

_____

_____

_____

_____

_____

_____

_____

Notes

AREA IS ADDITIVE: FINDING AREAS OF RECTILINEAR FIGURES

Materials

- Unit squares placed in containers for small groups
- Work mats (colored paper or fun foam)
- Recording sheet for each student

Organization (physical)

- **Getting Started:** Distribute a container of unit squares to each group of students.
- **Winding Down:** Count and put the unit squares in the containers before collecting, checking to be sure none fell on the floor or got left behind.

Mathematical Purpose

Students decompose given figures into rectangles, developing the notion that area is additive. Students continue to **iterate** unit squares into each of the rectangles, further reinforcing the concept of area (the space covered on a figure or surface using square units).

Activity 4.5 Resources

- *Area Is Additive: Finding Areas of Rectilinear Figures* Recording Sheet

 To access resource visit resources.corwin.com/ MasteringMathManips/ K-3

Manipulative Illustrated

Unit Squares (available from multiple sources)

Steps

1. Distribute the recording sheet. Ask students to look at the figure and estimate how many unit squares will completely cover the figure with no gaps and no overlaps. Encourage them to share their estimates with their partners.

2. Next ask them to sketch a line to decompose the **figure** into two rectangles. Ask them to estimate how many unit squares will completely cover each of the rectangles with no gaps and no overlaps. Encourage them to share their estimates with their partners.

3. Ask students to use unit squares to cover the figure on the recording sheet with no gaps and no overlaps. Ask them to use one color for the large rectangle and a different color for the small rectangle. To support students' thinking, ask guiding questions such as the following:

   - *How many unit squares did it take to cover the large rectangle of the figure?*

   - *How many unit squares did it take to cover the small rectangle of the figure?*

   - *How many unit squares did it take to cover the entire figure?*

   - *What do you notice about the relationship between the totals for each rectangle and the total for the entire figure?*

4. Finally, ask students to use the Sketch a Picture strategy to connect concrete and visual representations. Then ask them to use the Caption Your Picture strategy to describe what is happening in each part of the figure.

5. Continue with similar opportunities, as needed (two more are provided on the recording sheet). This activity can be used to develop the notion of area as being additive when a figure is decomposed into smaller figures.

Why This Manipulative?

This activity further develops the notion that area is the amount of space that covers a figure or surface and that the basic unit of area is a square. And students will see that area can be partitioned into smaller pieces and then added to find the total. Using squares for this process lays a foundation for using multiplication to find the area of each rectangle and then adding these areas to find the total area. This also lays the foundation for finding surface area of figures in later years. You can also introduce these concepts with geoboards (see Activity 8.7 in this book).

Developing Understanding

As students decompose a rectilinear figure into smaller rectangles, they explore the additive nature of area. By asking students to repeat the activity of partitioning the figures, finding the areas of the smaller figures, and then adding those areas to find the area of the entire figure, teachers can help students start to generalize that area is always additive.

Featured Connection

In this activity, students use the Make a Sketch strategy to partition the original figure into rectangles and then each rectangle into square units, after doing so with concrete unit squares first. Then students use the Caption Your Picture strategy to translate the visual representations in each part of the figure to the symbolic and/or verbal representations. Because the process of finding the area of a rectilinear figure can be so complex, asking students to use multiple representations to guide their thinking is likely to assist them in seeing the relationship between addition, multiplication, and area. Recording their work using these two strategies will also serve as a record of their thinking to which they can refer when solving similar problems in the future.

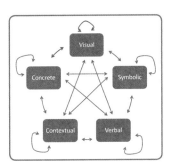

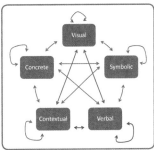

Source: Lesh, Post, & Behr (1987).

Notes

_____

_____

_____

_____

_____

Materials

- Unit squares placed in containers for small groups

- Work mats (colored paper or fun foam)

- Blank grid paper or a recording sheet for each student

Organization (physical)

- **Getting Started:** Distribute a container of unit squares to each group of students.

- **Winding Down:** Count and put the unit squares in the containers before collecting, checking to be sure none fell on the floor or got left behind.

Mathematical Purpose

Students model multiplication from the perspective of decomposing arrays into smaller rectangles, finding the products of the smaller rectangles, and then adding the products together to find the total area.

Steps

Activities 4.3 and 4.4 centered on building arrays or area models to represent multiplication. This activity builds on students' understanding of the area model as a representation of multiplication as they explore the distributive property.

1. Show the students a 3 × 6 array. Ask guiding questions such as the following to begin the discussion about using multiplication to find the number of squares in a rectangular array.

   - *Is there a way to know how many squares are in this array without counting them all?*

   - *How many rows are there?*

   - *How many squares are there in each row?*

   - *Is there a way to split the array into two smaller rectangles to help you know the total number of squares without counting?*

2. Ask students to use the Build the Equation strategy as they work in pairs to create a 3 × 6 array and to find all the different ways to decompose it into two smaller rectangles using the same number of squares. Examples of what students may do appear as follows. To support students' thinking, ask guiding questions such as these:

   - *Did you decompose horizontally or vertically?*

   - *How do you know both smaller figures are rectangles? [This concept is very important.]*

   - *Can you decompose a different way?*

   - *How many different ways can you find to decompose the array into two smaller rectangles?*

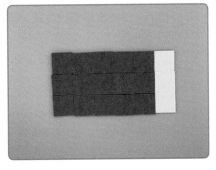

Activity 4.6 Resources

- *Distributive Property of Multiplication Over Addition* Recording Sheet (grid paper may be better, especially if the lines are light blue or gray)

- *Distributive Property of Multiplication Over Addition* Activity Video

online resources To access resources visit resources.corwin.com/ MasteringMathManips/ K-3

Manipulative Illustrated

Unit Squares (available from multiple sources)

3. Ask students to use the Make a Sketch and Caption Your Picture strategies to record their arrays and to label each section of their rectangles. They should record their actions on grid paper, noting the multiplication equation for each smaller rectangle as well as the calculations for the larger array.

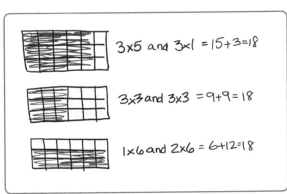

3x5 and 3x1 = 15+3=18

3x3 and 3x3 = 9+9=18

1x6 and 2x6 = 6+12=18

4. Using guiding questions, lead students in a conversation about which decomposition would be easiest to calculate mentally using multiplication facts they already know. This might include arrays that are 3 × 5 and 3 × 1 *or* arrays that are 3 × 3 and 3 × 3.

5. Ask students to work in pairs to use unit squares to represent other arrays that can be decomposed into two (or more) rectangles that would make multiplication easier. Examples may include 3 × 4, 3 × 7, 3 × 8, 4 × 6, 6 × 7, 4 × 8, 6 × 7, 6 × 8, and 7 × 9. Encourage students to think of the most strategic ways to decompose these arrays using multiplication facts they already know.

Why This Manipulative?

Unit squares are uniquely capable of representing the area model used for teaching multiplication. Because they are same-sized squares, they can be put together with no gaps and no overlaps to represent the arrays or area models so prevalent in teaching beginning multiplication (see the vocabulary discussion in Activity 4.4). They also allow students to easily decompose the larger rectangle into smaller rectangles with a simple slide, unlike other counters that don't fit together so nicely.

Note that this activity might also be replicated using two-color counters or linking cubes, though neither is suitable for making the connection to the area model.

Developing Understanding

When students begin exploring the use of decompositions of arrays for the purposes of applying the distributive property, explicitly point out that the goal in this activity is to help with mental math, using multiplication facts they already know. Therefore, the decompositions should focus on factors that are easier to multiply than the original factors. For example, when multiplying 6 × 8, simpler factors to work with would be 5 × 8 and 1 × 8 *or* 3 × 8 doubled. It's probably less helpful to decompose into 4 × 8 and 2 × 8 since those facts aren't typically as easily recalled as the former.

Featured Connection

In this activity, students first use the Build the Equation strategy to translate the equation into an array with unit squares. Next, students use the Make a Sketch strategy in conjunction with the Caption Your Picture strategy to help them connect between the concrete, visual, and symbolic representations. When sketching their actions, students should indicate how they first created the full array with squares and then decomposed the array into smaller rectangles. Then they can caption each part of the model with a multiplication equation and/or words. And finally, they can name the entire model with the original multiplication equation. The emphasis should center on using and connecting the multiple representations to facilitate deeper understanding and use as a guide for similar problems.

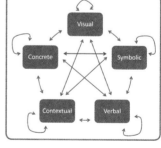

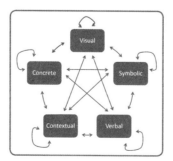

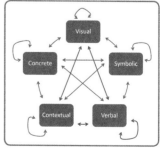

Source: Lesh, Post, & Behr (1987).

Notes

SAME AREA AND DIFFERENT PERIMETERS

| K | 1 | 2 | **3+** |

Materials

- Unit squares placed in containers for small groups
- Work mats (colored paper or fun foam)
- Recording sheet for each student

Organization (physical)

- **Getting Started:** Distribute a container of unit squares to each group of students.
- **Winding Down:** Count and put the unit squares in the containers before collecting, checking to be sure none fell on the floor or got left behind.

Mathematical Purpose

Students use unit squares to represent areas of figures as they examine what happens to the perimeter when the area changes and what happens to the area when the perimeter changes.

Activity 4.7 Resources

Same Area and Different Perimeters Recording Sheet

 To access resource visit resources.corwin.com/ MasteringMathManips/ K-3

Manipulative Illustrated

Unit Squares (available from multiple sources)

Steps

1. Distribute squares to students and ask them to count out 12 squares.

2. Ask students to work individually or in pairs to create as many different arrays as they can using those 12 squares. They should record each array as it is created. To support students' thinking, ask guiding questions such as the following:

   - *How many squares are in each figure?*
   - *What is the area of each figure?*
   - *If the area is always the same, what is happening with the perimeter?*

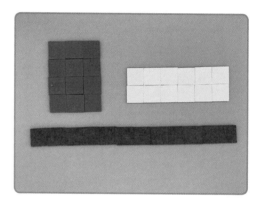

3. Ask students to use the Make a Sketch and Create a Diagram strategies to create a table on the recording sheet that shows the area and perimeter for each figure they sketched. To support their thinking, ask questions such as the following:

   - *What do you notice about the areas of the figures?*
   - *What do you notice about the perimeters?*
   - *Which arrangements have the smallest perimeters?*
   - *Which arrangements have the largest perimeters?*
   - *What patterns do you notice?*
   - *Do you think this would be true for other numbers?*

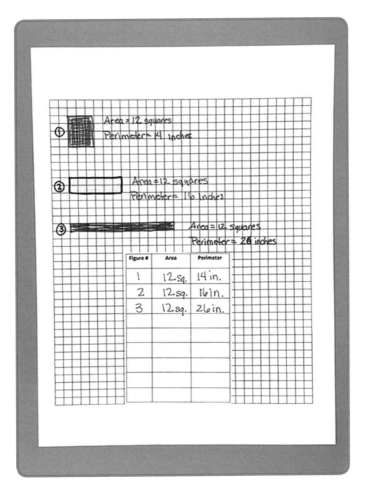

4. Repeat with other numbers of unit squares that lend themselves nicely to making multiple arrays (e.g., 16, 20, 24). Ask students guiding questions to create generalizations.

5. *Extension:* Ask students to repeat this activity, but this time keep the perimeter constant. Reflect on what happens to the area when the squares are arranged differently.

Why This Manipulative?

Unit squares provide the perfect tool for examining the concept of area. By creating rectangles with no gaps and no overlaps, students lay the foundation for more symbolic work with area later on, when square units are assumed but no longer visualized. Experimenting with different arrangements with the same number of squares allows students to explore the relationship between area and perimeter, as well.

Developing Understanding

The problem-solving and pattern detection opportunities are great in activities such as this, provided students have the prerequisite understandings of perimeter and area as their own measurable attributes. Students sometimes confuse the concepts of area and perimeter, often because we try to teach them at the same time. Students do best when the two are taught separately.

Perimeter is best understood as an extension of linear measurement, and teaching as such avoids later confusion.

Activity 2.10 in this book demonstrates one way in which linking cubes might be used to develop the notion of perimeter as a linear measurement prior to asking students to work with unit square configurations as they appear in this lesson.

This points to the idea that you may find it helpful to also teach area as its own attribute prior to working with students on putting the concepts of area and perimeter into the same lesson. Activities 4.3, 4.4, and 4.5 in this book may assist you in accomplishing that goal. Then, once the two concepts are understood independently, bring them together in an activity such as this to help students see how one impacts the other.

Featured Connection

In this activity, students use the Make a Sketch and Create a Diagram strategies to connect the concrete representations created with the unit squares to visual and symbolic representations in the table. Students should verbalize that the areas represent the number of

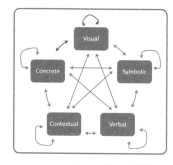 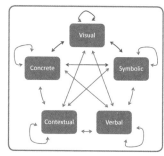

Source: Lesh, Post, & Behr (1987).

unit squares in each figure, while the perimeters represent the linear distance around the outside of each figure. By recording their work in a table, they might be able to begin making generalizations about the relationship between area and perimeter when the area remains the same but the configuration of the square units changes.

Notes

_____

_____

_____

_____

_____

_____

_____

_____

CLOSING REFLECTION: UNIT SQUARES

How do I use unit squares in my classroom now? What concepts do I use them to teach?

_____

_____

_____

_____

_____

_____

What new ways have I found to use unit squares to better support student understanding?

_____

_____

_____

_____

_____

_____

What are my goals to make unit squares a more regular part of my instruction?

_____

_____

_____

_____

_____

_____

CHAPTER 5
Base-Ten Blocks

INTRODUCTION

Understanding Base-Ten Blocks

Base-ten blocks are designed to model the base-ten place-value system. Base-ten blocks are proportional manipulatives (meaning the scale between the pieces is precise), and they are typically pre-grouped (meaning each piece beyond the unit represents a collection of pieces that come already grouped—students do not actively group them, which makes "trading" necessary). The typical set of base-ten blocks includes four types of pieces: a small unit cube, a rod, a flat, and a large cube. The latter three types (rods, flats, and large cubes) are typically etched to show the underlying components. Base-ten blocks are used in single-color (all the shapes are the same color) or multicolor sets. If using a multicolor set, take care that your students see value rather than color. Some sets are designed so the pieces interlock and you can construct larger pieces from smaller ones, allowing students to avoid the "trading" process, which can get in the way of true base-ten understanding.

Base-ten materials are particularly effective in teaching these topics:

- Place value, both whole numbers and decimals
- Comparing and ordering numbers
- Whole-number operations

Introducing Base-Ten Blocks to Students

Encourage learners to explore the materials using the *Notice and Wonder Thinking Routine* (described in the introductory chapter) before starting to teach with them by providing students time to explore the manipulatives and to list what they notice and what they wonder either on a class chart or on an individual graphic organizer. Students may notice that the pieces are etched to show the smaller components. They may notice they can build the larger pieces from smaller pieces if they have sufficient supply. They may wonder why there are two pieces in a cube shape, one small and one large. Use this opportunity to collect informal assessment data regarding your students' place-value understanding.

Regarding the developmental progression for K–3 students, it's important to note that young learners in Grades K–1 will do best by working with groupable manipulatives such as linking cubes, **bundled** straws, or KP® Ten-Frame Tiles. The activities in this chapter can be easily adapted using these alternatives.

Key Ideas With Base-Ten Blocks

- Work with base-ten materials is particularly important because it sets the stage for work with algebra tools in middle school. The use of these parallel tools and structures helps students see the connections between arithmetic and algebra.

- It may feel artificial in the primary grades to separate the names of the pieces (*unit, rod, flat,* and *cube*) from their values (1, 10, 100, and 1,000) when the pieces are almost always used with the unit (small cube) as 1 (the whole). However, when students work with decimals in later years, this separation pays off because it is easier to transition to using the flat or the (large) cube as the whole, allowing smaller pieces to represent tenths, hundredths, or even thousandths.

- Because most base-ten blocks are **pre-grouped** manipulatives and require trading, young learners will benefit from using groupable manipulatives such as **linking cubes** when first exploring **unitizing** principles such as working with groups of ten.

Things to Consider About Base-Ten Blocks

- Base-ten blocks help build number sense, in part, because they are proportional. Students develop a sense of scale as they internalize the relationships between and among the different pieces. For example, they may realize the large cube is 1,000 times the volume of the small unit cube.

- Base-ten blocks are flexible because the four types of pieces show a relationship of 10 times larger or smaller across the different types. Although we tend to assign the unit cube a value of 1 in the early grades, each piece can be assigned a value other than 1, including either whole numbers or decimal fractions. This flexibility facilitates work with different number sets. For example, if the flat (rather than the unit cube) is assigned a value of 1, then the rods represent tenths, and the unit cubes represent hundredths.

- Students benefit greatly when we separate the name of the piece from its value (e.g., labeling the pieces as units, rods, flats, and cubes rather than ones, **tens**, **hundreds**, and thousandths). In primary classrooms, this typically means *calling the small cube the "unit" and giving it a value of 1.* Rods (or longs) have a value of 10 in this system, flats represent 100, and the (large) cube has a value of 1,000. In this way, the value of each piece can be changed as students explore place value in other ranges by redefining the "unit" and, therefore, the value of each piece. This shift typically occurs in Grades 4 and above, though laying the foundation in Grades K–3 will serve students well.

Alternatives to Commercial Base-Ten Blocks

Early learners, especially in Grades K–1, often use a groupable manipulative before base-ten blocks are introduced. Ten linking cubes can be attached as a rod that is ten units long, or ten coffee stirring sticks can be bundled with a small rubber band. Ten beans can be glued to a craft stick. Ten counters can be placed on a ten frame. Ten O-shaped cereal pieces can be put on dry spaghetti. In these ways, young learners see the transition from ten ones to one group of ten, especially if some kind of "cover" is provided so that the single objects are no longer visible, but can be checked to ensure there are still ten "inside."

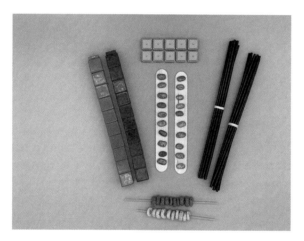

As students move from working with just ones (within ten) to working with ones and tens, the proportional nature of base-ten materials is important for developing good number sense. Typical commercial base-ten sets are built on a centimeter unit cube. This means centimeter grid paper provides a good alternative for units (a 1 × 1 square), rods (a 1 × 10 rectangle), and flats (a 10 × 10 square). We suggest you copy grid paper onto heavy paper, such as card stock, to make it sturdier. You may also consider cutting out units, tens, and hundreds from needlepoint mesh or plastic canvas.

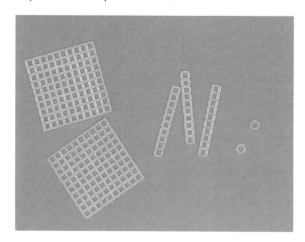

Because these pieces do not have volume, it is difficult to represent a cube ($10 \times 10 \times 10$) with grid paper. A typical paper milk carton ($\frac{1}{2}$ gallon or 2 liters) is approximately a 10×10-cm base and can be cut so it stands 10 cm high to easily create more large cubes.

Some lesser-known manipulatives do an even better job of conveying the nesting principle of the base-ten system than base-ten blocks. For example, KP® Ten-Frame Tiles use "lids" to group ten single tiles into one group of ten and to group ten groups of ten into one group of one hundred.

And finally, many classrooms include the abacus-like tool known as a rekenrek. The rekenrek includes beads, typically red and white, arranged in groups of five. The beads can be used to develop number concepts and operations, helping students focus on using 5 and 10 as benchmark numbers.

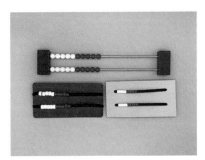

Working With Virtual Base-Ten Blocks

Virtual base-ten materials can have a number of functional advantages over their concrete counterparts. First, as with most virtual tools, there is an endless supply. Second, the online versions of base-ten blocks typically provide an additional feature in that the rods, flats, and large cube can be grouped or broken apart with the click of a button as students work with them. This may facilitate a clearer notion of the nesting principle of the base-ten system. For example, one group of ten can be concurrently thought of as ten ones, and students can go back and forth between those representations. A rod dragged from the tens column to the ones column might automatically appear as ten units. Ten units grouped together with the select tool might automatically appear as a rod. Third, students can explore the creation of larger units. What happens if you stack ten large cubes one atop the other? What is the value of this "super-rod"? The shapes of the pieces (unit cube, rod, flat) repeat in each period of the place-value system, helping students see how the system grows as they work with larger values.

"TEN ONES AND SOME MORE ONES" VS. "ONE TEN AND SOME MORE ONES"

| K | 1 | 2 | 3+ |

Materials

- One bag of unit cubes and rods for each pair of students (20 unit cubes and one rod)

- Work mat for each pair of students (a piece of fun foam or construction paper)

- Blank paper

Organization (physical)

- **Getting Started:** Distribute one container or bag with 20 unit cubes and one rod to each pair of students.

- **Winding Down:** Count and put the base-ten blocks back in the containers before collecting, checking to be sure none fell on the floor or got left behind.

Mathematical Purpose

Students represent teen numbers as "ten ones and some more ones" or as "one ten and some more ones."

Manipulative Illustrated

Base-Ten Blocks (available from multiple sources)

Steps

Part A: Teen numbers as "ten ones and some more ones"

1. Ask each pair of students to count out 13 unit cubes onto their work mat. Ask them to recount to make sure there are exactly 13. Then ask them the following questions: How do you know there are 13 on your mat? Can you arrange them in a way to prove there are 13? Is there another way to arrange them to prove there are 13?

2. Next, talk about the importance of 10. We each have 10 fingers. We each have 10 toes. There are 10 one-digit numbers. What else comes in sets of 10?

3. Ask students to arrange their 13 unit cubes on their work mats to show 10 ones and 3 more ones. Ask:

   - *Where do you see 10 on your mat?*

   - *Where do you see 3 on your mat?*

   - *How much is 10 and 3 altogether?*

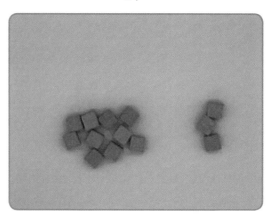

4. Write the number 13 for all to see. Ask: Do you see a connection between the way the number 13 looks and the way your unit cubes look on your work mat?

5. Continue with other teen numbers.

6. Ask each student to fold a blank sheet of paper into four sections. Then have the students sketch one arrangement in each section, labeling the section with the number that was represented.

Part B: Teen numbers as "one ten and some more ones" (same as Part A, with an extension in Step 3)

1. Building off of Part A, now give students one rod and three extra unit cubes and ask them to make a second representation of 13.

2. Encourage them to line up the 10 unit cubes from the first mat next to the rod to verify they hold the same value. Ask:
   - *Where do you see 10 on your new mat?*
   - *Where do you see 3 on your new mat?*
   - *How are the blocks on the two mats the same?*
   - *How much is 10 and 3 altogether?*

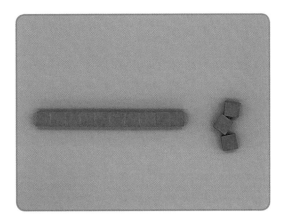

3. Write the number 13 for all to see. Ask: Do you see a connection between the way the number 13 looks and the way your unit cubes look on your work mat?

4. Continue with other teen numbers. Ask each student to fold a blank sheet of paper into four sections. Then have the students sketch one arrangement in each section, labeling the section with the number that was represented.

Why This Manipulative?

As students begin to visualize teen numbers as inclusive of "one group of ten and some more ones," base-ten blocks provide the opportunity to show the numbers in both forms. This lays a foundation for students to internalize the notion that one ten is concurrently ten ones. Although groupable manipulatives are more appropriate for helping students gain insights into the nesting structure of place value when they start regrouping, base-ten blocks do well to represent numbers when no regrouping is required.

Developing Understanding

Be sure to ask guiding questions to ensure that students connect each representation to the number 13 as well as connect the two representations to each other. In the opening stage, students were asked to group the unit cubes in a variety of ways to prove they had 13 on their mats. This flexibility with numbers will prove to be very useful over time. That said, students also need to conclude that groups of ten are most useful for representing our number system, as evidenced by the connection between written multi-digit numbers and the number of groups created.

Featured Connection

Use the Make a Sketch strategy and Name Your Model strategy to connect the concrete, pictorial, and abstract representations for teen numbers. When sketching base-ten blocks, encourage students to use simple figures, such as a line for a rod and an X for a unit cube. Students do not need to draw literal representations of the objects.

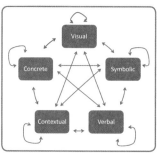 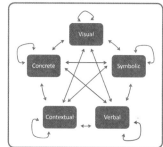

Source: Lesh, Post, & Behr (1987).

Notes

_____

_____

_____

_____

_____

_____

_____

_____

_____

_____

_____

_____

Notes

Materials

- Bags of base-ten blocks (20 unit cubes, 10 rods, and 1 flat) for each pair of students
- 1 six-sided die for each pair of students
- 5.2 *Race to 100* game board for each pair of students

Organization (physical)

- **Getting Started:** Distribute one container or bag with 20 unit cubes, 10 rods, and 1 flat to each pair of students.
- **Winding Down:** Count and put the base-ten blocks back in the containers before collecting, checking to be sure none fell on the floor or got left behind.

Mathematical Purpose

Students will develop a greater understanding of the nesting structure of the base-ten system by trading for the next-sized base-ten piece whenever possible.

Activity 5.2 Resources

Race to 100 Game Board

 To access resource visit resources.corwin.com/ MasteringMathManips/ K-3

Manipulative Illustrated

Base-Ten Blocks (available from multiple sources)

Steps

Notes: One of the limitations of base-ten blocks is the need to "trade" whenever regrouping is needed. This cooperative game helps students begin to work with the trading sequence. Also, note that this "game" is cooperative between partners, not competitive. Pairs of students may race against other pairs to get to 100 the quickest. However, with young children, this competition may detract from the thinking inherent with the game. Therefore, you may want to de-emphasize the competition.

1. Introduce "Race to 100" to students. Game directions:

    - *Player 1 rolls the die and places that many unit cubes in the ones place.*
    - *Player 2 rolls the die and places that many unit cubes in the ones place.*
    - *If there are 10 or more unit cubes in the ones place, Player 2 trades 10 ones for 1 ten (encourage students to line up 10 unit cubes next to the rod to be sure they count correctly).*
    - *Play continues back and forth, with each player trading 1 rod for 10 unit cubes each time it is possible.*
    - *Play continues until 10 rods are collected and can be traded for 1 flat.*

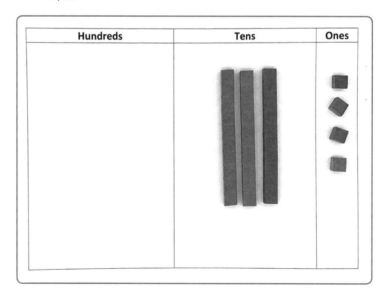

2. During game play, ask guiding questions to ensure students are thinking about the math. Ask:

- *How many unit cubes are in the ones place? Why?*
- *How do you know when to make a trade?*
- *How many rods are in the tens place?*
- *Are you close to making a trade?*

Why This Manipulative?

Base-ten blocks represent the base-ten place-value system, especially when students are viewing and naming numbers in their many forms. Because base-ten blocks are pre-grouped, students must internalize the nesting structure of "10 ones in 1 ten," "10 tens in 1 hundred," and so on. Trading is an artificial way to understand how the magnitude grows from one place to the next, so the practice afforded students in this activity helps them better understand the nature of the manipulative as well as the grouping-by-tens nature of the base-ten place-value system.

Developing Understanding

Because the trading groups-of-ten nature of base-ten blocks can be cumbersome, it can distract students from the nesting nature of the base-ten place-value system. Students may also find themselves inadvertently trading for the wrong number of unit cubes if they miscount. Therefore, precision is critical. Use this activity to reinforce such precision by asking students to line up 10 unit cubes next to the rod each time to ensure proper counting. This will have the added benefit of helping students internalize the importance of groups of ten, a principle that exists in every place, both very large (whole numbers) and very small (decimal fractions).

Note that the virtual version of base-ten blocks tends to have a grouping feature that helps get around the issue of miscounting.

Featured Connection

This activity lends itself to using the Create a Diagram strategy as students place the base-ten pieces onto the game board. The game board itself is a diagram that organizes the base-ten pieces in a systematic way. With this strategy, we are highlighting the connection between the concrete and visual representations. In this case, the base-ten blocks are the concrete objects, and the game board is the diagram. Much like a place-value chart, the game board keeps the base-ten pieces in their proper spaces, corresponding to the places where the digits that represent them are placed. Because base-ten block pieces are

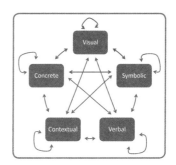

Source: Lesh, Post, & Behr (1987).

proportional, it's not necessary to keep them in place-value order to know their quantity. However, using charts like this helps students connect what they are seeing with the blocks to the positions in which the digits will appear in the numerals.

Materials

- Base-ten blocks app or physical base-ten blocks (unit cubes and rods for two-digit numbers; unit cubes, rods, and flats for three-digit numbers)

- Work mats (fun foam or construction paper)

- Blank paper

Organization (virtual)

- **Getting Started:** Ensure students know how to use the virtual base-ten blocks; review annotation tools, taking screenshots, and so on.

- **Winding Down:** Take screenshots to save student work.

Mathematical Purpose

Students demonstrate multiple ways for building numbers with base-ten blocks.

Manipulative Illustrated

Number Pieces app from Math Learning Center: https://apps .mathlearningcenter.org/number -pieces/

Steps

1. Ask students to represent the number 43 with base-ten blocks. Then ask them to work with a partner to show 43 with base-ten blocks in another way. Then ask two pairs to work together to show 43 in four different ways. Ask:

   - *How did you represent 43 the first time?*

   - *What did you do to represent it in other ways?*

   - *Are you sure every way you've built represents the number 43?*

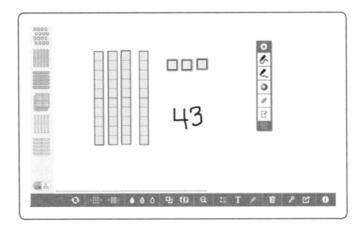

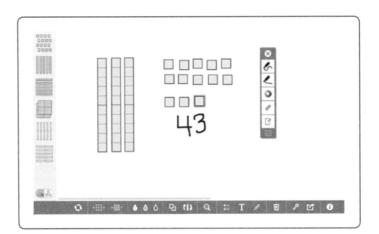

2. Ask each student to fold a sheet of paper into four sections and sketch 43 in four different ways, writing an equation to match. Ask:

   - *Are you sure each sketch represents 43?*

   - *What symbol did you use for rods?*

   - *What symbol did you use for unit cubes?*

3. Repeat with other two- or three-digit numbers.

Why This Manipulative?

Base-ten blocks represent the magnitude of growth based on powers of ten. Because there are four distinct pieces, students can work with four digits anywhere on the number scale. That said, in the primary grades, most students will use the base-ten blocks to represent ones, tens, and hundreds with an occasional reference to thousands. To leave room for later development with shifting the places (e.g., using the flat as one whole, rods as tenths, and unit cubes as hundredths), be sure to call the base-ten pieces by their names and not their values. For example, rods may be assigned a value of 10, but they should be called "rods" and not "tens."

Developing Understanding

This activity lays the foundation for renaming numbers as students transition into modeling operations. Knowing how to rename numbers using different place-value pieces will support students in building conceptual understanding of regrouping. Be sure to frequently discuss different ways or versions of naming numbers outside of the context of addition and subtraction so that this becomes a natural process.

Featured Connection

Use the Make a Sketch and Create a Diagram strategies to highlight the connection between concrete and symbolic representations of two- and three-digit numbers. In this case, students use base-ten blocks to demonstrate a number in several ways and then sketch each configuration as well as label it with an equation. Furthermore, students might use the Create a Diagram strategy to label each sketch rather than writing equations. In the example that follows, the diagram appears in the form of a number bond. This is a great

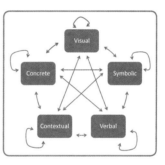 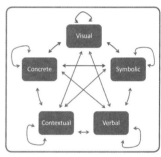

Source: Lesh, Post, & Behr (1987).

connection since students typically use number bonds in the early years to represent addends for smaller numbers. By using number bonds to represent place value, this diagram can help students make visual and mental connections to what they learned in earlier years.

Materials

- Base-ten blocks app or physical base-ten blocks (unit cubes and rods for two-digit numbers; unit cubes, rods, and flats for three-digit numbers)

- Whiteboards or other erasable writing surface

Organization (virtual)

- **Getting Started:** Ensure students know how to use the virtual base-ten blocks; review annotation tools, taking screenshots, and so on.

- **Winding Down:** Take screenshots to save student work.

Mathematical Purpose

Students distinguish between "places" and "values" of numbers as they identify the values of base-ten blocks that are arranged in unconventional ways. Furthermore, students will engage in subitizing by instantly recognizing quantities without counting (see Activity 1.2 for an early learning example of subitizing).

Steps

1. This teacher-led activity may be done as a whole-group or small-group activity.

2. Arrange three rods and four unit cubes on your device, hidden from students. Be sure to mix up the pieces so that rods and unit cubes are *not* sorted and arranged in the traditional "places."

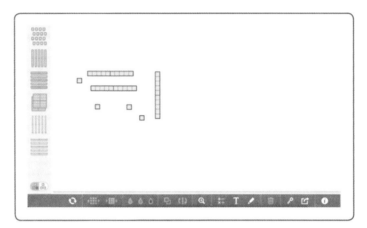

3. Reveal the arrangement for about three seconds and then cover it again. Students should use the Name Your Model strategy to write down the numeral that matches the quantity they saw. After all students have written a numeral, flash again for them to check and/or refine their answers. Repeat once more, if needed.

4. Reveal the blocks to the students and leave the arrangement where they can see it. Check in with students to learn what they wrote, using a modified version of the Caption Your Picture strategy as they describe what they saw using place-value language. To facilitate students' thinking, ask guiding questions such as the following:

   - *What number did you see represented? How do you know?*

   - *Could it have been arranged another way?*

   - *Was it arranged in the same order as the digits in the written number?*

5. Repeat with additional two- or three-digit numbers.

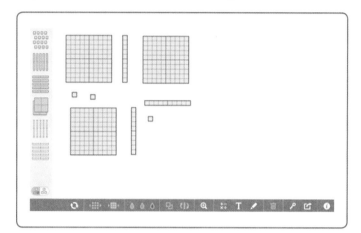

6. *Extension 1:* For each arrangement, use the Make a Sketch strategy to help students connect the concrete to the visual representations. When sketching, students may use squares, lines, and *X*s to represent flats, rods, and unit cubes.

7. *Extension 2:* Students may repeat this activity in small groups, taking turns playing the teacher role.

Why This Manipulative?

Because base-ten blocks represent powers of ten, they are a great tool for representing the digits in base-ten numbers. Because they are proportional, the blocks themselves need not be placed in left-to-right order (e.g., hundreds, then tens, then ones). Rather, they can be scattered so that students must attend to the magnitude of each size, mentally putting together hundreds with hundreds, tens with tens, and ones with ones. Students can then record the number, in which place does matter since the placement of the digits determines their magnitude, in contrast to the blocks with which the size or shape determines the value.

Developing Understanding

This activity resembles the subitizing activities used in primary classrooms (instant recognition of quantity without counting by ones). This activity should be teacher-led in the beginning so that students only see the blocks for a few seconds and then record or verbalize the quantities.

An added feature may be to flash the arrangement once, have students record the number, then flash it one or two more times for students to revise their written numbers, if needed. This provides

Activity 5.4 Resources

• *Representing Numbers as Quick Images* Activity Video

 To access resource visit resources.corwin.com/ MasteringMathManips/ K-3

Manipulative Illustrated

Number Pieces app from Math Learning Center: https://apps .mathlearningcenter.org/number -pieces/

students with the opportunity to estimate their totals and then to revise those estimates to achieve greater precision.

The important vocabulary in this activity centers on the distinction between place and value, noting that with written numbers, the place, or position, of each digit determines its value. Because base-ten blocks are proportional, the attribute of place is not critical in order to detect their value. However, with numerals, place is non-negotiable. By helping students see that distinction, they will better grasp the notion of "place" as position and the idea of "value" as how much a digit represents based on its position. After several teacher-led episodes, students may take turns playing the "teacher" in small groups.

Featured Connection

In this activity, students use the Name Your Model and Caption Your Picture strategies to represent the pictured quantity both in writing and verbally. With these strategies, we are highlighting the connection between the visual, symbolic, and verbal representations. First,

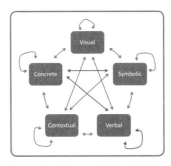 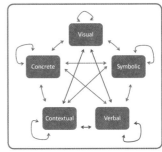

Source: Lesh, Post, & Behr (1987).

students name their models when they record the numeral to match the quantity that was flashed. And that is just the start. Not only should students name the represented number, but they should also describe how they arrived at that number using place-value language. Although this activity uses verbal descriptions, you may certainly ask students to record their descriptions in writing, as well.

Notes

_____

_____

_____

_____

_____

_____

_____

_____

Notes

COMPARING TWO-DIGIT NUMBERS

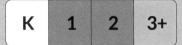

Materials

- Base-ten blocks in bags or tubs (unit cubes and rods for two-digit numbers; unit cubes, rods, and flats for three-digit numbers)

- One work mat per student (fun foam or construction paper)

- Blank paper for recording

- One copy of comparing numbers cards per student (one-, two-, or three-digit numbers—see directions on the cards sheet)

Organization (physical)

- **Getting Started:** Distribute one container of base-ten blocks to each student or pair of students.

- **Winding Down:** Count and put the base-ten blocks back in the containers before collecting, checking to be sure none fell on the floor or got left behind.

Mathematical Purpose

Students compare numbers using base-ten blocks by directly comparing the number of base-ten pieces in each place.

Activity 5.5 Resources

Comparing Numbers Cards

 To access resource visit resources.corwin.com/ MasteringMathManips/ K-3

Manipulative Illustrated

Base-Ten Blocks (available from multiple sources)

Steps

1. Preparation: Ask students to cut apart the comparing numbers cards (one sheet per student).

2. Ask each student to flip over one card and build that number on an individual work mat using the "simplest" version (the number of pieces matches the digit in each place). Support students' thinking by asking guiding questions such as the following:

   - *Did you represent each digit with its corresponding pieces?*

   - *How do you know you represented it correctly?*

   - *Did you represent it using the "simplest" version?*

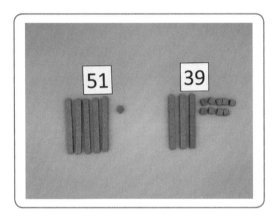

3. Ask students to work with their partners to compare their numbers, identifying which is greater and which is lesser. Support students' thinking by asking guiding questions to help them realize that once they compare the "bigger" pieces, no further comparisons are needed with the smaller pieces. Translate this to looking at the digits in the numbers.

   - *Which number is greater?*

   - *Which is lesser? How do you know?*

   - *Which pieces helped you figure out which number was greater and which was lesser?*

   - *Did you have to compare the smaller pieces?*

   - *How might this help you when comparing numerals? [Reference the number cards.]*

4. Ask students to use the Make a Sketch strategy to create visual representations of the base-ten blocks. They should also use the Name Your Model strategy by writing an inequality statement with the two numbers using either < or >.

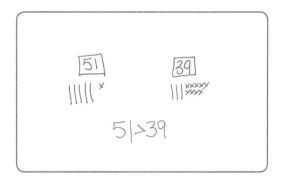

Why This Manipulative?

Base-ten blocks represent each digit in a number using proportionally sized pieces. Therefore, students can visually distinguish the magnitude each digit represents. For this activity, the rods (tens) are 10 times larger than the units (ones). Therefore, when students are comparing numbers that have different digits in the tens place, they can visually see that the number with the greater number of rods is the greater number without having to compare the units. That said, if they are comparing two numbers where the tens place is the same, then they *do* need to compare the units to determine which number is greater and which is lesser.

Developing Understanding

As in the previous activity, be sure to emphasize the distinction between "value" and "place." With the base-ten blocks, value is determined by the size or shape of each piece. However, with written numbers, the magnitude is determined by the place in which the digit appears. As you work with young learners, using the base-ten blocks to build and compare numbers gives you the opportunity to help them see that comparing the largest pieces is the best place to start. This way, they can determine which number is greater simply by comparing the larger pieces, provided they are not equivalent. You will also want to use guiding questions to help students generalize from the manipulatives to the digits in the numerals. Making this connection is well worth the time it takes to build concrete understanding and connect it to the abstract symbols.

Also, for the purposes of this activity, remind students to build the numbers in their "simplest" version, using the fewest number of base-ten block pieces needed by matching the number of pieces to the quantity represented in each digit. Comparing numbers built with base-ten blocks is easiest when the number of each piece corresponds with the digits.

Featured Connection

Students engage in three connection strategies during this activity. First they use a modified version of the Build the Equation strategy when they begin with the symbolic (number cards), and then they build corresponding concrete representations. After making their comparisons, they use the Make a Sketch and Name Your Model strategies to record their work. The combining of these three strategies supports students' thinking as they grapple with the complex mental processes involved in working with place value. Because students must concurrently attend to magnitude, place, and value when learning to compare numbers, these three strategies help them connect the concrete, visual, and abstract representations in an effort to build conceptual understanding.

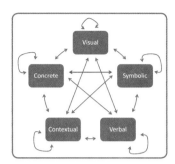

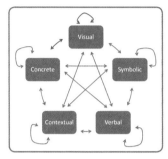

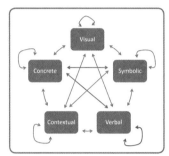

Source: Lesh, Post, & Behr (1987).

Notes

_____

_____

_____

_____

_____

_____

_____

_____

_____

_____

Notes

Materials

- Virtual base-ten blocks (or physical base-ten blocks and a work mat)
- Comparing numbers cards (same cards as used in previous activity—select one set of cards to use, based on the number set you're using with your students)

Organization (virtual)

- **Getting Started:** Ensure students know how to use the virtual base-ten blocks; review annotation tools, taking screenshots, and so on.
- **Winding Down:** Take screenshots to save student work.

Mathematical Purpose

Students count up or down by hundreds, tens, or ones, depending on the selected number set, using visual representations to help them conceptualize what is happening when they count up and down by "place."

Activity 5.6 Resources

Comparing Numbers Cards

 To access resource visit resources.corwin.com/ MasteringMathManips/ K-3

Manipulative Illustrated

Number Pieces app from Math Learning Center: https://apps .mathlearningcenter.org/number -pieces/

Steps

Note: The examples here use three-digit numbers. You can change the numbers based on the number sets in which students are currently working by using a different set of the provided number cards.

1. Demonstrate the activity with the entire class. The directions follow the process for three-digit numbers. You will want to modify if working with two- or one-digit numbers.

   a. Flip over one card.

   b. Represent that number with base-ten blocks. The following example shows 345.

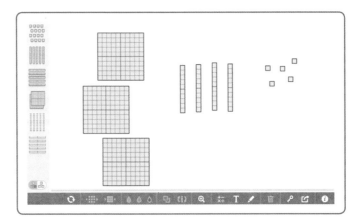

   c. Ask the students to count up by hundreds, beginning with the selected number. For each count, place one more flat on the work mat until they get to nine flats and some more. In the following example, students would count, "345, 445, 545, 645, 745, 845, 945."

   d. When they get to nine flats and some more, stop and count backward by one hundred until there are no more flats. In this example, students would count, "945, 845, 745, 645, 545, 445, 345, 245, 145, 45."

   e. *Optional:* Repeat this process with the same number, only this time counting up and down by tens, placing/removing a rod on the work mat each time. In this example, students would count "345, 355, 365, 375, 385, 395, 405, 415, 425 …"

   f. *Optional:* Repeat this process with the same number, only this time counting up and down by ones, placing/removing a unit cube on the work mat each time. In this example, students would count, "345, 346, 347, 348, 349, 350, 351 …"

g. *Extension:* Ask students to "play" one more round by flipping over a card and writing the number. Then ask them to record the count as they count up (or down) by hundreds, tens, or ones. Ask students to talk about what they notice in the number patterns and how those compare with the base-ten block patterns created during this activity.

2. Ask students to work in pairs or small groups to play this counting game using the number cards and counting numbers (up/down by hundreds, tens, and/or ones) you provide along with the base-ten blocks app (or physical base-ten blocks). Ask guiding questions: How do you know which digit to pay attention to? Is it easier to count up or to count down by hundreds, tens, or ones?

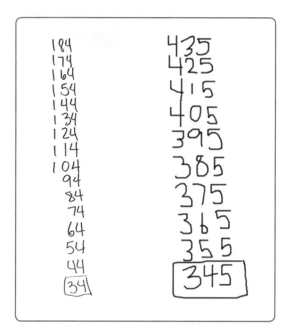

Why This Manipulative?

Because base-ten blocks represent the magnitude of each place in the number system (up to four places), they can be used to help students visualize the changes happening in each relative place. The base-ten blocks provide a visual for what it looks like when numbers are increasing by hundreds vs. tens vs. ones. This assists students to engage in meaningful skip counting rather than depending solely on the verbal pattern cues.

Developing Understanding

The teacher demo will be critical in helping students understand how to go about "playing" this counting game (we use the word *game* lightly here—this is not a competitive activity unless you make modifications). Be sure students are using the base-ten blocks to correctly model the changes occurring as they count up and down by different magnitudes. This will assist students as they internalize the concept rather than simply counting by rote memorization.

The conversation that takes place during the initial demonstration plays a critical role in developing understanding. As with other place-value activities, young learners are grappling with connecting the abstract and verbal patterns with what they concretely represent. Taking the time to have students practice counting forward and backward by different places while providing visual cues will be well worth the time, with deeper understanding being the dividend.

Featured Connection

This activity uses a modified version of the Build the Equation strategy as students begin with the abstract (number cards), building that number with concrete/visual representations. Furthermore, by adding additional number pieces to the concrete model, students make a connection to the verbal patterns. These connections are further enhanced when students record their counting using number sequences during the extension step.

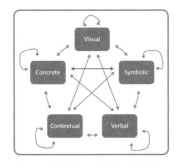

Source: Lesh, Post, & Behr (1987).

Notes

_____

_____

_____

_____

_____

_____

_____

_____

_____

_____

_____

_____

_____

Notes

Materials

- Base-ten blocks in bags or tubs (unit cubes and rods for one- and two-digit numbers; unit cubes, rods, and flats for three-digit numbers)
- Work mats (fun foam or construction paper)

Organization (physical)

- **Getting Started:** Distribute one container of base-ten blocks to each student or pair of students.
- **Winding Down:** Count and put the base-ten blocks back in the containers before collecting, checking to be sure none fell on the floor or got left behind.

Mathematical Purpose

Students explore concrete representations for addition with regrouping using base-ten blocks.

Manipulative Illustrated

Base-Ten Blocks (available from multiple sources)

Steps

Note: The examples here focus on two-digit addition. You can change the numbers based on the number sets in which students are currently working.

1. Ask pairs of students to work together to add 32 + 57 using base-ten blocks, with one student representing 32 and the other representing 57. Support students' thinking by asking guiding questions such as the following:

   - *What is the meaning of addition?*
   - *What are we doing when we're adding these two numbers? What action is taking place?*

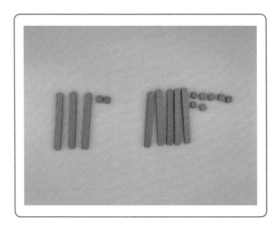

2. Ask students to combine their pieces onto one mat, putting the tens with the tens and the ones with the ones. Support their thinking by asking guiding questions such as these:

   - *What is the total? How do you know?*
   - *Is the number represented in its simplest version? [Each digit must be directly represented by the number of pieces that represent the magnitude of that place.]*

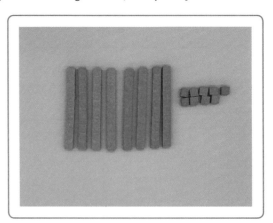

3. Ask students to clear their mats and to now represent 45 + 27 using base-ten blocks, with one student representing 45 and the other representing 27. Ask students to combine their pieces onto one mat, putting the tens with the tens and the ones with the ones. Support their thinking by asking guiding questions such as these:

- *What is the total? How do you know?*

- *Is the number represented in its simplest version? [Each digit must be directly represented by the number of pieces that represent the magnitude of that place.]*

- *Do you need to group anything together to represent the total in its simplest version?*

4. Repeat with additional numbers as needed, asking guiding questions to help students make generalizations as to when regrouping is needed.

Why This Manipulative?

Because base-ten blocks represent the place-value system using proportionally sized pieces, they can be used to represent arithmetic operations in base ten, representing the values in each place. This works quite well when no regrouping is necessary. However, when regrouping is necessary, as is often the case with multi-digit addition, the trading process can hinder some students' ability to see ten ones as concurrently existing as one group of ten. For that reason, groupable manipulatives, such as KP Ten-Frame Tiles or connecting cubes, may present a better option.

Developing Understanding

When using base-ten blocks for adding that requires regrouping, a review of the trading process may be helpful. Consider using the Activity 5.2 "Race to 100" game to help prepare students for using trading. Discuss that the act of "trading" is used with base-ten blocks to help them see that ten unit cubes can also be represented by one rod. This discussion can be avoided, as mentioned earlier, if you use groupable manipulatives, instead.

Featured Connection

Use the Build the Equation strategy to connect the symbolic and concrete representations. First, students translate the numbers on their number cards to concrete representations. Then they combine their concrete representations to show the action of the original equation.

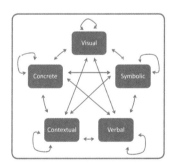

In addition, you may choose to use the Create a Word Problem strategy at the end of this lesson to remind students that math represents real-world contexts. With this strategy, we are highlighting the connection between the concrete and contextual representations and adding tremendous value to students' understanding of the addition process. Eventually, you will want to repeat this activity and connect it to the Make a Sketch and Name Your Model strategies as well, connecting all three of Piaget's categories for representation: concrete, visual, and symbolic.

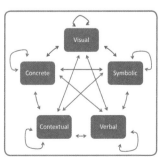

Source: Lesh, Post, & Behr (1987).

Materials

- Virtual base-ten blocks (or physical base-ten blocks and work mats)

Organization (virtual)

- **Getting Started:** Ensure students know how to use the virtual base-ten blocks; review annotation tools, taking screenshots, and so on.

- **Winding Down:** Take screenshots to save student work.

Mathematical Purpose

Students explore concrete representations for subtraction with regrouping using base-ten blocks.

Activity 5.8 Resources

- *Subtracting With Base-Ten Blocks* Activity Video

 To access resource visit resources.corwin.com/ MasteringMathManips/ K-3

Manipulative Illustrated

Number Pieces app from Math Learning Center: https://apps .mathlearningcenter.org/number -pieces/

Steps

Notes: The examples here focus on two-digit subtraction. Change the numbers based on the number sets in which students are currently working. Also, this example requires that students are already familiar with naming and representing numbers in various ways, as explored in Activity 5.7.

1. Ask pairs of students to work together to solve 56 – 24 using base-ten blocks, with one student representing 56 and the other creating a space to "receive" the removed blocks (if using physical blocks, a second work mat will suffice). Support students' thinking by asking guiding questions such as the following:

   - *What is the meaning of subtraction?*

   - *What are we doing when we're subtracting one number from another?*

   - *What action is taking place?*

   - *Why did we create a "receiving" space on the screen?*

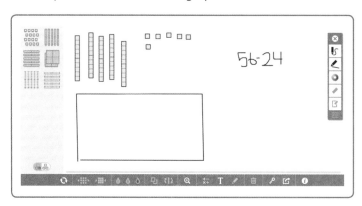

2. Ask students to move 24 pieces into the receiving space. Support their thinking by asking guiding questions such as these:

   - *How many pieces are left on the original mat?*

   - *How do you know this is correct?*

   - *Is the number represented in its simplest version? [Each digit must be directly represented by the number of pieces that represent the magnitude of that place.]*

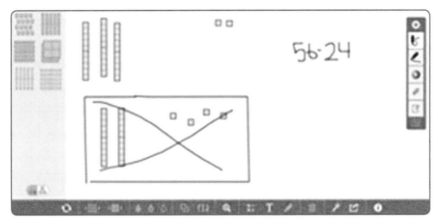

3. Ask students to clear their screens. Ask them to represent 56 – 28 using base-ten blocks, with one student representing 56 and the other creating a space to "receive" the removed blocks (if using physical blocks, a second work mat will suffice). Support students' thinking by asking guiding questions such as the following:

- *Is 56 represented in a version that will allow you to easily remove 28?*

- *Is there a friendlier version of 56 that will assist with this action [e.g., 4 rods and 18 unit cubes]? [Note: There is no need to talk about "borrowing" or "regrouping"—just renaming 58 as 40 and 18 will suffice for young learners.]*

- *Now that you've made a "friendlier number," how will you subtract now?*

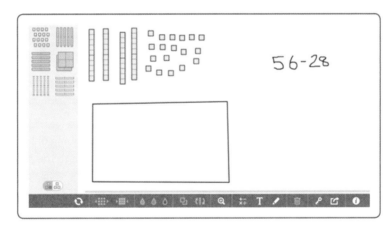

4. Ask students to proceed with the subtraction process, moving pieces that represent 28 onto the empty mat and covering them with a piece of paper.

5. Repeat with additional numbers as needed, continuing to ask guiding questions to help the students make generalizations as to when regrouping is needed.

Why This Manipulative?

Because base-ten blocks represent the place-value system using proportionally sized pieces, they can be used to represent arithmetic operations in base ten, representing the values in each place. This works quite well when no regrouping is necessary. However, when regrouping is necessary, as is often the case with multi-digit subtraction, the trading process can hinder some students' ability to see ten ones as concurrently existing as one group of ten. For that reason, using a virtual base-ten blocks model or a groupable manipulative, such as KP Ten-Frame Tiles or connecting cubes, may present a better option.

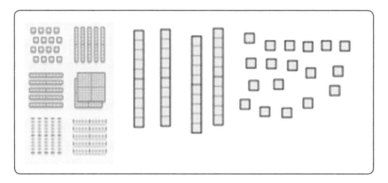

Developing Understanding

When using base-ten blocks, the "regrouping by trading" action can be confusing for students. The process introduced here requests that students first build a "friendly" version of the minuend so they will have enough of the corresponding pieces when they go to subtract. This avoids the need to "trade" for more pieces in the middle of the process.

Featured Connection

Use the Build the Equation strategy to connect the symbolic and concrete representations. First, students translate the minuend from their number cards to concrete representations. Then they use their concrete representation of the minuend to show the action of removing the subtrahend from the concrete/visual representation as indicated in the original equation.

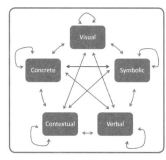

Source: Lesh, Post, & Behr (1987).

In addition, you may choose to use the Create a Word Problem strategy at the end of this lesson to remind students that math represents real-world contexts. With this strategy, we are highlighting the connection between the concrete and contextual representations and adding tremendous value to students' understanding of the addition process. Eventually, you will want to repeat this activity and connect it to the Make a Sketch and Name Your Model strategies as well, connecting all three of Piaget's categories for representation: concrete, visual, and symbolic.

Notes

_____

_____

_____

_____

_____

_____

Notes

Materials

- Base-ten blocks in bags or tubs (unit cubes and rods; work mats made of fun foam or construction paper)
- Recording sheet for each student

Organization (physical)

- **Getting Started:** Distribute one container of base-ten blocks to each student or pair of students.
- **Winding Down:** Count and put the base-ten blocks back in the containers before collecting, checking to be sure none fell on the floor or got left behind.

Mathematical Purpose

Students look for patterns as they multiply by a single-digit number and then multiply by the corresponding multiple of ten.

Activity 5.9 Resources

Multiplying by Multiples of Ten Recording Sheet

 To access resource visit resources.corwin.com/ MasteringMathManips/ K-3

Manipulative Illustrated

Base-Ten Blocks (available from multiple sources)

Steps

1. Ask students to represent 3 × 4 using unit cubes. For this activity, the order matters—they should create three groups with four unit cubes in each group. To support their thinking, ask guiding questions such as the following:

   - *How many groups are there?*
   - *How many unit cubes are in each group?*
   - *How many unit cubes are there altogether?*

2. Next, ask students to represent 3 × 40 using rods. For this activity, the order matters—students should create three groups with four rods in each group. Ask guiding questions:

   - *How many groups are there?*
   - *How many rods are in each group?*
   - *How many rods are there altogether?*
   - *What is the value of each group?*
   - *What is the total value?*

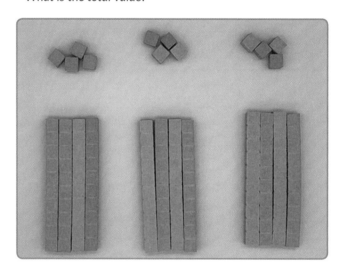

3. Distribute the recording sheet. Ask students to use the Create a Diagram strategy by completing the table on the recording sheet. Encourage them to use base-ten blocks to help them complete the first section of the table.

5.9 Multiplying by Multiples of Ten Recording Sheet

Use base ten blocks to multiply each pair of expressions. Complete each row of the table below and look for patterns.

#	Multiply	Product	#	Multiply	Product
1	3 x 4	12	2	2 x 5	10
1	3 x 40	120	2	2 x 50	100
3	4 x 2	8	4	5 x 3	15
3	4 x 20	80	4	5 x 30	150
5	3 x 2	6	6	4 x 4	16
5	3 x 20	60	6	4 x 40	160
7	3 x 3	9	8	2 x 2	4
7	3 x 30	90	8	2 x 20	40

For each pair, what patterns do you notice?

4. Ask students to repeat this process for the rest of the pairs of expressions on the table.

5. After students have finished the task, bring them back together to discuss their findings. Facilitate the student conversation by asking guiding questions such as these:

   » *What did you notice as you did this task?*

   » *Did you notice any patterns as you multiplied one-digit numbers and then multiplied by a corresponding group of ten?*

   » *What did the blocks look like when you did this?*

   » *What did the numbers (products) look like when you did this?*

Why This Manipulative?

Because base-ten blocks represent the place-value system using proportionally sized pieces, they can be used to represent arithmetic operations in base ten. In this case, students are able to represent and compare the **products** when multiplying by ones and by the corresponding multiples of ten, looking for generalizable patterns in the process. Far too often, students blindly learn the pattern to "tack on a zero" when multiplying by ten, a practice that fails when students apply it to decimals. This activity helps students visualize the idea that they are multiplying by a different magnitude of ten, resulting in a product that is 10 times that of the original product.

Developing Understanding

By using guiding questions to help students recognize the connection between multiplying by a number and multiplying by the corresponding multiple of ten, you may lead them into discovering an all-important pattern. Through discovery and discussion, you are guiding students to see the relationship between multiplying single-digit numbers and corresponding groups of ten. The goal is to help students lean into this pattern. At this point in time, it's important that students avoid the generalization that they simply "tack on a zero" to the product. This generalization will come as they develop fluency with multiplying by tens, but it is not where they should start.

Featured Connection

Use the Create a Diagram strategy to highlight the connection between the concrete and symbolic representations. By translating the concrete representation with the base-ten blocks to the symbolic representations on a table, students will be more likely to generate patterns that emerge from this work. This connection can play a huge role in guiding students toward discovering the pattern that emerges rather than simply learning the "rule" of tacking on a zero.

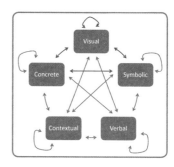

Source: Lesh, Post, & Behr (1987).

Notes

_____

_____

_____

_____

_____

_____

_____

_____

_____

_____

_____

_____

CLOSING REFLECTION: BASE-TEN BLOCKS

How do I use base-ten blocks in my classroom now? What concepts do I use them to teach?

_____

_____

_____

_____

_____

What new ways have I found to use base-ten blocks to better support student understanding?

_____

_____

_____

_____

_____

What are my goals to make base-ten blocks a more regular part of my instruction?

_____

_____

_____

_____

_____

CHAPTER 6
Pattern Blocks

INTRODUCTION

Understanding Pattern Blocks

Pattern blocks are sets of wood or plastic blocks used to illustrate both geometric and numerical concepts. The set typically includes six different pieces: yellow hexagon, red trapezoid, blue rhombus, green triangle, orange square, and tan rhombus. The blocks are proportional and have a standard edge length, making them well suited for creating geometric designs and for illustrating measurement principles. Add-on pieces are available and represent $\frac{1}{4}$ and $\frac{1}{8}$ of the yellow hexagon.

Pattern blocks are particularly effective in teaching these concepts:

- Geometric vocabulary
- Geometric attributes
- Perimeter
- Spatial relationships
- Fraction concepts
- Equivalent fractions
- Fraction operations

Introducing Pattern Blocks to Students

Introduce pattern blocks as composed of six pieces. As much as possible, encourage students to use the geometric names rather than the colors. Use the *Notice and Wonder Thinking Routine* (described in the introductory chapter) to support students' exploration of the pattern blocks. Students may notice that the edges are the same length for all of the pieces except for the trapezoid, which has one side with a length 2 times that of all other edges. Students may recognize the proportional sizes of the pieces. They may wonder what kinds of designs they can make.

Key Ideas With Pattern Blocks

- Pattern blocks offer a playful way to develop spatial relationships. Provide many opportunities for students to use pattern blocks as they solve puzzles and other activities. Many of these are available in print and electronic form. In addition, online virtual manipulatives such as the Math Learning Center's Pattern Shapes app provide puzzles for the students to fill with pattern blocks.

- Because pattern blocks are proportional and un-grouped, they afford students excellent opportunities for engaging in fraction work.

- Perimeter is frequently taught alongside area with a focus on using iterated square units to concurrently focus on both area and perimeter. This frequently causes confusion for students. Using pattern blocks to focus on perimeter affords students the opportunity to center their focus on the linear measurement of perimeter without attending to the square units that "cover" area. Because the unit length of pattern blocks is consistent, they are a perfect tool for helping students learn perimeter.

- When using pattern blocks to explore fraction concepts and operations, avoid using the hexagon as the "whole," or unit, too frequently. Use this tool to develop flexibility with unit, encouraging students to use the smaller pieces or multiple pieces to define the "whole" or unit.

- Several activities in Chapter 7 of this book, "Fraction Manipulatives," can also be accomplished using pattern blocks. Don't miss out on the amazing ways in which pattern blocks can be used to represent fractions.

Things to Consider About Pattern Blocks

- Even after decades of use, pattern blocks usually come in standard colors.

- Students tend to name the pattern-block pieces by their colors rather than their geometric names. Encourage use of the latter.

- The unit lengths of the sides of each shape are consistent, making pattern blocks a great tool for exploring many tools such as perimeter.

- The proportional nature of the pieces makes pattern blocks a great tool for exploring proportional relationships, including fractions and whole numbers.

Alternatives to Commercial Pattern Blocks

There are dies available for die-cut machines that will cut pattern blocks. These might be cut from card stock or fun foam, providing completely adequate pieces. There are also many patterns available online and in books that can be printed and precut for classroom use.

Working With Virtual Pattern Blocks

Although concrete manipulatives afford the greatest benefits, virtual pattern blocks possess several benefits as well. They include an unlimited supply of each piece, and they usually include a snap tool that helps the pieces fit into place. Some sites add protractors and other measurement tools to explore concepts such as angle measurement and perimeter.

Virtual pattern blocks are especially useful as they provide an unlimited number of pieces. When looking for an online version of pattern blocks, you may find it useful to look for an app that has a writing tool so students can annotate their work.

Materials

- Large container of pattern blocks for each group of students
- Work mats (fun foam or heavy paper)
- Recording sheet for each student

Organization (physical)

- **Getting Started:** Distribute a container of pattern blocks to each group of students.
- **Winding Down:** Ask students to tidy up their workspace, being sure that all pattern blocks are accounted for and placed back in the container.

Mathematical Purpose

In this activity, students use pattern blocks to compose or decompose shapes that are equivalent to the yellow pattern-block piece. Activities such as this provide the foundation for developing spatial sense for future work in geometry.

Activity 6.1 Resources

How Many Ways to Compose a Hexagon? Recording Sheet

 To access resource visit resources.corwin.com/ MasteringMathManips/ K-3

Manipulative Illustrated

Pattern-Block Pieces (available from multiple sources)

Steps

1. Ask each student to take out one yellow hexagon. Using the hexagon as a base, ask them to cover it with other pattern blocks with no gaps and no overlaps.

2. Ask students to keep going, making as many unique equivalent hexagons as possible. To support their thinking, ask guiding questions such as the following:
   - *How many sides does a hexagon have?*
   - *How many angles does a hexagon have?*
   - *How many unique hexagons do you think you can make?*

3. Students continue to cover hexagons until they find all of the possible combinations with no repeats.

4. Ask students to use the Make a Sketch strategy to show their work on the recording sheet. Note that there are more hexagons on the sheet than are needed.

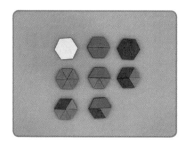

5. *Extension:* This is a great activity for children beyond first grade when used as an introductory activity for using pattern blocks for either geometry or **fractions**. If you are using it for that purpose, be sure to ask guiding questions that incorporate the vocabulary and concepts that will be covered in future lessons.

Why This Manipulative?

Pattern blocks provide a pleasing aesthetic when working with geometric and spatial skills. They fit together in various arrangements and allow students to explore concepts of angle, unit length, translations, composing and decomposing, and so on. In this activity, students explore ways in which pattern blocks fit together to create regular hexagons equivalent to the yellow hexagon piece. Virtual pattern blocks may also be a great tool for this activity since they have the benefit of an endless supply for every shape, and they have a snap tool that fits the pieces into place on the screen. Students can take screenshots of their arrangements when they're finished, or they can still engage in the Make a Sketch activity to transfer their work to a new representation.

Developing Understanding

Building spatial sense through the manipulation of shapes is an essential stage for geometric thinking. As students "play" with geometric shapes, they informally build understandings about geometric attributes. Encourage students to rotate, flip, and shift shapes in many different positions as they explore how many ways they can make unique hexagons equivalent to the yellow piece.

During this activity, you may want to reinforce many geometric concepts. First, most geometry standards include much terminology; you can use the pattern blocks to develop geometry vocabulary during this activity. Second, the notion of composing and decomposing shapes is prevalent throughout the K–3 standards, and you can use this hexagon task to promote spatial reasoning. Third, many geometric attributes can be reinforced with this activity across the grade levels.

Finally, this activity provides a unique opportunity for using geometry as a springboard for problem solving. As students engage with geometric concepts, the task asks them to find all possible combinations of blocks to create hexagons, providing you with the opportunity to engage students in higher-level thinking.

Featured Connection

Use the Make a Sketch strategy in this activity to highlight the connection between the concrete and visual representations. Learning to sketch pattern blocks may prove challenging for young learners. Many children might find it easier to trace the pattern blocks rather than to sketch them freehand. The provided recording sheet may help students with the process since the large hexagons are predrawn. You might point out that simply putting a dot at the midpoint of each hexagon may make sketching easier. Provide students many opportunities to practice, coaching them along the way.

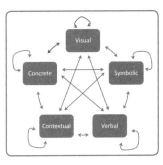

Source: Lesh, Post, & Behr (1987).

Notes

_____

_____

_____

_____

_____

_____

_____

COMPOSING AND DECOMPOSING LARGER FIGURES WITH PATTERN BLOCKS

| K | 1 | 2 | 3+ |

Materials

- Large container of pattern blocks for each group of students
- Pattern-block puzzles collected from online or commercial resources (example provided)
- Pattern-Block Puzzle Pages (several for each group of students)
- Recording sheet for each student

Organization (physical)

- **Getting Started:** Distribute a container of pattern blocks to each group of students. Provide pattern block puzzles and the recording sheet.
- **Winding Down:** Ask students to tidy up their workspace, being sure that all pattern blocks are accounted for and placed back in the container.

Mathematical Purpose

In this activity, students use pattern blocks to compose predrawn composite figures, similar to using puzzle pieces to complete a picture.

Activity 6.2 Resources

Composing and Decomposing Larger Figures With Pattern Blocks Recording Sheet

 To access resource visit resources.corwin.com/ MasteringMathManips/ K-3

Steps

1. Ask students to select a shape to fill with pattern blocks. To support their thinking, ask guiding questions such as the following:

    - *How many blocks do you think will fill this shape?*
    - *What pieces did you use?*
    - *How many of each piece did you use?*
    - *Could you have filled this puzzle a different way?*

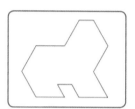

2. Distribute the recording sheet. Ask students to use the Create a Diagram strategy to translate the total number of pattern-block pieces on a table, called a "recipe card," once the shape is filled.

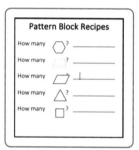

3. Once students are finished recording their results, ask them to fill the same puzzle a different way and record the results on another recipe card.

4. Ask students to continue filling the pattern-block puzzle with different configurations of pattern blocks until at least two recipe cards are filled.

5. Repeat this activity with different pattern-block puzzles over the course of several days by creating designs with other values. This activity may also be placed in a learning center.

6. *Extension 1:* This activity can be extended as a data collection and representation activity.

7. *Extension 2:* This is a great activity for children beyond first grade when used as an introductory activity for using pattern blocks. If you are using it for that purpose, be sure to ask guiding questions that incorporate the vocabulary and concepts that will be covered in future lessons.

Why This Manipulative?

Pattern blocks provide dynamic opportunities for students to build spatial sense through the manipulation of shapes. Because pattern blocks include the attribute of proportional dimension, students can move them into many different configurations and see that they fit together with no gaps and no overlaps. When using virtual versions of pattern blocks, the snap feature assists students with fitting the pieces together along their like-sized edges.

Developing Understanding

Physically manipulating geometric shapes, especially in the form of blocks and other physical toys, is an essential stage for geometric thinking. As students "play" with geometric shapes, they informally build understandings about geometric attributes.

This activity demonstrates one way that students can manipulate shapes, seeing how they fit together to compose new shapes. Although a plethora of pattern-block puzzles are available commercially and online, this lesson is provided to ensure teachers tap into these amazing opportunities for students to develop spatial skills while engaging in geometric puzzles. Just as with Activity 6.1, encourage students to rotate, flip, and shift shapes in many different positions as they explore different configurations for completing their pattern-block puzzles.

An additional component of this activity centers on the completion of a chart, or "recipe card," each time the students create new configurations. The provides a record of how the shapes were used and connects spatial reasoning to quantitative data. This activity can be extended to include data collection and representation concepts as well.

Featured Connection

In this activity, students use the Create a Diagram strategy to highlight the connection between concrete and symbolic representations, with the "recipe card" serving as the diagram. By engaging in this process multiple times on the same recording sheet, students will see that the same shape can be composed and decomposed in many different ways.

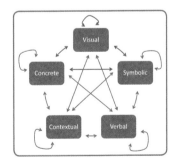

Source: Lesh, Post, & Behr (1987).

And by recording the data on tables, students will have a lasting record of how they went about doing this.

Manipulative Illustrated

Pattern-Block Pieces (available from multiple sources)

Note: A virtual version of pattern-block puzzles is available in the Math Learning Center Pattern Shapes app: https://apps.mathlearningcenter.org/pattern-shapes/

Materials

- Large container of pattern blocks for each group of students
- Work mats (fun foam or heavy paper)
- Recording sheet for each student
- *Optional:* Precut pattern-block pieces and glue for students to record their designs

Organization (physical)

- **Getting Started:** Distribute a container of pattern blocks to each group of students.
- **Winding Down:** Ask students to tidy up their workspace, being sure that all pattern blocks are accounted for and placed back in the container.

Mathematical Purpose

In this activity, students explore both spatial sense and number sense as they create pattern-block designs that total a given value.

Steps

1. Tell students that for today's task, each green triangle has a value of $1.

2. Ask students what the value of each of the other pattern-block pieces is, given that the value of a triangle is $1. To support their thinking, ask guiding questions such as the following:

    - *How many triangles are equivalent to one rhombus? One trapezoid? One hexagon?*

    - *How can you use that information to determine the value of each piece?*

3. Ask students to complete the values table on the recording sheet.

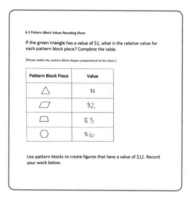

4. Ask students to use pattern-block pieces to create designs (composite shapes) that have a value of $12 (see the examples that follow). To support their thinking, ask guiding questions such as the following:

    - *How do you know that this design has a value of $12?*

    - *Can you write that as an equation?*

    - *What operation(s) might you use?*

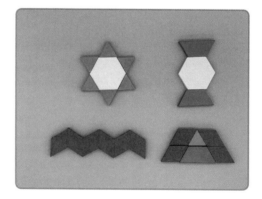

5. When time is up, ask students to work in pairs, describing their $12 designs to one another using both geometry and number sense vocabulary.

6. Ask students to use the Make a Sketch strategy to record their work. An alternative to sketching would be to glue precut paper pattern blocks onto the recording sheet. Also ask students to use the Name Your Model strategy to record equations that indicate the values for each design.

7. Repeat this activity over the course of several days by creating designs with other values. This activity may also be placed in a learning center.

Why This Manipulative?

Pattern blocks provide a pleasing aesthetic when working with geometric and spatial skills. Their proportional side lengths and common colors for each shape provide a foundation for students to compose and decompose figures to be used in a variety of contexts, including finding quantitative values, as in this activity. Furthermore, pattern blocks work well for this activity because they provide a foundation for creating multiple configurations for the same figure with easily identifiable pieces. Once again, these manipulatives provide a playful way for students to explore geometric and quantitative concepts.

Developing Understanding

Building spatial sense through the manipulation of shapes is an essential stage for geometric thinking. As students "play" with geometric shapes, they informally build understandings about geometric attributes.

As you lead students through this activity, encourage them to rotate, flip, and shift shapes in many different positions as they create their $12 designs. Sometimes they will find that the same figure can be composed with different pattern blocks. In addition, older students may come to realize that each of the designs they create for a given value has the same area (in this case, 12 triangles).

Activity 6.3 Resources

- *How Many Ways to Compose a Given Value?* Recording Sheet

 To access resource visit resources.corwin.com/ MasteringMathManips/ K-3

Manipulative Illustrated

Pattern-Block Pieces (available from multiple sources)

Featured Connection

In this activity, students use the Make a Sketch and Name Your Model strategies to connect the concrete representations they created with the pattern blocks to visual and symbolic representations. Sketching geometric figures that were created with concrete objects helps

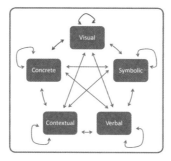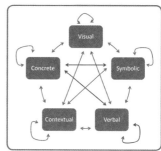

Source: Lesh, Post, & Behr (1987).

students further develop their spatial skills, and they are also able to keep a written record of the different designs that had the same value and, therefore, the same area. By connecting to symbolic representations of the values assigned to each design, students make an important connection between the geometry and number standards as well.

Notes

_____

_____

_____

_____

_____

_____

_____

_____

_____

_____

_____

_____

_____

Notes

Materials

- Large container of pattern blocks for each group of students
- Work mats (fun foam or heavy paper)
- Pattern-block puzzles (one or more puzzles per student, depending on your math goals)

Organization (physical)

- **Getting Started:** Distribute a container of pattern blocks to each group of students. Provide pattern-block puzzles and the recording sheet.
- **Winding Down:** Ask students to tidy up their workspace, being sure that all pattern blocks are accounted for and placed back in the container.

Mathematical Purpose

In this activity, students explore perimeter as the linear measurement that extends around the outside of a figure. Working on perimeter as its own concept, without connecting it to area, is very helpful for students since they often confuse area and perimeter.

Manipulative Illustrated

Pattern-Block Pieces (available from multiple sources)

Note: The Math Learning Center's Pattern Pieces app also provides nice puzzles for students to fill and then examine the perimeters: https://apps.mathlearningcenter .org/pattern-shapes/

Steps

1. Ask students what they notice about the sides of each of the pattern blocks. To support their thinking, ask guiding questions such as the following:

   - *What do you notice about the side lengths of all the pieces?*
   - *Do all the side lengths match up with different pieces?*
   - *Which ones match up? Which ones don't?*
   - *What do you notice about the longest side on the trapezoid and the sides of the other pattern-block pieces?*

2. Select one of the pattern-block puzzles from Activity 6.2 (see example pictured). Ask students to fill in the provided shape with pattern blocks. Encourage each student to use different pattern-block arrangements. You will use this later to point out that although the pattern blocks change, the perimeter remains constant.

3. Ask students to count the edges of the blocks that touch the perimeter of the figure. Note that if the long edge of a red trapezoid is touching the outside, it counts as two units since it is twice as long. Support students' thinking by asking guiding questions such as these:

   - *How did you count the units around the perimeter?*
   - *How did you know where to start and stop?*
   - *Will it be the same if you start in another spot?*
   - *What happens to the perimeter when the puzzle is filled in differently? [Point out that each student filled out the puzzle differently.]*

4. Ask students to use a modified version of the Caption Your Picture strategy to connect this concrete representation to a contextual, symbolic representation. Ask them to use the word *perimeter* as well as the number in their captions. Note that all students who used the same puzzle should name the same perimeter.

5. Continue with other puzzles, recording perimeters and discoveries on a blank sheet of paper folded into four equal sections.

Why This Manipulative?

Because pattern blocks are proportional and based on a common unit, they lend themselves well to an exploration of perimeter. Because square units are not used in this activity, resist the temptation to focus on area, using this time to emphasize perimeter as the linear measurement that goes around the outside of the figure.

Developing Understanding

A common misconception that frequently emerges from teaching perimeter and area at the same time can be avoided with activities such as this one, which only focuses on perimeter. Students can focus on the linear measurement around the perimeter of the figure without being concerned about square units or with the iteration of square units with no gaps and no overlaps, which is necessary for area. Note that measuring perimeters, such as with linking cubes in Activity 2.10, prior to measuring perimeters around figures such as in this activity may help students in cementing their understanding of perimeter prior to connecting it to area.

As you help students grapple with looking at the linear perimeter of the object as opposed to the area they covered, take time to explore the common unit length used with the pattern-block pieces. Focus students' attention on the side lengths rather than on the area of each piece. Students often miss the notion that perimeter is a measure of length, unlike area, which carries the attribute of "covering."

Featured Connection

In this activity, students use a modified version of the Caption Your Picture strategy to highlight the connection between the concrete and symbolic representations. As mentioned in the directions, students' captions should include both the word *perimeter* and the numerical value they determined to be the perimeter. By using this strategy, students are also likely to make a verbal connection to the perimeter of the pattern-block puzzle they created, helping them distinguish between representing area and representing perimeter.

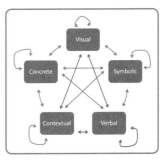

Source: Lesh, Post, & Behr (1987).

Notes

_____

_____

_____

_____

_____

_____

EQUIVALENT FRACTIONS WITH PATTERN BLOCKS

K	1	2	3+

Materials

- Virtual pattern-blocks app (or physical pattern blocks and work mats)
- Recording sheet for each student

Organization (virtual)

- **Getting Started:** Ensure students know how to use the virtual pattern blocks; review annotation tools, taking screenshots, and so on.
- **Winding Down:** Take screenshots to save student work.

Mathematical Purpose

In this activity, students engage in problem solving using pattern blocks as a fraction tool. This activity emphasizes the process of decontextualizing the math from a situation, using tools and strategies to "do the math," and then recontextualizing the solution to ensure it makes sense in the context from which it came. In addition, the third problem in this set requires that students shift away from using one hexagon as the "whole" in order to work with fourths.

Activity 6.5 Resources

Equivalent Fractions With Pattern Blocks Recording Sheet

 To access resource visit resources.corwin.com/ MasteringMathManips/ K-3

Steps

> Jake ate $\frac{2}{3}$ of a watermelon. Suzie picked a watermelon the same size as Jake's and cut it into 6 equal-sized pieces. If she wants to eat the same amount as Jake, how many pieces should Suzie eat?

1. Ask students to work with partners as they use pattern blocks to solve the first problem. Ask them guiding questions:

   - *Which pattern blocks will you use?*
   - *What will represent one whole?*
   - *Can you split that whole into both thirds and sixths?*
   - *How will you know how many pieces of watermelon Suzie will eat?*

2. As students use the virtual pattern blocks, ask them to use the Name Your Model strategy to show the equivalent fractions for each figure. Also ask students to label their figures to make the direct connection back to the contextual situation.

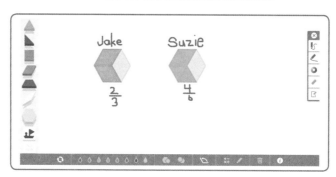

3. During the whole-group discussion, ask guiding questions to help students understand two major ideas:

   - *Discuss the notion of equivalent fractions—fractions that name the same amount, even though the number of pieces and size of those pieces is not the same. Provide a couple more examples, if needed.*
   - *Discuss that although students used equivalent fractions to solve the problem, when they answer the original question only the numerator (the number of pieces) is needed rather than a fractional answer.*

4. Ask students to read the next two situations and use pattern blocks to find the solution. Remind them to carefully attend to

the question to see if they need to answer with the fraction or just with the numerator. To support students' thinking, continue asking guiding questions such as those listed earlier.

Why This Manipulative?

Pattern blocks are often used to reinforce geometric thinking. However, as is shown here, pattern blocks can also be used to help students explore fractions. Although add-on pieces are available to represent fourths and eighths of the yellow hexagon, students might benefit from learning to shift to a different unit when solving problems, as illustrated as follows for Problem 3. The use of virtual pattern blocks is especially useful as students can add their annotations and then take a screenshot rather than needing to replicate their physical pattern blocks with sketches.

Developing Understanding

This activity focuses on using pattern blocks to solve fraction problems, a great way for students to work with equivalent fractions and other fraction concepts. Since the problems in this activity are presented in a contextual situation, the complexity is increased because students must decontextualize the math, work on the math to solve each problem, and then recontextualize the solutions to ensure that they make sense in the context. This is a complex process that develops over time.

With the problems included, students will need to grapple with the notion of unit. Especially for Problem 3, students will not be able to represent $\frac{2}{4}$ with pattern blocks if they stick to using just the single hexagon as the unit.

> Max drank $\frac{1}{2}$ gallon of water. Rajim wanted to drink the same amount, but his gallon was divided into 4 same-sized bottles. How many bottles should Jeff drink?

By creating a two-hexagon unit, students are then able to show $\frac{2}{4}$ with the red trapezoids, as pictured.

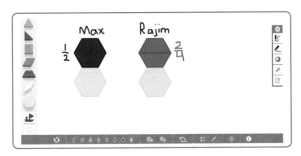

Manipulative Illustrated

Pattern Shapes app from Math Learning Center: https://apps.mathlearningcenter.org/pattern-shapes/

Featured Connection

In this activity, students use the Name Your Model strategy to highlight the connection between the concrete and symbolic representations. Since students are using pattern blocks to represent fractions, the symbolic representation is particularly important to emphasize the comparison of fractional values as opposed to the geometric properties of the pattern blocks.

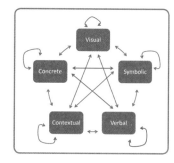

Source: Lesh, Post, & Behr (1987).

Notes

_____

_____

_____

_____

_____

_____

_____

_____

_____

_____

_____

_____

_____

_____

_____

Notes

Materials

- Virtual pattern-blocks app (or physical pattern blocks and work mats)
- Blank paper

Organization (virtual)

- **Getting Started:** Ensure students know how to use the virtual pattern blocks; review annotation tools, taking screenshots, and so on.
- **Winding Down:** Take screenshots to save student work.

Mathematical Purpose

Students compare fractions, attending to the fact that they must be fractions that are part of the same whole in order to be compared. In this activity, students will be asked to attend to the shift in unit for each problem in order to make comparisons.

Manipulative Illustrated

Pattern Shapes app from Math Learning Center: https://apps.mathlearningcenter.org/pattern-shapes/

Steps

> Compare $\frac{1}{2}$ and $\frac{1}{3}$

1. Post the fractions $\frac{1}{2}$ and $\frac{1}{3}$ for all to see. To learn what students already know about fractions, ask students to use a modified version of the Build the Equation strategy to sketch these two fractions and to explain what they know. To support their thinking, ask guiding questions such as the following:

   - *What do you know about the 1 and the 2 in $\frac{1}{2}$?*
   - *What do you know about the 1 and the 3 in $\frac{1}{3}$?*
   - *Which pieces are larger, halves or thirds?*
   - *How do you know?*

2. Once students have sketched and discussed the fractions, talk with the whole class about which is bigger, $\frac{1}{2}$ or $\frac{1}{3}$. During the discussion, point out the importance of the unit—the only way two fractions can be compared if they are naming parts of a same-sized whole. By way of example, ask students,

> Which is larger, $\frac{1}{2}$ of a pizza or $\frac{1}{3}$ of a pizza?

Of course, most students will say $\frac{1}{2}$. But then explain that that is only true if the pizzas are both the same size. What if we were comparing $\frac{1}{2}$ of a small pizza with $\frac{1}{3}$ of an extra-large pizza? We can't really compare the fractions because they're not naming parts of same-sized wholes.

3. Next, ask students to use a pattern-blocks tool (or physical pattern blocks) to compare $\frac{1}{2}$ and $\frac{1}{3}$ using common wholes, or units (we will use the word *unit* moving forward). The example that follows shows the comparing first with the yellow hexagon as the unit and then with the red trapezoid as the unit.

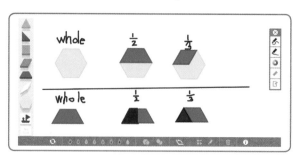

4. Next, ask students how they might combine shapes to create new units for comparing $\frac{1}{2}$ and $\frac{1}{3}$. One suggestion may be to combine them to make hexagons. Allow time for students to discover different ways of composing units that can then be used to demonstrate $\frac{1}{2}$ and $\frac{1}{3}$. The example that follows shows two possibilities.

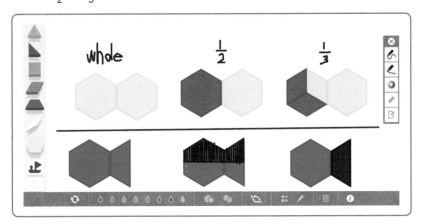

5. Continue the exploration with other fractions and other units. The point here is that the students playfully explore different ways of defining a unit to compare two fractions. Other fractions they explore may include fractions with common numerators, common denominators, or even more complex options. Here you see an example comparing $\frac{1}{3}$ and $\frac{2}{3}$, followed by a comparison of $\frac{5}{6}$ and $\frac{1}{2}$. Note that students may begin using the <, >, and = symbols as appropriate for the grade-level standards and math goals you are addressing.

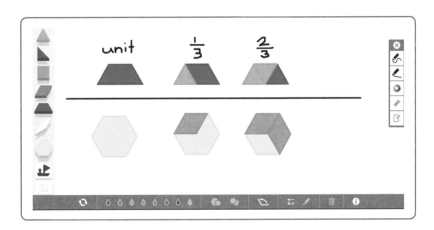

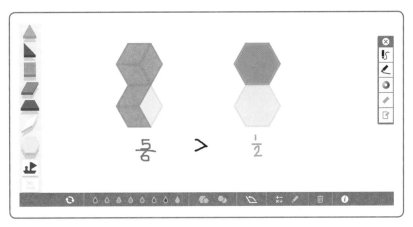

Why This Manipulative?

Because the different pieces are easy to differentiate, pattern blocks lend themselves well to creating models with flexible units to compare fractions. By comparison, fractions as pieces of circles, squares, rectangles, and bars can be difficult to differentiate without paying close attention to the markings and/or continuously comparing back to the largest piece.

Using a virtual tool, such as the Math Learning Center's Pattern Shapes app, provides additional support because the colors of the pieces can be changed, as seen in the examples. Furthermore, the annotation tool can be used to color in fractions that aren't available as pattern-block pieces (e.g., coloring $\frac{1}{2}$ of a red trapezoid). Of course, if using physical pattern blocks, you can provide precut paper shapes in those configurations, or you can purchase add-on sets that provide fourths and eighths of the yellow hexagon.

Developing Understanding

To compare fractions, students must ensure that the fractions they are comparing are related to the same whole. Therefore, this activity frequently shifts the "whole" so that when students compare fractions, they must relate back to the whole in order to make their comparisons. To support their thinking, be sure to ask many guiding questions, and teach the students to begin asking those questions of themselves. You may find it helpful to post an anchor chart that lists the guiding questions for comparing fractions. Possible prompts may include the following:

- *What fractions are you comparing?*
- *What is the whole to which the fractions are referring?*
- *How might you represent fractions that refer to the same whole?*
  - » *Fraction Pieces: Set out a matching "whole" for each fraction. Then create the fractions you are comparing on top of the wholes.*
  - » *Sketches: Sketch a matching "whole" for each fraction, and then shade in the fractions you are comparing.*
  - » *Number Lines: Draw a matching number line for each fraction and mark the fractions you are comparing.*

Featured Connection

In this activity, students use a modified version of the Build the Equation strategy since they are starting with the symbolic fractions and then building them out with pattern blocks. Although students are not technically building equations, they are working toward building inequalities by comparing fractions.

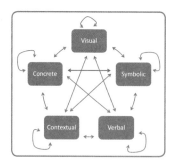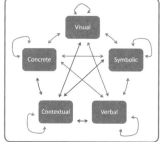

Source: Lesh, Post, & Behr (1987).

To extend this experience, you may also ask students to use a modified version of the Write a Word Problem strategy, providing examples for why a common unit is necessary for comparing fraction pieces. The pizza example was provided in Step 2.

CLOSING REFLECTION: PATTERN BLOCKS

How do I use pattern blocks in my classroom now? What concepts do I use them to teach?

_____

_____

_____

_____

_____

What new ways have I found to use pattern blocks to better support student understanding?

_____

_____

_____

_____

_____

What are my goals to make pattern blocks a more regular part of my instruction?

_____

_____

_____

_____

_____

CHAPTER 7

Fraction Manipulatives (Towers, Circles, Tiles/Bars, and Squares)

INTRODUCTION

Understanding Fraction Manipulatives

Commercial fraction manipulatives are available in a variety of shapes—the traditional circles, squares, oblongs, and three-dimensional square prisms that link together. These are proportional manipulatives (meaning the scale between the pieces is precise), and they are ungrouped (meaning each unit fraction piece is separate). Many commercial suppliers have a standard color sequence for the pieces so the corresponding values (e.g., **halves**, **thirds**, **quarters**) are always the same color in all tools from that supplier.

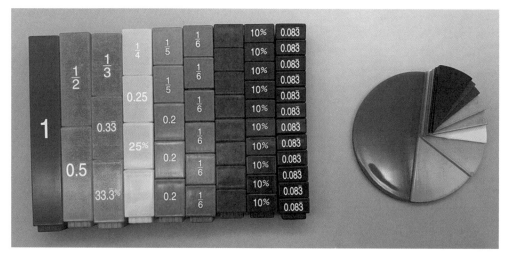

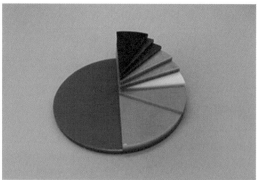

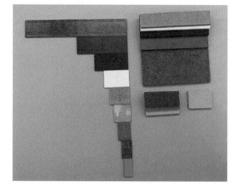

Fraction tools are particularly helpful for teaching these key ideas:

- Understanding unit fractions
- Understanding fractions as whole numbers and whole numbers as fractions
- Understanding composing and decomposing fractions
- Comparing and ordering fractions
- Fraction operations
- Fractions in context, such as time and money

Introducing Fraction Manipulatives to Students

In the primary grades, students work with these tools to introduce the idea of partitioning shapes, to understand unit fractions, and to represent fractional values. This is especially true since there is such a strong crossover between geometry standards and fraction standards in the early grades. If you use the *Notice and Wonder Thinking Routine* (described in the introductory chapter), students may make observations about the number of pieces and the labeling of those pieces (e.g., there are three one-third pieces) or about how the pieces fit together (all three of the lined-up one-thirds are the same length as all eight of the lined-up one-eighths). They may notice that the smaller the pieces become, the more same-sized pieces it takes to make a whole. Use this exploration as an informal assessment of your students' fraction understanding. What key ideas have they brought to your class? What key ideas do you need to establish or strengthen?

Key Ideas With Fraction Manipulatives

- Use a variety of shapes as your unit whole when representing fractions. This encourages students to think flexibly about the relationship between the various fractional values.

- Keep in mind that even in the early years, students should be working with fractions greater than one whole. They should be exploring what it means to have five thirds or three halves.

- Be aware of nuances that have implications in later years. For example, if you are working with children "making wholes" with two halves, three thirds, four fourths, and so on, be mindful that this connects with multiplying and dividing by 1 when working with equivalent fractions in the middle grades. Therefore, emphasize that two halves, three thirds, four fourths, and so on are different names for one whole.

- Deliberately help your students know how precisely to represent fractions. When building physical models, precision is helpful. Diagrams or sketches can be labeled; this means freehand sketches can be approximations of the actual values.

- Connect area fraction representations (as included in this chapter) with number line representations, especially in Grade 3.

- Be careful about simplifying fractions too quickly. Not only do many standards delay or skip this skill, but simplifying a fraction can hide the underlying mathematics from students.

- Although not explicitly stated, the fraction pieces used in most of these activities are interchangeable for other fraction pieces, including pattern blocks. Do not be limited by the actual pieces demonstrated.

Things to Consider About Fraction Manipulatives

- Depending on where you purchase fraction manipulatives, you may notice that color-coding across sets or shapes is always the same color for each value (whole, one-half, one-third, etc.). This can be helpful to the teacher ("take your pink pieces") but runs the risk that students will over-associate the color with the value and think that pink is always one-half.

- To work with mixed numbers, you will need more than one set per group if there's only one whole within a single set. Die-cut alternatives can be helpful here.

- Using a variety of fraction tools is helpful for students because it provides them with a wide range of references for the whole. If students only see circular examples (pizza, pie, or fraction circles) in class, they may struggle when they encounter fractions where the whole is not a circle. Rectangular models (fraction bars, tiles, or towers) are becoming more common because they link nicely to the number line.

- Fraction manipulatives can be labeled or unlabeled. Some sets may have decimal or percent labeling options as well. There is greater flexibility in unlabeled sets, or at least having a blank side on your fraction manipulatives, because you can change the value of the unit whole.

Alternatives to Commercial Fraction Manipulatives

Cutting strips to fold or tear your own set of fraction tiles from construction paper is an excellent activity for building understanding of unit fractions. That said, students benefit tremendously from the precision of commercial or die-cut alternatives. There are commercial dies available for a variety of fraction shapes. It is also possible to create your own sets of more precise fraction pieces on graph paper for some groups of denominators (halves, thirds, fourths, and sixths work well on a 1×12 rectangle, for example).

Other commercial manipulatives can also be used to represent fractional relationships. Base-ten blocks are excellent for representing tenths or hundredths when making the connection to decimals. Pattern blocks (with the yellow hexagon as the whole) represent halves, thirds, and sixths nicely. By using an add-on set of pattern blocks available from some manufacturers or by defining the whole as a shape other than one single hexagon, fourths and eighths are also possible. Furthermore, shifting the unit allows for additional configurations (e.g., if the unit is two connected hexagons, then the trapezoids become fourths). Tangrams provide a good example of fourths, eighths, and sixteenths, with one-half of a complete seven-piece set easy to identify as the two large triangles. Cuisenaire Rods® provide interesting fraction opportunities when each different color is identified as the whole and students are asked to identify the fractional name of each of the other rods in relation to the stated whole.

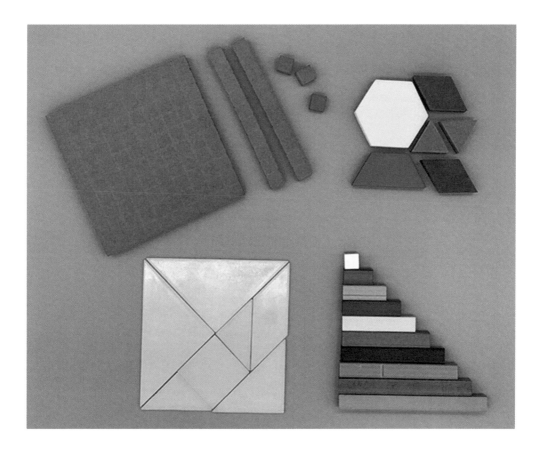

Working With Virtual Fraction Tools

Virtual fraction tools continue the benefit of an endless supply of all the pieces, particularly as students are counting by unit fractions when they learn to add and subtract. When using virtual fraction tools, be careful that the pieces cannot be rescaled so the fractions fall out of relationship with the whole. It is helpful for pieces to snap together (wedge-to-wedge for circles and end-to-end for more linear models) so that students can easily find a whole. Consider how the whole is represented and how easily students can see equivalent values (e.g., that $\frac{1}{2}$ is the same length as $\frac{2}{4}$ and $\frac{4}{8}$).

Notes

_____

_____

_____

_____

_____

_____

_____

WHOLE NUMBERS AS FRACTIONS WITH CIRCLES AND RECTANGLES

Materials

- Unmarked fraction circle (or square) pieces placed in zip-top bags~one per student (Select the type of fractions depending on the grade level and math goal with which you are working; If fraction pieces are marked, simply ask students to flip them over so they can only see the blank side.)

- Work mats for each student (fun foam or heavy paper)

- Blank paper for recording

Organization (physical)

- **Getting Started:** Distribute a container with bags of fraction circle or square pieces to each group of students.

- **Winding Down:** Count and put the fraction circle or square pieces back in the bags prior to placing them in the containers before collecting, checking to be sure none fell on the floor or got left behind.

Mathematical Purpose

In this activity, students use unit fractions to compose one whole, using fraction pieces to represent their thinking as they "count by unit fractions."

Steps

Part 1: How to make one whole with fraction pieces

1. Ask students to remove their fraction pieces from the bags and put them together into "wholes." To support students' thinking, ask questions such as the following:

    - *What kind of fractions are in this [point] circle?*

    - *How many fourth-sized pieces does it take to make a whole?*

    - *How many half-sized pieces does it take to make a whole?*

    Continue with other sizes.

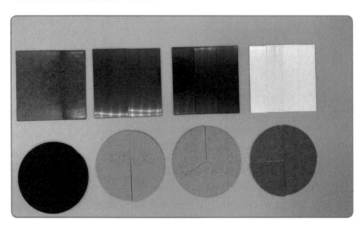

2. Together, use the "see it, touch it, say it" strategy to count by unit fractions (see Activity 1.1). For example, when counting by fourths, touch each piece, one at a time, while counting by units, "One fourth, two fourths, three fourths, four fourths ... it takes four fourths to make a whole."

3. If recording fraction symbols fits with your math goal (e.g., third grade), you may also ask students to use the Make a Sketch strategy to record their fraction pieces and to write the unit fractions on each piece. Furthermore, you may also want students to use the Caption Your Picture strategy to record the "whole" as a sum of unit fractions.

4. Repeat with other-sized fraction pieces.

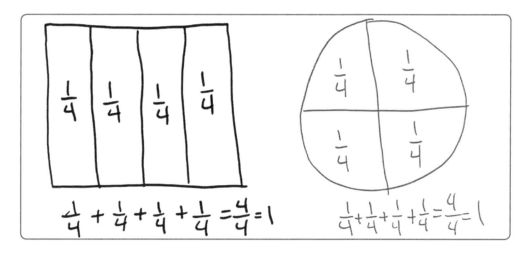

$\frac{1}{4} + \frac{1}{4} + \frac{1}{4} + \frac{1}{4} = \frac{4}{4} = 1$

Part 2: How to make many wholes with fraction pieces

5. Ask students to put all their fraction pieces back in their bags except the halves. This time, students push all their half-sized pieces together and then begin putting them together into multiple wholes.

6. Again, use the "see it, touch it, say it" strategy to count by unit fractions. For example, when counting by halves, touch each piece, one at a time, while counting by units, "One half, two halves makes one whole. One half, two halves, three halves, four halves makes two wholes. One half, two halves, three halves, four halves, five halves, six halves makes three wholes …"

7. Again, if recording fraction symbols fits with your math goal (e.g., third grade), you may also ask students to use the Make a Sketch strategy to record their "wholes" composed of fraction pieces and to write the unit fractions on each piece. Furthermore, you may also want students to use the Caption Your Picture strategy to record one whole, two wholes, three wholes, and four wholes with unit fractions.

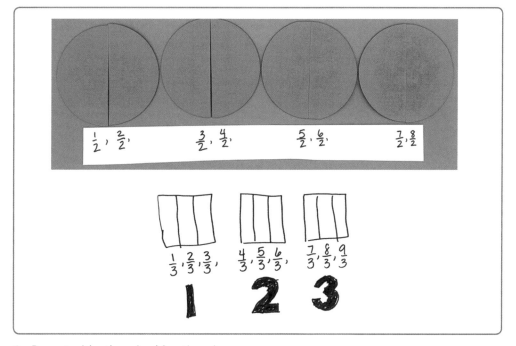

8. Repeat with other-sized fraction pieces.

Why This Manipulative?

Fraction circles, like fraction squares, provide students with the opportunity to see when they have arrived at a whole without necessarily needing a referent close by, as would be the case with fraction bars or rectangles. This is helpful in the early stages of fraction understanding where students are simply playing with shapes and not yet working with symbols. Note that for halves, thirds, and sixths, pattern blocks would also work for this activity.

Developing Understanding

Provide students with the opportunity to explore fraction pieces prior to engaging in composing whole units. Students should compare and contrast ways in which unit fractions can be sorted and then combined to create whole units. Furthermore, students should recognize that like-sized pieces should be combined to form the whole, and the whole needs to be defined ahead of time. For example, in the cases illustrated in this lesson, students need to know that the circle and the square are the whole units (as opposed to a half-circle or a non-square rectangle).

This activity may also be used to discover other fraction concepts such as the relationships between the fractional pieces and "one whole," the notion that same-sized pieces have the same fraction name, and the concept that the size of the pieces is related to the number of pieces it takes to make a circle or square that is equivalent to one whole.

Featured Connection

In this activity, all students are making a connection between the concrete and verbal representations as they use the "see it, touch it, say it" strategy described in Activity 1.1. In addition, for those who are working on recording unit fractions, students use the Make a Sketch

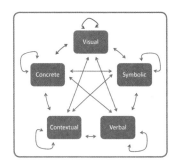 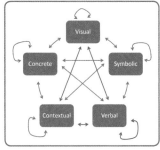

Source: Lesh, Post, & Behr (1987).

and Caption Your Picture strategies to connect concrete representations to visual and symbolic representations. Making these connections provides important scaffolding to future fraction work as it encourages students to develop a mental structure of the visuals represented by the symbols.

Notes

_____

_____

_____

_____

Notes

_____

_____

_____

_____

_____

_____

_____

_____

_____

_____

_____

_____

_____

_____

_____

_____

_____

_____

_____

_____

_____

Materials

- Fraction tower pieces placed in zip-top bags (one whole, two halves, three thirds, and four fourths) for each student; you may include other-sized pieces as well, depending on your grade level and math goal
- Activity sheet for each student

Organization (physical)

- **Getting Started:** Distribute fraction tower pieces to students.
- **Winding Down:** Ask students to put the fraction towers back together prior to placing them in zip-top bags to ensure all pieces are included.

Mathematical Purpose

In this activity, students compare fractions equivalent to one whole, viewing them as equal amounts, while using fraction towers and number lines to represent contextual situations.

Activity 7.2 Resources

"One" as a Fraction Activity Sheet

 To access resource visit resources.corwin.com/ MasteringMathManips/ K-3

Manipulative Illustrated

Fraction Towers (available from multiple sources)

Steps

> Juan and Corrina each had same-sized brownie bars. Juan's was still whole, but Corrina's was cut into four equal pieces. Who had more? How do you know?

1. Ask students to read the first problem, either together or separately. Ask guiding questions to assist students in focusing on the context such as the following:

   - *What is this math story about?*
   - *What are the quantities, relationships, and/or actions taking place?*
   - *What is the question asking?*

2. Ask students to use fraction tower pieces to represent the first problem with fraction towers, either individually or in pairs. Ask guiding questions such as these:

   - *How did you know which fraction tower pieces to use?*
   - *What did you notice about each of the whole brownie bites?*
   - *Which one had more? How do you know?*

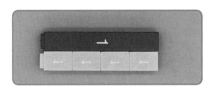

3. Ask students to represent the situation with fractions and with number lines. Ask guiding questions such as these:

   - *How do you write the whole brownie that was cut into four pieces as a fraction?*
   - *How can you represent that on a number line?*

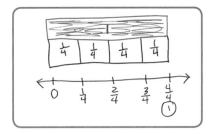

4. As students are ready, ask them to continue with the other problems, following the same sequence.

Why This Manipulative?

Fraction towers provide the opportunity for students to compare fractions using a bar model, which translates nicely into number line work. Furthermore, fraction towers establish the whole and each fractional part proportionally and precisely. This is helpful for young learners as they grapple with basic concepts of fractions such as (1) fraction pieces that name the same amount of the whole must be the same size, and (2) the number pieces that comprise the whole determine the size of those pieces.

Note that this activity may also be suitable for fraction circles, fraction squares, fraction bars, and fraction strips. You may also use pattern blocks if you restrict the denominators to numbers that work well with pattern blocks (halves, thirds, and sixths).

Developing Understanding

Provide students with the opportunity to explore the fraction towers prior to engaging in problem solving. Students should compare and contrast the function of fraction towers with that of fraction tiles and fraction circles. Furthermore, students should connect the use of fraction towers to number lines, noting that fractions can lend themselves to being viewed as a distance model, like number lines, though many students still view them as area models.

Be sure to guide students in noticing some of the fraction concepts that can be envisioned with the fraction towers, including the relationships between the fractional pieces and "one whole," the notion that same-sized pieces have the same fraction name, and the concept that the size of the pieces is related to the number of pieces it takes to make a bar that is equivalent to one whole. These ideas are typically developed in first and second grade and then formalized in third grade.

Featured Connection

This activity focuses on the Create a Diagram strategy to highlight the connection between the concrete objects and visual and symbolic representations. This connection occurs as the students use the fraction towers to represent the word problem. Then they use **open number line** representations to show their understanding by marking the whole and partitioning the whole into equal-sized pieces to show how those pieces fit together to make another whole. Finally, students use fraction symbols to indicate the parts that comprise a whole on the number line (e.g., $\frac{1}{4}, \frac{2}{4}, \frac{3}{4}, \frac{4}{4}$).

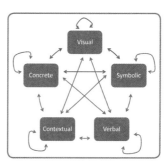

Source: Lesh, Post, & Behr (1987).

Notes

_____

_____

_____

_____

Materials

- Fraction circle pieces without markings (one whole, two halves, three thirds, and four fourths) in zip-top bags for each student; you may include other-sized pieces as well, depending on your grade level and math goal

- Spinner, paper clip, and pencil for each pair of students

Organization (physical)

- **Getting Started:** Place a set of fraction circles in each bag. Include two halves, three thirds, and four fourths in each bag (you may include other fraction types for different grade levels and math goals); demonstrate how to use the spinner.

- **Winding Down:** Put the fraction pieces together into circles to ensure all pieces are together and place them in a zip-top bag.

Mathematical Purpose

In this activity, students represent and count unit fractions using fraction circle pieces. By using fraction circles, students are able to recognize unit fractions as individual pieces (how many) and their relative size to the whole (how much).

Steps

1. Ask students to remove the fraction circle pieces from their bags, leaving them in an unsorted pile. If the fraction circle pieces have fractions written on them, ask students to flip them upside down so they cannot see the written fractions. Remind students that in order to know the value of each piece, one must define the whole. In this case, the "whole" is one full circle.

2. Describe the directions for the game, modeling as appropriate.

   a. Partner 1 spins the spinner and selects one of the fraction circle pieces from the unsorted pile.

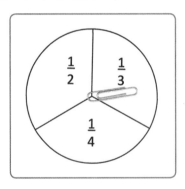

   b. Partner 2 spins the spinner and selects one of the fraction circle pieces from the unsorted pile.

   c. Partners continue taking turns, adding one piece to their circles on each turn, as indicated on the spinner. When constructing circles, halves go with halves, thirds with thirds, and fourths with fourths.

   d. If a partner spins a fraction that is no longer available in the unsorted pile, that turn is lost.

e. The winner is the first partner to complete all three circles.

f. After the game is completed, each student should flip over the pieces, one at a time, counting the fractions with each flip. For example, when counting the fourths, the student would say something like this: "One fourth, two fourths, three fourths, four fourths—four fourths makes one whole circle!"

3. Ask guiding questions during the game play:

- *How can you tell which piece represents one half? One third? One fourth?*

- *How many halves make a whole circle? Thirds? Fourths?*

- *I can see you have three $\frac{1}{4}$-sized pieces. How might we name those pieces when they're all together?*

- *What if I have five $\frac{1}{2}$-sized pieces? What would that look like? What would I call that?*

Why This Manipulative?

Fraction circles are ideal for this lesson since students can clearly tell when the whole circle is completed. Other fraction manipulatives, such as fraction bars or fraction squares, are not so obviously "complete" when the whole shape is constructed. Pattern blocks also work well for this game if one is focusing on halves, thirds, and sixths.

Developing Understanding

This learning game provides opportunities for students to work with unit fraction pieces, one at a time. Be sure to identify one circle as the "whole" for this activity. This lays an important foundation for students as they become flexible with defining units. Encourage students to call all the pieces by their unit fraction names before, during, and after game play.

When talking about the pieces, be sure to talk about them in terms of their size ("$\frac{1}{2}$-sized pieces," "$\frac{1}{4}$-sized pieces," etc.). This helps students recognize that each piece has an identity as one piece that

Activity 7.3 Resources

Representing and Counting Unit Fractions Spinner

online resources To access resources visit resources.corwin.com/ MasteringMathManips/ K-3

Manipulative Illustrated

Paper Fraction Circle Pieces (available from multiple sources) has a specific size as compared to the whole. When talking about how many they have, use language such as "I can see you have three $\frac{1}{4}$-sized pieces." This helps students begin to distinguish between the count (how many of the same-sized pieces) and the actual size of the piece relative to the whole. Students will eventually connect these ideas to the notion of numerators and denominators. When appropriate, begin asking these questions as students are playing (see previously suggested guiding questions).

Featured Connection

Use the Name Your Model strategy to highlight the connection between the concrete and symbolic representations. As students complete their "wholes," they should write an equation to go with each. For younger children, they may simply think of the pieces as halves, thirds, or fourths and name their models accordingly. For example, they may write 1 third + 1 third + 1 third = 3 thirds. For students in third grade, they may begin naming their models using unit fractions. For example, they may write

$\frac{1}{3} + \frac{1}{3} + \frac{1}{3} = \frac{3}{3} = 1$ whole.

Source: Lesh, Post, & Behr (1987).

Notes

_____

_____

_____

_____

_____

_____

_____

_____

_____

_____

_____

Notes

ACTIVITY 7.4

ITERATING UNIT FRACTIONS TO MAKE A WHOLE

| K | 1 | 2 | 3+ |

Materials

- Virtual pattern blocks or physical pattern blocks
- Recording sheet for each student

Organization (virtual)

- **Getting Started:** Ensure students know how to use the virtual pattern blocks; review annotation tools, taking screenshots, and so on.
- **Winding Down:** Take screenshots to save student work.

Mathematical Purpose

In this activity, students iterate unit fractions to make a whole. Note that for each question, the whole is redefined, providing students with the opportunity to grapple with the notion of how many pieces will fit on each whole and what is the unit fraction value of each piece.

Activity 7.4 Resources

- *Iterating Unit Fractions to Make a Whole* Recording Sheet

 To access resource visit resources.corwin.com/ MasteringMathManips/ K-3

Manipulative Illustrated

Pattern Shapes app from Math Learning Center: https://apps .mathlearningcenter.org/pattern -shapes/

Steps

1. Ask students to work in pairs to compare the relative sizes and values of each pattern block. Ask guiding questions such as the following:

   - *If the yellow hexagon is the whole, what's the value of each triangle?*
   - *If the red trapezoid is the whole, what's the value of each triangle?*
   - *If the blue rhombus is the whole, what's the value of each triangle?*

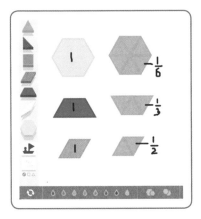

2. Ask students to cover a rhombus with triangles. Record the answers on the first row of the recording sheet. Ask guiding questions such as the following:

   - *How many triangles does it take to cover a rhombus?*
   - *What is the unit fraction that describes each triangle?*

3. Ask students to individually or with a partner complete the recording sheet.

214

Why This Manipulative?

Pattern blocks are proportional, ungrouped, and unmarked. This makes them ideal for fraction concepts, especially when developing the notion that redefining the unit changes the relative value of all other pieces. Please note that in this book, pattern blocks have their own chapter (see Chapter 6), and fraction lessons are included there as well. However, this single lesson is included in the fraction chapter as a reminder that pattern blocks can be used as fraction pieces every bit as much as fraction circles, fraction squares, and fraction bars.

Developing Understanding

By first defining the whole as a yellow hexagon, the students can easily determine that a red trapezoid comprises $\frac{1}{2}$ of the yellow hexagon, a blue rhombus comprises $\frac{1}{3}$ of the yellow hexagon, and a green triangle comprises $\frac{1}{6}$ of the yellow hexagon. Next, as the unit is redefined as one blue rhombus, students must change their orientation and now see that the green triangle is $\frac{1}{2}$ of the blue rhombus. Next, when defining the red trapezoid as the whole, students see that the green triangle comprises $\frac{1}{3}$ of the red trapezoid, though they may find it more difficult to determine that the blue rhombus comprises $\frac{2}{3}$ of the red trapezoid. Note that this final point (comparing the trapezoid to the rhombus) does not appear on the recording sheet, but it may be given to students as a bonus.

In this activity, students are being asked to combine two major ideas: iterating unit fractions to make a whole *while* attending to the identified whole. This lays an important foundation for fraction work now and in the future: The fractional value of each piece is **unknown** until it is related to the whole.

Featured Connection

In this lesson, students use the Create a Diagram strategy to highlight the connection between the pattern blocks and the abstract or visual representations that emerge when creating a table. Students should work carefully to place the correct information in the table, attending to the questions down the left-hand side of the recording sheet and the labels across the top. Most importantly, students must use precision to be sure they answer the questions in the first column with whole numbers and the second column with fractions.

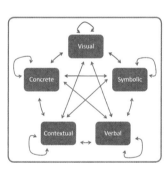

Source: Lesh, Post, & Behr (1987).

Notes

_____

_____

_____

_____

_____

Materials

- Fraction tile pieces in zip-top bags (one per student); include one whole, two halves, three thirds, four fourths, six sixths, and eight eighths
- Fraction equivalence cards
- Whiteboards and markers (one per pair of students)

Organization (virtual)

- **Getting Started:** Ensure students know how to use the virtual fraction pieces; review annotation tools, taking screenshots, and so on.
- **Winding Down:** Remind students to take screenshots to save their work.

Mathematical Purpose

In this activity, students compare equivalent fractions, viewing them as equal amounts, while using fraction tiles to compare.

Activity 7.5 Resources

Fraction Equivalence Cards

 To access resource visit resources.corwin.com/ MasteringMathManips/ K-3

Manipulative Illustrated

Fractions from Math Learning Center: https://apps .mathlearningcenter.org/fractions/

Steps

1. Ask each student to take out the tile that represents one whole. The one-whole tile will be the base for building fractions during this activity.

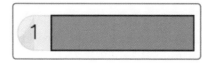

2. Ask each student to flip over one card and to use fraction tiles to build the fraction named on the card. To support students' thinking, ask guiding questions such as the following:

   - *How did you know how many pieces to use?*
   - *How did you know which size pieces to use?*

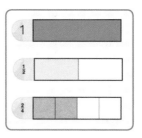

3. Ask students to record a statement about their fractions on a whiteboard using <, =, or >. To support their thinking, ask guiding questions such as these:

   - *How could you tell whether or not the two fractions were equivalent?*
   - *What do you notice about the numerators when the fractions are equivalent?*
   - *What do you notice about the denominators when the fractions are equivalent?*
   - *What do you notice about the fraction symbols when they are equivalent?*

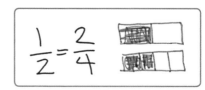

4. Repeat the first three steps until time is up. The team with the most points wins the game.

Why This Manipulative?

Fraction tiles without markings provide an excellent way for students to compare fractions because they are already proportional. By first defining the whole, students are able to determine to relative values of the remaining fraction tiles by comparing their relative sizes to the wholes. And because each fractional piece is purposefully built to represent a unit fraction, students gain insights into building an understanding of iterating unit fractions to build any given fraction.

Developing Understanding

Comparing fractions is always dependent on defining a common whole, and doing so at the beginning of this lesson sets students up for deeper understanding of the comparative nature of fractions. Allowing time at the beginning of the lesson for students to organize their fraction tile pieces affords them the opportunity to develop and/or extend their understanding of building fractions from unit fractions.

Be sure to point out that in every example in this activity, the denominators of the fractions being compared are the same, while the numerators are different. This emphasizes the importance of the numerator as the count (how many pieces) and the denominator as the size of the piece (the unit of measure). Because the denominators are the same in each pair of fractions, the students' descriptions should include comparisons about the number of each-sized fraction piece. For example, since the pieces are the same size in both fractions, the number of pieces will determine which fraction represents a greater and which represents a lesser amount.

When incorporating the Write a Word Problem strategy, the notion of starting with a same-sized whole becomes a critical understanding. Because this activity begins with fraction bars based on same-sized wholes, students may not pick up on this very important notion. When introducing a context such as pizza or craft felt, students are forced to realize that they can only compare two fractions when they are naming parts of same-sized wholes.

Featured Connections

This activity already asks students to use the Name Your Model strategy to highlight the connection between the fraction tiles and the equations or inequalities that compare them. Students should become increasingly comfortable using the symbols <, >, and = when writing comparison statements.

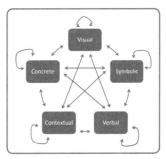 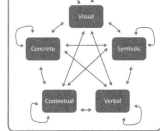

Source: Lesh, Post, & Behr (1987).

To further connect students' understanding to the models, you might also incorporate the Write a Word Problem strategy into this activity. After the activity is completed, ask students to take up to three of their comparison statements and describe what this could mean in real life. For example, if the students had $\frac{1}{2} = \frac{2}{4}$ as one of their comparisons, they might use the context of apples to compose a problem such as "Kim has $\frac{1}{2}$ of an apple, and Sara has $\frac{2}{4}$ of an apple. Who has more?" They could then illustrate the word problem to show that one $\frac{1}{2}$-sized piece and two $\frac{1}{4}$-sized pieces are the same amount, provided the original apples were the same size. This could be repeated with any of a variety of contexts, noting that both fractions must represent part of a same-sized whole.

COMPARING FRACTIONS WITH LIKE NUMERATORS

K	1	2	3+

Materials

- Fraction bars (one set per student, stored in a zip-top bag)—include one whole, two halves, three thirds, and four fourths in each bag; you may include other-sized pieces as well, depending on your grade level and math goal
- Fraction cards (one sheet per pair of students)
- Whiteboards and markers for each student

Organization (physical)

- **Getting Started:** Place a set of fraction bars in each bag; ask students to cut apart the game cards along the *dark* lines, mix them, and place them in a pile, facedown.
- **Winding Down:** Put the fraction pieces together into "wholes" to ensure all pieces are together and then place them in a zip-top bag.

Mathematical Purpose

In this activity, students will compare fractions with like denominators as they work with partners to build fractions with fraction bar pieces. The model emphasizes the importance of the numerator as the count (how many pieces) and the denominator as the size of the piece (the unit of measure).

Steps

1. Ask students to work in pairs for this activity. Individual students should have their own bag of fraction pieces.

2. Ask students to use the longest bar to define "one whole" for today's purpose. Support their thinking with questions like the following:
   - *Why is it important to identify the whole?*
   - *How does knowing the whole help us know the value of all the other pieces?*

3. Ask students to put together the fraction tiles so they have a row of halves, a row of thirds, and a row of fourths.

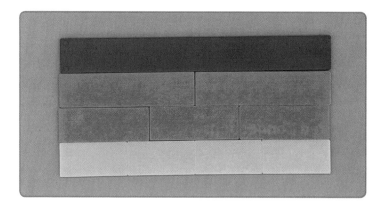

4. Ask each student to flip over one card and build one of the fractions. Ask guiding questions such as these:
   - *How did you know which sized pieces to use?*
   - *How did you know how many pieces to use?*

5. Ask students to compare their fractions. Ask guiding questions such as these:
   - *Which fraction is greater?*
   - *Which fraction is smaller?*
   - *How do you know?*

6. Ask students to record a comparison statement using < or > on their whiteboards. Ask guiding questions such as these:

    *   *How did you know how to write that?*

    *   *How do you know which way the arrow points?*

    *   *How do you read that inequality out loud?*

7. Repeat this process with the remaining cards.

Why This Manipulative?

Fraction tiles without markings provide an excellent way for students to compare fractions because they are already proportional. By first defining the whole, students are able to determine the relative values of the remaining fraction tiles by comparing their relative sizes to the wholes. And because each fractional piece is purposefully built to represent a unit fraction, students gain insights into building an understanding of iterating unit fractions to build any given fraction.

Developing Understanding

Comparing fractions is always dependent on defining a common whole, and doing so at the beginning of this lesson sets students up for deeper understanding of the comparative nature of fractions. Allowing students time at the beginning of the lesson to organize their fraction tile pieces affords them the opportunity to develop and/or extend their understanding of building fractions from unit fractions.

Be sure to point out that in every example in this activity, the numerators of the fractions being compared are the same, while the denominators are different. This emphasizes the importance of the numerator as the count (how many pieces) and the denominator as the size of the piece (the unit of measure). Because the numerators are the same in each pair of fractions, the students' descriptions should include comparisons about the size of the fraction pieces. For example, when starting with the same whole, halves and thirds are larger than fourths, and halves are larger than thirds. So if they have the same number of pieces, the pieces that are larger-sized will represent a greater amount.

Activity 7.6 Resources

Comparing Fractions With Like Numerators Fraction Cards

 To access resource visit resources.corwin.com/ MasteringMathManips/ K-3

Manipulative Illustrated

Fraction Tiles Without Labels (available from multiple sources)

Featured Connections

During this activity, students are already asked to use the Name Your Model strategy to highlight the connection between the fraction pieces and the comparison statement.

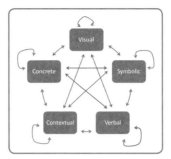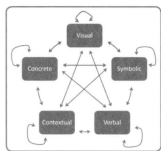

Source: Lesh, Post, & Behr (1987).

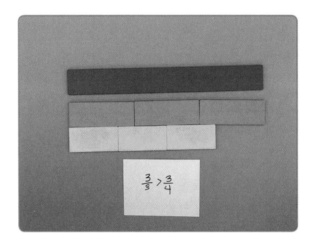

To further the experience, use the Create a Diagram strategy to highlight the connection between the fraction bars and number lines. Together, each pair of students should create a single number line and then mark the two fractions along the number line as a way to show which is greater and which is less than.

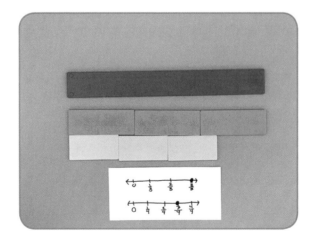

Notes

_____

_____

Notes

COMPARING FRACTIONS WITH LIKE DENOMINATORS

| K | 1 | 2 | 3+ |

Materials

- Fraction bars (one set per student, stored in a zip-top bag)—include one whole, two halves, three thirds, and four fourths in each bag; you may include other pieces as well, depending on your grade level and math goal

- Fraction cards (one sheet per pair of students)

- Whiteboards and markers for each student

Organization (physical)

- **Getting Started:** Place a set of fraction bars in each bag; ask students to cut apart the game cards along the *dark* lines, mix them, and place them in a pile, facedown.

- **Winding Down:** Put the fraction pieces together into "wholes" to ensure all pieces are together and then place them in a zip-top bag.

Mathematical Purpose

In this activity, students will compare fractions with like denominators as they work with partners to build fractions with fraction bar pieces. The model emphasizes the importance of the numerator as the count (how many pieces) and the denominator as the size of the piece (the unit of measure).

Steps

1. Ask students to use the longest bar to define "one whole" for today's purpose. Ask the following guiding questions:

    - *Why is it important to identify the whole?*

    - *How does knowing the whole help us know the value of all the other pieces?*

2. Ask students to put together the fraction tiles so they have a row of halves, a row of thirds, and a row of fourths.

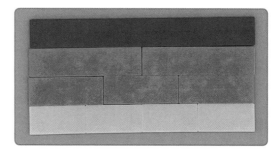

3. Ask each student to flip over one card and build one of the fractions. Ask guiding questions such as these:

    - *How did you know which sized pieces to use?*

    - *How did you know how many pieces to use?*

4. Ask students to compare their fractions, using guiding questions such as these:

    - *Which fraction is greater?*

    - *Which fraction is smaller? How do you know?*

5. Ask students to record a comparison statement using < or > on their whiteboards. Ask guiding questions such as these:

    - *How did you know how to write that?*

    - *How do you know which way the arrow points?*

    - *How do you read that inequality out loud?*

6. Repeat this process with the remaining cards.

Why This Manipulative?

Fraction tiles without markings provide an excellent way for students to compare fractions because they are already proportional. By first defining the whole, students are able to determine to relative values of the remaining fraction tiles by comparing their relative sizes to the wholes. And because each fractional piece is purposefully built to represent a unit fraction, students gain insights into building an understanding of iterating unit fractions to build any given fraction.

Developing Understanding

Comparing fractions is always dependent on defining a common whole, and doing so at the beginning of this lesson sets students up for deeper understanding of the comparative nature of fractions. Allowing students time at the beginning of the lesson to organize their fraction tile pieces affords them the opportunity to develop and/or extend their understanding of building fractions from unit fractions.

Be sure to point out that in every example in this activity, the denominators of the fractions being compared are the same, while the numerators are different. This emphasizes the importance of the numerator as the count (how many pieces) and the denominator as the size of the piece (the unit of measure). Because the denominators are the same in each pair of fractions, the students' descriptions should include comparisons about the number of each-sized fraction piece. For example, since the pieces are the same size in both fractions, the number of pieces will determine which fraction represents a greater and which represents a lesser amount.

Featured Connections

During this activity, students are already asked to use the Name Your Model strategy to highlight the connection between the fraction pieces and the comparison statement. The emphasis is on comparing the denominators since the numerators are always the same in each pair of fractions.

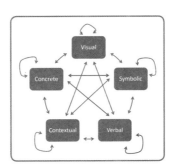

To further the experience, use the Caption Your Picture strategy to highlight the connection between the fraction bars and verbalizations of their comparisons. For example, when comparing $\frac{1}{4}$ and $\frac{3}{4}$, a student might say something like "$\frac{3}{4}$ is greater than $\frac{1}{4}$ because there are more of the same-sized pieces."

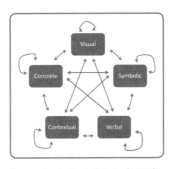

Source: Lesh, Post, & Behr (1987).

Activity 7.7 Resources

Comparing Fractions With Like Denominators Fraction Cards

Comparing Fractions with Like Numerators Fraction Cards

 To access resources visit resources.corwin.com/ MasteringMathManips/ K-3

Manipulative Illustrated

Fraction Bars Without Labels (available from multiple sources)

Listen for students to begin identifying the language pattern as they talk about more or less of the same-sized pieces.

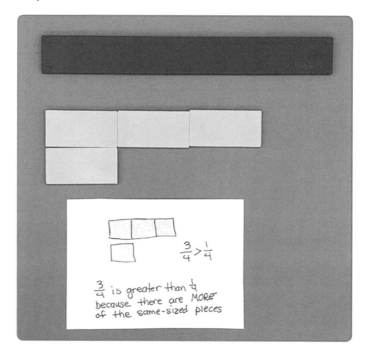

Notes

_____

_____

_____

_____

_____

_____

_____

_____

_____

_____

_____

Notes

Materials

- One set of construction paper strips per student (one colored strip for each unit fraction and one for the whole)

- One zip-top bag per student

Organization (physical)

- **Getting Started:** This activity is easiest if the strips are cut to 2″ × 24″ from 18″ × 24″ construction paper. Black is good for the whole as it is difficult to write on. Stack the colors of paper and cut in sets if possible. If using smaller paper strips, it is more difficult to create smaller unit fractions. Have extra strips on hand, especially for colors in the thirds and fifths families.

- **Winding Down:** At the end of the activity, have students put their fraction bar set in a plastic bag for safekeeping.

Mathematical Purpose

In this activity, students fold and tear paper strips to create unit fraction sets. This builds understanding of the relationship between the size of the piece and the number of partitions of the whole. Students can also use the set to support other fraction work, noting that the set will not be as precise as a commercial set of fraction materials.

Steps

1. Distribute a set of paper strips to each student. If you want the class to use the same color for each unit fraction, tell the students this from the beginning. It is helpful in this case to make a written key (on the board or a shared screen) available to students while they work.

2. Ask the students to take the black strip and label it "one whole." Ask the students to take a second color strip and think about how they could represent one half, supporting their thinking with questions like these:

   - *What does one half mean? How many pieces will you partition the entire strip into?*

   - *Is there more than one way to identify half of the strip? How many different ways can you identify?*

3. Tell students that for this activity, the strips will be partitioned like a bar model, folding and tearing parallel to the shorter side. It is important to tear the partitions rather than cut with scissors so that the orientation remains correct when the pieces approach a square. Construction paper will tear nicely if folded firmly before tearing.

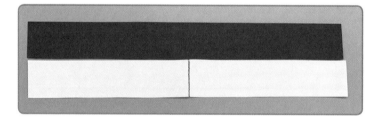

4. Continue to partition strips into additional unit fractions. It can be helpful to work in batches of related denominators. One strategy is to create halves, fourths, and eighths first. Then fold thirds and use those to create sixths and twelfths. Fold fifths and create tenths from them. For folding thirds and fifths, teach students to make a fan or zigzag fold, adjusting the segments to be as even in length as possible before pressing the folds into the paper and tearing.

Support students' thinking by asking guiding questions like these:

- *How might you create thirds without using a ruler?*

- *Why is it important to make the sections as even as possible?*

- *Why are we creating thirds and sixths [halves, fourths, and eighths; fifths and tenths] together? How do these numbers relate to each other in ways that make folding easier?*

- *What do you notice is happening to the size of each piece as you create more pieces from a given whole strip?*

5. Encourage students to label one side of each unit fraction piece so the values can be readily determined without reassembling the whole.

6. These paper fraction bar sets can be used to represent fractions, to compare fractions, and to create equivalent fractions. When comparing fractions, note that visual comparisons of fractions that are almost equal might not be accurate, depending on the error in the student's work. Sets of equivalent fractions might not be exactly equal for the same reason.

Why This Manipulative?

The active construction of a manipulative set helps students understand the pieces in the set. Students see that the whole is the same each time because they began with a set of congruent paper strips. They actively experience the fact that there's much more folding and tearing to make a set of twelfths than to make a set of halves. There are more pieces from the unit whole, and each piece of value $\frac{1}{12}$ is smaller. While students will benefit in future lessons from the precision of commercial fraction bars or tiles, there is great learning in constructing a set for themselves.

Developing Understanding

This activity helps students ground their sense of unit fractions in concrete experiences. There is great pride in doing mathematics with tools students have made themselves because students have ownership over the entire process. Students will recognize that the pieces might not fit together exactly, as shown in the accompanying photo, and can transition smoothly from these personal fraction bar sets to more precise commercial tools.

Students can use these fraction pieces to mark fractions on a number line or for activities that involve comparing and ordering fractions. Be careful with tasks where precision is important because there is error in these handmade tools.

Featured Connection

Students use the Name your Model strategy when they label each piece of their newly constructed fraction bar set. As shown in the picture, the fraction pieces can be labeled in different ways, depending on the language focus of the lesson.

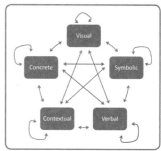

Source: Lesh, Post, & Behr (1987).

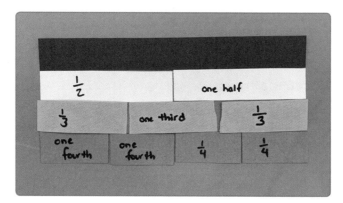

Notes

_____

_____

_____

_____

_____

_____

_____

_____

_____

Notes

_____

_____

_____

_____

_____

_____

_____

_____

_____

_____

_____

_____

_____

_____

_____

_____

_____

_____

_____

_____

_____

FRACTIONS ON THE CLOCK (QUARTERS AND HALVES)

| K | 1 | 2 | 3+ |

Materials

- Fraction circle pieces in zip-top bags, one per student
- Paper **analog clocks**, approximately the same diameter as the fraction circles
- Blank paper

Organization

- **Getting Started:** Ask students to take out the whole circle, halves, thirds, and fourths (you may also want to have them use sixths and twelfths, depending on your objective).

- **Winding Down:** Put the fraction pieces together into "wholes" to ensure all pieces are together and then place them in a zip-top bag.

Mathematical Purpose

In this activity, students relate fraction circle pieces to clock reading, specifically focusing on half-hours and quarter-hours.

Activity 7.9 Resources

- *Fractions on the Clock (Quarters and Halves) Activity Video*

To access resource visit resources.corwin.com/ MasteringMathManips/ K-3

Steps

1. Ask students to place one $\frac{1}{2}$-sized fraction circle on the clock face. Point out to students that for the sake of this lesson, if part of a number is covered, we will consider the entire number covered (e.g., see the 12 and 6 in the accompanying photo). Ask guiding questions such as the following:

   - *How many halves would fit on the clock?*

   - *What numbers are covered up if the half-circle covers the right side of the clock?*

   - *What numbers are covered up if the half-circle covers the left side of the clock?*

   - *What does it mean if we say it is "half past 4"?*

Continue to ask questions like this until the students understand the "half past" language.

2. Ask students to place one $\frac{1}{4}$-sized fraction circle on the clock face. Remind students that for the sake of this lesson, if part of a number is covered, we will consider the entire number covered (e.g., see the 12 and 6 in the accompanying photo). Ask guiding questions such as the following:

   - *How many quarters [fourths] would fit on the clock?*

   - *What numbers are covered up if the quarter-circle covers the upper-right side of the clock?*

   - *What numbers are covered up if the quarter-circle covers the lower-right side of the clock?*

   - *What does it mean if we say it is "a quarter past 4" or "a quarter till 6"?*

Manipulative Illustrated

Fraction Circles (available from multiple sources)

Continue to ask questions like this until the students understand the "quarter past" and "quarter till" language.

3. Ask students to fold a blank sheet of paper into four equal sections and to sketch four clock faces. Then, ask them to (1) color in the first half of the hour, (2) color in the second half of the hour, (3) color in the first quarter of the hour, and (4) color in the last quarter of the hour. In each section, ask them to write a sentence that describes the time using fraction language.

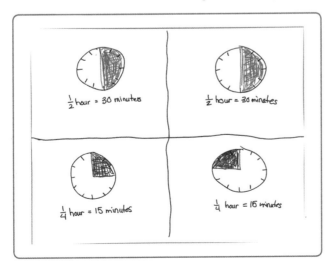

4. Students may continue explorations with sixths and twelfths, as appropriate. Continue to ask guiding questions that lead students to use fractional language in reference to clock reading.

Why This Manipulative?

When learning to tell time on a clock, students often attend to the perimeter of the clock rather than the area. Using fraction circles to identify half-hours and quarter-hours on the clock face helps students make the connection between fractions and telling time on an analog clock.

Developing Understanding

When learning to tell time on an analog clock, students' learning is greatly enhanced when they attend to the area of the clock face rather than just the perimeter. By placing fraction circle pieces on a precut and labeled paper clock, students can visualize and connect half-hours and quarter-hours to the fractions they've been studying. The goal is for students to connect the fraction language with the time span it represents. For example, a half-hour is equivalent to 30 minutes, and a quarter-hour is equivalent to 15 minutes.

In addition, students may begin to realize that fractions of an hour do not necessarily need to begin or end at the "top" of the clock face. Guide students in seeing, for example, that a half-hour may begin at the 2 and end at the 8, still representing a 30-minute segment of time. This can be done for both half-hours and quarter-hours.

Furthermore, although we do not conventionally talk about "third-hours," students may benefit from using the one-third-sized fraction circle pieces to visualize that 20-minute segments of time can be thought of as thirds of an hour.

Featured Connection

This activity features the Make a Sketch strategy as students first use the fraction circle pieces to represent fractions of hours and then sketch an analog clock with the fractions of hours shaded in. This connection is key for students as they work toward understanding how the numerals on a clock face correspond with fractions of an hour, specifically quarter-hours and half-hours. Note that for this activity, it is easiest for students to write the numerals on the outside of the clock face rather than on the inside (e.g., not splitting the 1 and 2 of the 12 into two different halves).

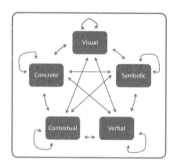

Source: Lesh, Post, & Behr (1987).

Elicit students' ideas by asking guiding questions such as the following:

- *Which numbers correspond to the quarter-hour fractions?*

- *Which numbers correspond to the half-hour fractions?*

- *Can you see other half-hours on the clock besides the one that begins at the top and continues to the bottom [12 and 6]?*

CLOSING REFLECTION: FRACTION MANIPULATIVES

How do I use fraction manipulatives in my classroom now? What concepts do I use them to teach?

_____

_____

_____

_____

_____

What new ways have I found to use fraction manipulatives to better support student understanding?

_____

_____

_____

_____

_____

What are my goals to make fraction manipulatives a more regular part of my instruction?

_____

_____

_____

_____

_____

Chapter 8
Tangrams and Geoboards

INTRODUCTION

Understanding Tangrams and Geoboards

Tangrams are seven-piece puzzles used to develop spatial sense and fraction concepts. These pieces are comprised of one **square**, one **parallelogram**, two small isosceles triangles, two medium isosceles triangles, and one large isosceles triangle. These seven pieces can fit together like puzzle pieces in a variety of ways, most commonly to form a single square.

Geoboards are a family of tools designed to help students think about shapes. The flat board has pegs arranged in a grid, and students use rubber bands to create shapes on the board. The traditional geoboard has an array of 25–100 pegs arranged in a square grid. Some boards have pegs in a circular arrangement on the back of the board. Other boards have pegs arranged in an isometric grid.

For the purposes of this chapter, tangrams and geoboards have been combined since they are being used to illustrate many of the same concepts. Furthermore, they frequently come out into the daylight at about the same time since they are frequently used when teaching the same instructional units. The emphasis in this chapter centers on analyzing geometric attributes and using them to develop number and operations concepts.

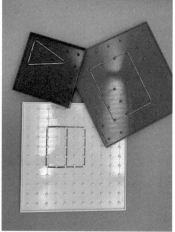

Tangrams and geoboards are most effective for teaching the following ideas:

- Geometric attributes
- Geometric relationships
- Geometric vocabulary
- Area
- Fractions
- Representing shapes and **attributes**

Introducing Tangrams and Geoboards to Students

Tangrams: Introduce tangrams as puzzles comprised of seven pieces. These pieces can be put together in a variety of ways, using two or more pieces. Encourage students to try making squares, triangles, or rectangles with two, three, four, five, six, or seven pieces. In addition, a variety of commercial puzzle books are available to provide even more options.

Geoboards: For many teachers, the use of rubber bands is nerve-wracking. Remind students about the appropriate use of mathematical tools before you distribute materials, and trust your own ability to distinguish a band that slips from a band intentionally aimed at a target. Some teachers provide a fixed number of bands to each student to limit the risk.

Use the *Notice and Wonder Thinking Routine* (described in the introductory chapter) to support students' exploration of the tangrams and the geoboards.

- *Tangrams:* Students may notice the number of pieces and the colors for each puzzle. They may wonder how the pieces might be put together to form shapes or pictures.
- *Geoboards:* Students may notice the quantity of pegs or the arrangement of the pegs. They may explore the number of squares they can find on the board or whether they can make certain shapes. You might ask them: How many different types of triangles can you make? Is there any triangle you cannot make?

Key Ideas With Tangrams and Geoboards

- Provide ready-made tangram and geoboard puzzles in your learning centers. These puzzles are available from many sources, including online downloads and published books. There are also several apps that provide opportunities for student exploration. Check out the Tangram Builder on Mathigon (https://mathigon.org/tangram) or the Tangram app on Toy Theater (https://toytheater.com/tangram).

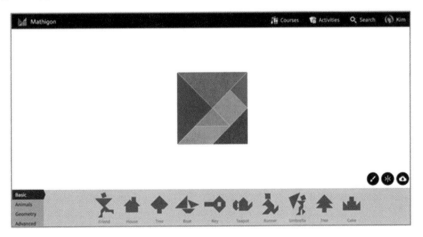

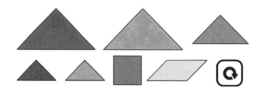

- Tangram puzzles and geoboards can be used to reinforce both fraction and geometric principles. Be sure to emphasize both of these concepts, making connections between the geometry and fraction standards that appear in your standards framework.

- Remind students that squares are special rectangles that have the attribute of same-sized edges. This is an important relationship that is often overlooked as students progress through the grades, as many have a misconception that squares and rectangles are completely unrelated.

Things to Consider About Tangrams and Geoboards

- Tangrams typically come in a variety of colors, each seven-piece puzzle being a different color. For management purposes, you may want to put them in bundles so that students who sit near one another each have a different-colored set.

- There are many different kinds of geoboards, each supporting different kinds of mathematical thinking. Explore using a variety of geoboard tools to support the full range of your standards.

- Depending on how you place bands on the geoboard, the side of a shape might not be a single segment, but the two sides of the stretched band. It is worth talking to students about this as a limit of the tool so they understand that the side of a shape created on the geoboard might not look exactly like the shape we sketch or create with other tools.

- Consider how you will manage the bands. Set your classroom expectations and manage the materials in ways that support your students successfully using the tool.

- Recognize that if you use the circular side of the geoboard, you will get a many-sided **polygon**, not an actual circle, when stretching a band around the pegs.

Alternatives to Commercial Tangrams and Geoboards

Making Tangrams: Tangrams can be cut from commercial die-cut machines. Fun foam is a great alternative to the commercially made plastic sets. You may also use heavy paper. Students can also make their own tangrams; see Activity 8.2 for instructions.

Making Geoboards: Geoboards can be constructed from squares of plywood or foam-core board with strong pins or small nails arranged on the appropriate grid. It is helpful to use a paper template to place the pins or nails consistently when creating homemade boards.

Working With Virtual Tangrams and Geoboards

Virtual Tangrams: Although less frequently found than other manipulatives apps, students can use virtual tangrams to create larger shapes and figures much as they do with the physical pieces. Look for apps that have a "snap" tool and that do not allow shapes to be resized so that students can easily manipulate the online pieces without worrying about changing their proportional values.

Virtual Geoboards: Students can use virtual geoboards for many of the same experiences. The way students construct shapes might be different, tracing around the perimeter rather than stretching a band from one **vertex**. Shapes might also appear differently, with single-edge segments rather than the double-edge segments that bands can create.

Notes

_____

_____

_____

_____

_____

_____

_____

_____

_____

_____

_____

_____

_____

_____

COMPOSING AND DECOMPOSING SHAPES WITH TANGRAMS

K	1	2	3+

Materials

- Bagged tangram puzzle for each student
- Work mat for each student (fun foam or heavy paper)
- Recording sheet for each student

Organization (physical)

- **Getting Started:** Distribute bagged tangram puzzles to each student; if possible, provide a different-color set to students in each group.
- **Winding Down:** Ask students to count out all seven pieces as they place them back in the bags before placing the bags back in the storage container.

Mathematical Purpose

Students will compose larger figures from smaller shapes.

Activity 8.1 Resources

Composing and Decomposing Shapes With Tangrams Recording Sheet

 To access resources visit resources.corwin.com/ MasteringMathManips/ K-3

Manipulative Illustrated

Plastic Tangram Pieces (available from multiple sources)

Steps

1. Ask students to remove the tangram pieces from the bag. Ask them to work with a partner to name all of the shapes that are in the bag. Then ask them to sort the pieces by shape. To support students' thinking, ask guiding questions such as the following:

   - *How many pieces are there altogether?*
   - *Can you name and describe the pieces?*
   - *What is the name of each of your sorting categories?*
   - *What do you notice about the triangles?*

2. Next, ask students if they can put any pieces together to make a square. Give them a few moments to find several different configurations.

3. Next, ask students to try putting pieces together to make a triangle. Give them a few moments to find several different configurations.

4. Next, ask students to try putting pieces together to make a rectangle. Give them a few moments to find several different configurations.

5. Distribute the recording sheet. Ask students to use the Create a Diagram strategy to record their findings as they create different-sized squares, non-square rectangles, and triangles as directed on the chart. Continue to ask guiding questions as students work on this task.

6. *Extension:* Students can connect their work with tangrams on geoboards, re-creating the different tangram pieces and composing larger figures from smaller shapes.

Why This Manipulative?

Tangrams provide an exceptional opportunity for students to explore spatial and geometric attributes. In this activity, students are introduced to the seven basic tangram pieces. Because tangrams are proportional, having similar side lengths and areas, students can use them to create other geometric figures as well as nonstandard geometric figures such as those found in books, online apps, and other electronic sources. Students may also explore representations of the tangram pieces using other geometry-based manipulatives such as geoboards.

Developing Understanding

Practice this activity ahead of time to ensure proper use of geometric vocabulary as well as clear direction-giving. Encourage students to use the geometric vocabulary as you model it, as well as to discuss the relative shapes and sizes of each piece. One relationship that likely needs to be specifically addressed is the relationship between squares and rectangles: All squares are rectangles, but not all rectangles are squares. Squares are a special class of rectangle that has the extra attribute of four congruent edges.

Featured Connection

In this activity, students use the Create a Diagram strategy to highlight the connection between physical and symbolic representations. In this instance, the chart is used as a record-keeping strategy to help students track which larger figures they were able to compose with specific numbers of smaller shapes. If you desire, you may also ask students to use the Make a Sketch strategy so they can keep a record of the actual pieces and configurations they created.

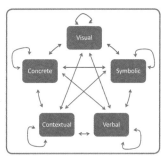

Source: Lesh, Post, & Behr (1987).

ACTIVITY

8.2

EXAMINING GEOMETRIC
RELATIONSHIPS BY
BUILDING A TANGRAM SET

| K | 1 | 2 | 3+ |

Materials

- Tangram pieces, one set per bag, as a point of reference
- 4 × 4 square for each student (plus extras for additional practice) cut from heavy paper or card stock
- One zip-top bag per student
- Scissors

Organization (physical)

- **Getting Started:** Pass out one 4 × 4 square and one zip-top bag to each student. Place sets of tangrams on the tables for students to reference as needed.
- **Winding Down:** Have students put the tangram pieces back together to make a square and then count out all seven pieces as they put them back in the zip-top bags.

Mathematical Purpose

Students will decompose larger figures into smaller shapes, examining the relationships between those shapes in the process.

Steps

You may find it helpful to watch the video of this activity and practice the process for cutting the tangram pieces prior to engaging with students. The following instructions follow the steps in the video. For each step, ask students to follow your instructions. Then, at the end, students may use these tangram pieces to create puzzles and answer questions just as they did with the commercial tangram sets.

1. Fold and cut the square in half along the diagonal.

2. Fold one of the large triangles along the line of symmetry and cut along the crease. Put both triangles in the zip-top bag.

3. Turn the other medium triangle so that the longest edge is at the bottom. Fold the right angle down so that the vertex points at the midpoint of the longest edge and cut along the crease. Place the medium triangle in the zip-top bag.

4. Fold the trapezoid along the line of symmetry and cut along the crease.

5. Fold one small trapezoid along the midpoint of the longest edge and cut along the crease. Place the small triangle and the square in the zip-top bag.

6. Fold the other small trapezoid so that the "toe" touches the top of the "laces" and cut along the crease. Place the small triangle and the parallelogram in the zip-top bag.

7. Remove the pieces from the zip-top bag. Count to ensure there are seven pieces. Now put the pieces back together into the original-sized square.

8. Review the task just completed by asking guiding questions such as the following:

   - *What do you notice about the pieces we just cut?*
   - *What did you notice about the shapes of the pieces?*
   - *What did you notice about the sizes of the pieces?*
   - *How might you be able to use these paper tangrams to learn if some of the pieces are the same size, even though they may be different shapes?*

9. *Extension 1:* Ask students to use the Make a Sketch and Caption Your Picture strategies to show the relationships they discovered between the areas of the different shapes (see the "Developing Understanding" section).

10. *Extension 2:* Use these pieces in subsequent days to do additional tangram puzzle tasks such as reviewing Activity 8.1 or creating new tangram puzzles.

Why This Manipulative?

Making paper tangrams allows students to explore the attributes of the tangram pieces by decomposing the large square into its smaller shapes rather than the typical activity of using the smaller shapes to compose the larger square. Because students did the cutting, they are more likely to be able to think about the relationships among and between the smaller shapes. Comparing the paper tangrams to the commercial sets will also give them the opportunity to think about the similarity, given that the paper tangrams are larger, but still proportional to the plastic or foam tangrams.

Developing Understanding

Students cutting their own tangram pieces provides a great opportunity for them to work and think in the "opposite direction" since they are, in essence, decomposing the square into its tangram pieces rather than using the small pieces to compose the large square.

Both during and after this activity, encourage students to use the geometric vocabulary as you model it. Even more importantly, use guiding questions such as the ones provided to help students think about and discuss the relative shapes and sizes of each piece. Students often find it shocking to realize that the medium triangle, square, and trapezoid all have the same area. You might suggest that they either fold their paper pieces or use the smallest triangle to show this relationship if they do not come up with comparison strategies on their own. You might also find it helpful to look at Activity 8.5 for a more detailed examination of working with same-sized pieces that have different shapes.

Once this activity is completed, you may want to place a stack of extra squares and student-friendly directions in a learning center so that students can continue to cut their own tangram pieces over the next several days as many students enjoy repeating this activity several times.

Activity 8.2 Resources

- *Examining Geometric Relationships by Building a Tangram Set* Activity Video

 To access resource visit resources.corwin.com/ MasteringMathManips/ K-3

Manipulative Illustrated

Hand-Cut Tangrams (with link to video)

Featured Connection

The nature of the connections between representations is slightly different for this activity than for others in this book. This activity connects the concrete to concrete representations as the students compare their paper tangram pieces to their commercially made

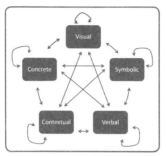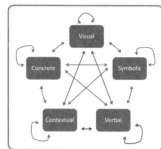

Source: Lesh, Post, & Behr (1987).

tangram pieces, both of which are concrete. If additional representations are desired, you may ask students to use the Make a Sketch and Caption Your Picture strategies to make connections between concrete, visual, and verbal representations as they show the relationships between the pieces that they discovered along the way.

Notes

_____

_____

_____

_____

_____

_____

_____

_____

_____

_____

_____

_____

Notes

FINDING RELATIVE VALUES
OF TANGRAM PIECES

| K | 1 | 2 | 3+ |

Materials

- Bagged tangram puzzle for each student
- Work mat for each student (fun foam or heavy paper)
- Recording sheet for each student

Organization (physical)

- **Getting Started:** Distribute bagged tangram puzzles to each student; if possible, provide a different-color set to students in each group.
- **Winding Down:** Ask students to count out all seven pieces as they place them back in the bags before placing the bags back in the storage container.

Mathematical Purpose

Students will explore the relative values between given shapes.

Activity 8.3 Resources

Finding Relative Values of Tangram Pieces Recording Sheet

 To access resources visit resources.corwin.com/ MasteringMathManips/ K-3

Manipulative Illustrated

Tangram Pieces (available from multiple sources)

Steps

1. Students will be working in groups of four. They will need to have access to different-colored tangram pieces for this activity. If each student has a different-color set, they will be able to trade pieces as needed.

2. Ask students to each put their tangram pieces together into one large square (one square per student). Either during or after they do this, ask guiding questions such as the following to preview this activity:

   - *What do you know about the shapes of the tangram pieces?*
   - *What do you know about the sizes of the tangram pieces?*
   - *Which tangram pieces are the same shape?*
   - *Which tangram pieces are the same size?*

3. Ask the students to work together in groups to solve this riddle.

   > If the smallest triangle has a value of 1, what is the value of each of the rest of the pieces?

   To support students' thinking, ask questions such as the following:

   - *How many small triangles would fit inside a square?*
   - *How many small triangles would fit inside a medium triangle?*
   - *How many _____ would fit inside a _____?*
   - *How might the little triangle or other pieces help you determine the value of each piece?*

4. Distribute the recording sheet. Ask students to use the Make a Diagram strategy to record their thinking.

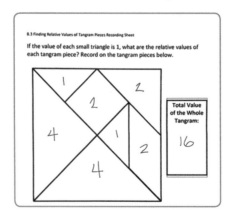

5. Once students have found the value of each piece, ask them to find the value of the whole large square. Then ask them to explain the steps they used to solve this problem.

6. *Extension 1:* Ask students to create the tangram piece shapes on a geoboard as another way to explore the fractional or whole-number relationships between and among the tangram pieces.

7. *Extension 2:* Repeat this activity with a focus on fractions. Ask students to answer the following riddles:

a. If the square has a value of 1, what is the value of the smallest triangle?

b. If the medium triangle has a value of 1, what is the value of the smallest triangle?

c. If the large triangle has a value of 1, what is the value of the smallest triangle?

d. If the square has a value of 1, what is the value of the smallest triangle?

e. If the parallelogram has a value of 1, what is the value of the smallest triangle?

Why This Manipulative?

Because tangram pieces are consistently proportional to one another, their relative sizes do not change, regardless of the size of the original large square. This makes them very useful for asking students to explore the relative sizes of the tangram pieces. As an extension, students may also create the tangram pieces on a virtual (or physical) geoboard to explore the relationships between the pieces using a different concrete representation.

Developing Understanding

Using the attribute of area to determine relative values may be challenging for some students while intuitive for others. This activity helps students connect geometric and quantitative skills in a way that is beneficial for both domains. Note that Activity 6.3 has a similar focus, so you may want to connect the use of pattern blocks and tangrams for finding relative values.

As students work to determine the value of each piece, guide them to lay the small pieces on top of the larger pieces with no gaps and no overlaps to determine their relative values. The small triangle will likely be the most-used piece, though you may want to urge students to use "known values" besides the small triangle since they won't have enough small triangles to cover more than a figure with a value of 4 (assuming students are working in groups of four).

When students are engaging in the fractions extension, they will once again need to put their tangram pieces together if they need a concrete representation to find fractional values.

Featured Connection

During this activity, students use the Create a Diagram strategy to highlight the connection between the concrete, visual, and symbolic representations. As students use the tangram pieces to determine the quantitative relationships, they record their work and describe their thinking using both numbers and words.

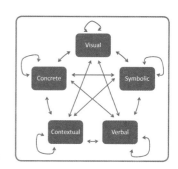

Source: Lesh, Post, & Behr (1987).

FINDING HALVES, THIRDS, AND FOURTHS ON A GEOBOARD

Materials

- Geoboards
- Bands
- Recording sheet for each student

Organization (physical)

- **Getting Started:** Distribute a board and bands to each student or group of students; review expectations for using bands and boards with students, as needed.

- **Winding Down:** Return boards and bands to storage.

Mathematical Purpose

Students will decompose rectangles (including squares) into halves, thirds, and fourths.

Activity 8.4 Resources

- *Finding Halves, Thirds, and Fourths on a Geoboard* Recording Sheet

 To download visit resources.corwin.com/ MasteringMathManips/ K-3

Manipulative Illustrated

Geoboards (available from multiple sources)

Steps

1. Ask students to create a rectangle on their geoboards. Ask them to check in with their tablemates to be sure everyone has a rectangle.

2. Ask students to hold up their geoboards for all to see. To support students' thinking, ask guiding question such as the following:

   - *Did everyone make the same rectangle?*
   - *Are the rectangles all the same size?*
   - *Are the rectangles all the same shape?*
   - *Did anyone make the special rectangle called a square?*

$\frac{1}{2}$ or halves

---

3. Next, ask students to use a different-colored band to split their rectangles into halves. Remind them that both halves must be the same size (but not necessarily the same shape; this will be explored in Activity 8.5).

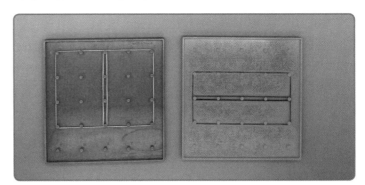

4. Ask students to record their partitioned rectangles on the recording sheet. *Optional:* Ask students to label each section with a unit fraction if that fits with your grade-level standards and math goals.

5. Ask students to make another shape on their geoboards and partition it in half. The new shape may be a rectangle, but it does not have to be. Once they've created that shape, ask them to record the partitioned shape on their recording sheet.

6. Ask students to continue this process until they've completed the recording sheet.

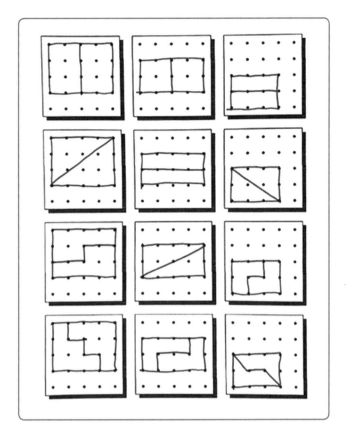

7. Bring students together to discuss what they notice and what they wonder when they view all of the different ways they showed halves with their geoboards.

8. Repeat this activity for other fractional parts, including fourths, thirds, or whatever fits with your grade-level standards and math goals.

Why This Manipulative?

Geoboards can be used to support students' understanding of fractions using area models, specifically with polygons. The ability to move bands to morph from one figure to another facilitates playfulness as students explore partitioning shapes into fractional parts. The advantage to using a geoboard is that the student will typically be starting with the whole and then partitioning it into fractional pieces, which tends to be the opposite action from building with fraction pieces and pattern blocks. That said, you may want to connect this activity to those that are introduced in the pattern blocks (Chapter 6) and fraction pieces (Chapter 7) chapters in this book.

Developing Understanding

As mentioned earlier, using geoboards offers students a great opportunity to partition shapes into fractional parts as opposed to building fractions up from pieces. Work with students to create initial shapes that will be easily partitioned into halves, thirds, or fourths (or other-sized fractions, depending on the grade-level standards and math goals you're working toward). They need not be limited to rectangles and squares.

Furthermore, a big idea that should be drawn out is that there are many ways to represent the same fraction using different units and different configurations. Use guiding questions and multiple examples to help students understand this principle. Be intentional as you guide students in using the sketches on the recording sheet to help them explore all the different ways they were able to create different shapes that can be partitioned into the same fraction pieces (e.g., different shapes all partitioned into fourths).

This activity may be used to support Activity 6.6 in this book, where students use pattern blocks to explore the need for a common unit when comparing fractions.

Featured Connection

In this activity, students use a modified version of the Build the Equation strategy by starting with a fraction and then building representations of that fraction on the geoboard. Although students are not building equations in this case, they are still starting with a symbolic representation and then building it with the concrete geoboards.

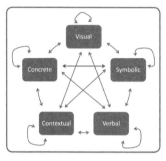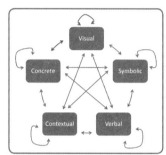

Source: Lesh, Post, & Behr (1987).

Furthermore, students use the Make a Sketch strategy to transfer their discoveries on the geoboard to paper. The collective sketches serve as a record for students to look at later in the activity, helping them to make generalizations based on their work.

Notes

_____

_____

_____

_____

_____

_____

_____

_____

_____

Notes

_____

_____

_____

_____

_____

_____

_____

_____

_____

_____

_____

_____

_____

_____

_____

_____

_____

_____

_____

_____

_____

_____

Materials

- Virtual geoboards (or physical geoboards and bands)
- Recording sheet for each student

Organization (virtual)

- **Getting Started:** Ensure students know how to use the virtual geoboards; review annotation tools, taking screenshots, and so on.
- **Winding Down:** Take screenshots to save student work.

Mathematical Purpose

Students will partition rectangles into fractional pieces, noting that same-sizes pieces need not be the same shape.

Activity 8.5 Resources

- *Same-Sized Parts Need Not Be the Same Shape* Recording Sheet

 To access resources visit resources.corwin.com/ MasteringMathManips/ K-3

Manipulative Illustrated

Geoboards (available from multiple sources)

Steps

1. Ask students to create a rectangle on their geoboards. Ask them to check with their tablemates to ensure everyone has a rectangle.

2. Ask students to partition the rectangle into fourths. If their rectangle does not facilitate the partitioning into equal-sized fourths, they may change the shape of the original rectangle. Ask them to check with their tablemates to ensure everyone has a rectangle correctly partitioned into fourths.

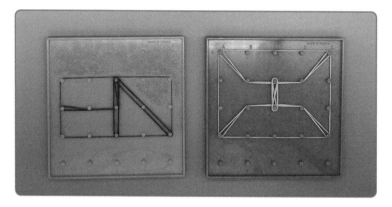

3. Ask students to use the Make a Sketch strategy to record their figures on their recording sheets.

4. Ask students to keep the same rectangle, but to partition it into fourths a different way. To support students' thinking, ask guiding questions such as the following:

   » *Are your fraction sections all the same size?*

   » *Can you make fraction pieces that are the same size but different shapes?*

   » *How do you know they are the same size if they are different shapes?*

5. Ask students to record their new partitioned rectangles and share with their partners.

6. Ask students to continue partitioning the same rectangle in different ways until their recording sheet is filled. Continue asking guiding questions, encouraging students to partition their fourths in unique and not-same-shape ways. Ask them to explain how they know the fourths are the same size, even if they are different shapes.

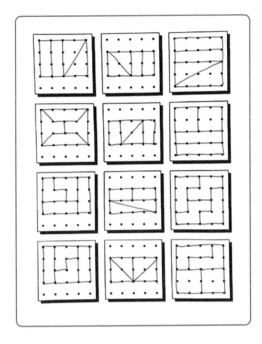

7. Bring students together to discuss what they notice and what they wonder when they view all of the different ways they showed fourths with their geoboards.

8. Repeat this activity for other fractional parts, including halves, thirds, or whatever fits with your grade-level standards and math goals.

Why This Manipulative?

Geoboards can be used to support students' understanding of fractions using area models, specifically with polygons. The ability to move bands to morph from one figure to another facilitates playfulness as students explore partitioning shapes into fractional parts.

The advantage of using a geoboard over other fraction manipulatives is that the student will typically be starting with the whole and then partitioning it into fractional pieces, the opposite of what typically happens with the others. That said, you may want to connect this activity to those that are introduced in the pattern blocks (Chapter 6) and fraction pieces (Chapter 7) chapters in this book.

If you would like to use virtual geoboards with more pegs, check out the Didax and Mathigon virtual manipulatives sites.

Developing Understanding

As mentioned earlier, using geoboards offers students a great opportunity to partition shapes into fractional parts as opposed to building fractions up from pieces. Work with students to create initial shapes that will be easily partitioned into halves, thirds, or fourths (or other-sized fractions, depending on the grade-level standards and math goals you're working toward). They need not be limited to rectangles and squares.

Furthermore, for this activity, a big idea that should be drawn out is that the parts must be the same size, but they need not be the same shape. Use guiding questions and multiple examples to help students understand this principle. Be intentional as you guide students in using the sketches on the recording sheet to help them explore all the different ways they were able to partition the same shape into the same-sized-but-different-shaped fractional pieces (e.g., fourths in different configurations).

Featured Connection

In this activity, students use a modified version of the Build the Equation strategy by starting with a fractional symbol and then building representations of that fraction on the geoboard. Although students are not building equations in this case, they are still starting with a symbolic representation and then building it with the concrete geoboards.

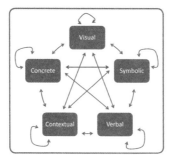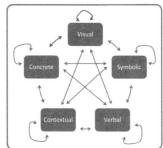

Source: Lesh, Post, & Behr (1987).

In addition, students use the Make a Sketch strategy to transfer their discoveries on the geoboard to paper. The collective sketches serve as a record for students to look at later in the activity, helping them to make generalizations based on their work.

Notes

_____

_____

_____

_____

_____

_____

_____

_____

_____

_____

_____

Notes

Materials

- Virtual geoboards (or physical geoboards and bands)
- Recording sheet

Organization (virtual)

- **Getting Started:** Ensure students know how to use the virtual geoboards; review annotation tools, taking screenshots, and so on.
- **Winding Down:** Take screenshots to save student work.

Mathematical Purpose

Students compare the attributes of various polygons using geoboards.

Activity 8.6 Resources

Comparing Polygons on the Geoboard Recording Sheet

 To access resources visit resources.corwin.com/ MasteringMathManips/ K-3

Manipulative Illustrated

Geoboard app from Math Learning Center: https://apps .mathlearningcenter.org/geoboard/

Steps

1. Ask students to represent a rectangle on their geoboards. Ask guiding questions such as the following:

   - *How would you describe your rectangle?*
   - *How do you know it's a rectangle?*
   - *Does it look like the other rectangles the students in your group made?*
   - *How is this rectangle different from your previous one?*

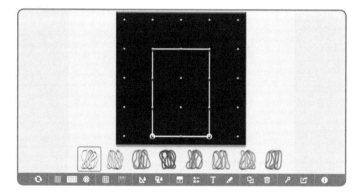

2. Ask students to use the Make a Sketch strategy to record their rectangles on one of the geoboards on the recording sheet.

3. Ask students to make a different rectangle on their geoboards. Continue asking guiding questions.

4. Repeat the activity with additional rectangles, asking students to verify that each one is uniquely different from the others.

5. When students have completed their recording sheets, have them work with a partner to explain how they know each rectangle is uniquely different from the others. Give them freedom to revise their work if their partners find any rectangles that are not unique.

6. Repeat this activity on another day with another shape (triangles, pentagons, hexagons, etc.).

Why This Manipulative?

Geoboards provide a unique perspective on representing and comparing geometric figures. The ability to move bands to morph from one figure to another facilitates playfulness as students explore the attributes of various figures. Virtual geoboards, such as pictured in this activity, have the added advantage of showing the bands as a single line rather than as a double line, making the geometric figures appear with greater precision. This activity might be enhanced by starting with a tangram piece, such as the square, and having students create squares with different configurations on the geoboard.

Developing Understanding

Students often have limited ideas about the shapes covered in the primary grades, in part because they are not exposed to the plethora of arrangements in which each category can appear. Provide students with ample time to explore many, many different configurations for each shape type, helping them to explore some important ideas often missed in the primary grades:

- Help students think about shapes other than the "regular" polygons when a category is mentioned (e.g., a pentagon always looks like home plate, a hexagon always looks like a yellow pattern block, or an octagon always looks like a stop sign).

- Help students realize that polygons, especially triangles and squares, can sit at any orientation. They need not be sitting on their "base" (e.g., a square can be tipped on one of its vertices).

- Help students understand that a square is a special kind of rectangle. Not all young children will fully grasp this, but the way you talk about it will make a difference in later grades.

Featured Connection

In this activity, students use the Make a Sketch strategy to connect concrete and visual representations. By sketching each polygon created, they are able to go back and reference all of the different configurations in one place, even when they no longer exist on the computer screen. Students may also use screenshots to collect their different polygons.

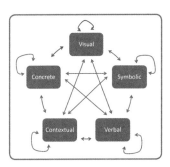

Source: Lesh, Post, & Behr (1987).

Notes

_____

_____

_____

_____

_____

_____

_____

Materials

- Virtual geoboards (or physical geoboards and bands)
- Recording sheet

Organization (virtual)

- **Getting Started:** Ensure students know how to use the virtual geoboards; review annotation tools, taking screenshots, and so on.
- **Winding Down:** Take screenshots to save student work.

Mathematical Purpose

Students decompose rectilinear figures into non-overlapping rectangles as they find the area of the figures using geoboards.

Activity 8.7 Resources

- *Finding the Area of a Rectilinear Figure on a Geoboard* Recording Sheet
- *Finding the Area of a Rectilinear Figure on a Geoboard* Activity Video

online resources ↖ To access resources visit resources.corwin.com/ MasteringMathManips/ K-3

Steps

1. Ask students to re-create the figure in Problem 1 on the Recording Sheet. Ask them to use a different-colored band to decompose the figure into rectangles. As students do this, look around the room to find different configurations made by the students.

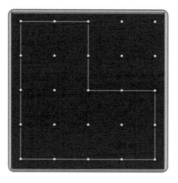

2. Select three or four students to share their geoboard designs, illustrating different ways the figure could be divided into rectangles. Ask students to discuss what they notice and what they wonder.

3. Next, ask students to determine the area of the figures. Remind students that area refers to the number of square units that cover a figure with no gaps and no overlaps. You may find it useful to re-create the figure with unit squares to remind students of the attributes of area. To support students' thinking, ask guiding questions such as the following:

   - *How would you find the area of each rectangle?*
   - *How can you use multiplication to represent the area of each rectangle?*
   - *What is the total area of the figure?*

4. Ask students to use the Make a Sketch and Name Your Model strategies to show their thinking on the recording sheet. They should include the partitioning, the areas for each section, and the area of the entire figure.

5. Ask students to work alone or in pairs to complete the other two problems, explaining their thinking with equations, numbers, and words.

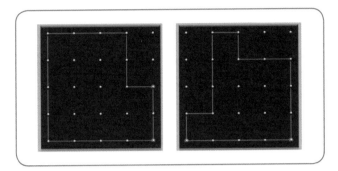

Why This Manipulative?

Geoboards provide a fantastic way for students to represent and analyze polygons. Because students can make polygons in various configurations, they are able to explore many geometric attributes and measurement processes. The ability to move bands to morph from one figure to another facilitates playfulness as students explore the attributes of various figures. This is especially helpful as students decompose rectilinear figures into rectangles and explore ways to find the area of each. This lays a foundation for work with area and surface area in future years.

Note that virtual geoboards have the added feature of showing a single line for each segment rather than the double line that appears from a band. Therefore, virtual versions of geoboards may be preferable in some cases.

In addition, note that the use of unit tiles may be useful to remind students of the attributes of area. Activities 4.4 and 4.5 in this book may be particularly useful as a connection to finding area on a geoboard.

Developing Understanding

This activity brings together several ideas explored over time: geometric attributes, decomposing polygons, the area model for multiplication, and arithmetic strategies such as multiplication and addition. Offer students support as they attempt to bring these many skills together into one problem-solving situation.

You may find it helpful to emphasize the many ways to decompose a rectilinear shape into multiple rectangles. Students may also benefit from a review of how to use multiplication to find the area of a rectangle. And finally, they may also benefit from a review of the concept of area itself, with a review of iterating square units (such as with unit squares) with no gaps and no overlaps, as mentioned earlier.

Manipulative Illustrated

Geoboard app from Math Learning Center: https://apps.mathlearningcenter.org/geoboard/

Featured Connection

In this activity, students use the Make a Sketch and Name Your Model strategies to connect the concrete representation on the geoboard to visual and symbolic representations. Because finding the area of a rectilinear figure involves several different skills,

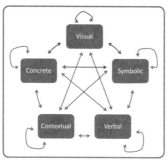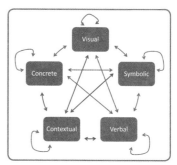

Source: Lesh, Post, & Behr (1987).

keeping record of their thinking along the way will help students transfer the understanding they developed from the manipulatives to the arithmetic processes used to find the areas of the rectangles and of the entire figure.

Notes

_____

_____

_____

_____

_____

_____

_____

_____

_____

_____

_____

_____

_____

CLOSING REFLECTION: TANGRAMS AND GEOBOARDS

How do I use tangrams and geoboards in my classroom now? What concepts do I use them to teach?

_____

_____

_____

_____

_____

What new ways have I found to use tangrams and geoboards to better support student understanding?

_____

_____

_____

_____

_____

What are my goals to make tangrams and geoboards a more regular part of my instruction?

_____

_____

_____

_____

_____

Chapter 9
Geometric Solids

INTRODUCTION

Understanding Geometric Strips and Solids

Geometric solids are sets of three-dimensional figures (either hollow or solid) designed to illustrate the various categories of three-dimensional shapes: cubes, **prisms**, **pyramids**, cones, **spheres**, and/or cylinders. Some hollow sets may have inserts to show altitude, slant height, or cross sections (e.g., cutting a circle, ellipse, or parabola from a cone), potentially making them useful even into high school. Some geometric solid sets are available with corresponding nets. In some cases, the various shapes within the set are built from the same units (e.g., the circular base of a cone is the same diameter as the sphere).

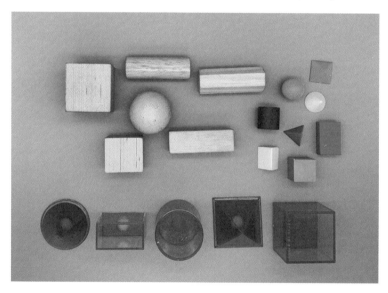

Geometric solids are particularly effective in teaching these topics:

- Attributes of two- and three-dimensional figures
- Relationships between two- and three-dimensional figures
- Geometric vocabulary
- Counting and cardinality (when counting and recording the number of faces, edges, vertices, etc.)

Introducing Geometric Strips and Solids to Students

Use the *Notice and Wonder Thinking Routine* (described in the introductory chapter) to introduce geometric solids to students. You will likely introduce each at a different time given that they address different areas of the curriculum. As students explore geometric solids, they may build composed shapes from the blocks. They may notice the relationships between the various pieces or count their faces, edges, and vertices. If the pieces are hollow and fill materials are available, they may fill the shapes and pour from one to another, wondering about volume.

Key Ideas With Geometric Solids

- Students often misunderstand significant ideas about two- and three-dimensional geometry because teachers use imprecise vocabulary, descriptions, and definitions about the shapes. Be sure to review two- and three-dimensional attributes and vocabulary prior to beginning your geometry unit.

- Geometric solids are easily found from a variety of sources. Look in discount and bulk catalogs, such as Oriental Trading Company, for inexpensive plastic shapes that can be put in the hands of all students.

- One very common misconception originating in the early grades that continues to plague students throughout elementary school is the notion that squares and rectangles are distinct from one another. In fact, a square is a special kind of rectangle that has equivalent sides. Similarly, a cube is a special kind of rectangular prism that has all square faces.

Things to Consider About Geometric Solids

- Think about two-dimensional figures appearing on the faces of the geometric solids. How might you help students discover this?

- Consider connecting what students know about two-dimensional figures to help them understand three-dimensional figures. In addition, be sure to model the use of clear and specific vocabulary that distinguishes three-dimensional figures from one another as well as from two-dimensional figures (Clements & Sarama, 2014).

- If you do not have commercial nets (two-dimensional patterns that fold into three-dimensional solids), think about how you might create nets for them by having students tape together two-dimensional shapes and fold them into three-dimensional figures. Research has shown that even in kindergarten, students are able to identify the relationships between two- and three-dimensional figures using nets (Clements & Sarama, 2014).

Alternatives to Commercial Geometric Solids

There are dies available for die-cut machines that will cut nets for many solid figures. If these are cut from card stock and assembled carefully, they can be reasonably sturdy. If one face is omitted, they can even be filled with sand or rice to explore volume. Sets of children's blocks often include a variety of three-dimensional shapes. They may not address the full range of solid figures in the curriculum but can be a good start. Everyday objects may also approximate a number of three-dimensional shapes. In addition, look in discount and bulk catalogs, such as Oriental Trading Company, for inexpensive sets of geometric solids. And finally, there are some commercial sets of shapes, such as Polydrons®, that snap together and apart so students can compose and decompose geometric solids and discover patterns in the process.

Working With Virtual Geometric Solids

As of this writing (in the summer of 2021), we have not found free virtual versions of these tools available on the sites we have reviewed in developing this book. Even when geometric solids appear on screen, ensuring primary students are visualizing the two-dimensional renderings as three-dimensional objects is questionable. For the purposes of this chapter, only physical geometric solids are described.

Notes

_____

_____

_____

_____

_____

_____

_____

_____

Notes

IDENTIFYING FACES OF GEOMETRIC SOLIDS AS TWO-DIMENSIONAL FIGURES

Materials

- Plastic three-dimensional solids
- Play dough or paint

Organization (physical)

- **Getting Started:** Distribute a bag of geometric solids and a bag of play dough to each pair of students.

- **Winding Down:** Ask students to count the solids into their bags prior to putting them away; ask students to check the zipper on their play dough bags to ensure they are completely sealed.

Mathematical Purpose

In this activity, students will compare and contrast the two-dimensional figures on the faces of three-dimensional figures.

Manipulative Illustrated

Geometric Solids (available from multiple sources)

Steps

1. Distribute one bag of geometric solids to each pair of students. Ask them to remove the solids and to discuss what they notice and wonder about the shapes. Ask guiding questions such as the following:

   - *What do you notice about these shapes?*
   - *Do any of them roll?*
   - *What shapes do you see on the flat sides or faces?*
   - *How many pointy vertices can you count?*
   - *What do you notice?*
   - *What do you wonder?*

2. Ask the students to work in pairs. One at a time, the students should choose a solid and describe it to their partner. Encourage them to focus on the two-dimensional shapes that comprise the faces. Continue until each student has had at least two turns.

3. Next, ask students to roll a piece of play dough into a flat "pancake." Ask students to select a geometric solid and to make an imprint of each flat face in the play dough. Ask guiding questions to support their explorations:

   - *What shapes do you see in the play dough?*
   - *Are there any prints that look the same?*
   - *How many prints are squares? Triangles? Circles?*
   - *Are there any solids that don't make shapes when you make a print?*

4. Ask students to compare their prints with those of other students. Students should identify the solid they used and show the two-dimensional prints they were able to create in the play dough.

5. Ask students to meet in small groups to discuss their discoveries. Assist students in their discussions, as needed, by asking similar questions as before:

   - *Which solids have square faces? Triangle faces? Circle faces?*
   - *Were you able to make a two-dimensional print with the curved surfaces?*

Why This Manipulative?

Geometric solids allow students to explore the attributes of both two- and three-dimensional figures. Most commercial sets of geometric solids are based on a common edge-length unit, making them easier to compare. And because the two-dimensional figures that appear on the faces of the solids consist of two-dimensional shapes with which most young children are familiar, this manipulative provides ample opportunity for students to develop their work with two-dimensional shapes while working with three-dimensional solids.

Developing Understanding

When talking with students about two- and three-dimensional figures, be sure to model precise vocabulary, descriptions, and definitions. Students' emerging understanding will take time, and yet precision from the very beginning is critical to emerging understanding. Table 9.1 is a set of definitions of the geometric solids that are most commonly available in primary classrooms. Be sure to embed these words into your discussions with students, encouraging them to "try them on for size."

Table 9.1 Definitions of Commonly Available Geometric Solids

Geometric Solid	Description
Cone	A three-dimensional figure with one curved surface, one flat surface (usually circular), one curved edge, and one vertex.
Cube	A three-dimensional figure with six congruent square faces. Cubes comprise a special category of prisms. Students often mistakenly call a cube a square.
Cylinder	A three-dimensional figure with one curved surface and two congruent circular bases.
Prism	A three-dimensional figure with two congruent and parallel faces that are polygons. The rest of the faces are parallelograms. Typical prisms used in primary classrooms include triangular prisms and rectangular prisms.
Pyramid	A three-dimensional figure with one base that is a polygon. The rest of the faces are triangles that meet at a single vertex. Students often mistakenly call a pyramid a triangle. Typical pyramids used in primary classrooms include triangular pyramids and rectangular pyramids.
Sphere	A three-dimensional figure with all points equally distant from the center. Students often mistakenly call a sphere a circle.

Featured Connection

Students use the Caption Your Picture strategy to describe the play dough prints they created during this activity. Students have already connected the concrete geometric solids to the play dough imprints they made. Next they will use verbal language to describe the play dough visuals. With enough guidance, students should begin navigating the distinction between the two-dimensional shapes printed on the play dough and the geometric solids with which they started.

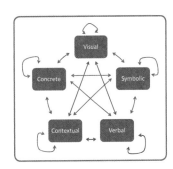

Source: Lesh, Post, & Behr (1987).

Materials

- Plastic or wooden geometric solids
- Opaque paper or fabric bags, approximately the size of a lunch bag

Organization (physical)

- **Getting Started:** Distribute a bag of geometric solids and a bag of play dough to each pair of students.
- **Winding Down:** Ask students to count the solids into their bags prior to putting them away; ask students to check the zipper on the play dough bags to ensure they are completely sealed.

Mathematical Purpose

In this activity, students use geometric vocabulary to describe the attributes of geometric solids hidden inside a bag.

Manipulative Illustrated

Geometric Solids (available from multiple sources)

Steps

1. Prior to "game time," review the geometric solids with students, and warm up with a quick around-the-circle description game. Hold up one geometric solid and ask students to think about words they would use to describe it. Ask them to then pair up with someone and say at least three things about that solid. Then bring students back together to generate a few key points. For example, if you held up a rectangular pyramid, the students might generate the following statements:

   - *It has a square on the bottom.*
   - *It has triangles on the sides.*
   - *It has a point [vertex] at the top.*

2. Repeat Step 1 for each geometric solid.

3. Next, ask students to work in pairs to play this noncompetitive "game."

4. Student A closes their eyes as Student B places one geometric solid inside an opaque bag.

5. Without looking, Student B describes the shape inside the bag using two- and three-dimensional geometric vocabulary and descriptions.

6. After at least four descriptions, Student A says, "Name that shape!" At that time, Student B names the shape that is inside the bag. Then Student B opens the bag to see if they are correct.

7. Students reverse roles and play again.

8. Play continues until time is up.

9. After individual students have had at least two chances to describe their shapes, bring the class back together to discuss what they noticed and what they might be wondering. Use this opportunity to further develop students' emerging precision with terminology and descriptive language. Facilitate this conversation by asking guiding questions such as the following:

   - *What did you notice when your partner was describing their shapes?*
   - *What did you notice when you were describing your shapes?*
   - *What was easy for you to describe?*
   - *What was difficult for you to describe?*
   - *What are you still wondering about geometric solids?*

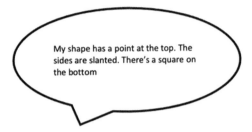

My shape has a point at the top. The sides are slanted. There's a square on the bottom

10. *Extension:* Ask students to each select one geometric solid and do a "treasure hunt" around the classroom, finding an object that has a shape similar to the solid they chose. In pairs, have students discuss how the objects they found are similar and how they differ from their selected geometric solid.

Why This Manipulative?

Geometric solids allow students to explore the attributes of both two- and three-dimensional figures. Most commercial sets of geometric solids are based on a common edge-length unit, making them easier to compare. And because the two-dimensional figures that appear on the faces of the solids consist of two-dimensional shapes with which most young children are familiar, this manipulative provides ample opportunity for students to develop their understanding of two-dimensional shapes while working with three-dimensional solids.

Developing Understanding

A key component of developing geometric thinking in the primary grades centers on using descriptive language and increasingly precise terminology. When talking with students about geometric solids, be sure to model precise vocabulary, descriptions, and definitions. For this activity, students may need support in using correct geometric terminology. You might want to refer to the Table 9.1 list of geometric solids and descriptions included with Activity 9.1.

When leading the conversations in this activity, students may need support in navigating their emerging use of geometric terminology. You may find it helpful to phrase questions that couch the vocabulary into the question. For example, instead of asking, "What is the name of your figure?" you may ask, "What can you tell me about the pyramid you are holding in your hands?"

Finally, as students describe their selected objects during the extension, support them with realizing that most objects are close to the geometric solids, but not exact. For example, if students selected the rectangular prism and then found a book that has a similar shape, they should recognize that the hard cover sticks out and that there is a "dent" next to the spine. Although the book resembles a rectangular prism, it also has physical features that "get in the way."

Featured Connection

In this activity, students are using a modified version of the Caption Your Picture strategy to connect verbal language to the manipulatives they are using. Although students are not asked to sketch or draw the geometric solids, they are asked to describe the hidden shapes using increasingly precise language. So, in essence, they are really captioning their actions and observations. As an extension, you may ask students to create sketches of their figures to the best of their abilities.

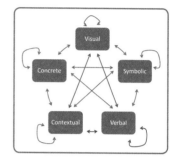

Source: Lesh, Post, & Behr (1987).

Notes

_____

_____

_____

_____

_____

_____

_____

_____

_____

_____

_____

Notes

Materials

- Plastic or wooden three-dimensional solids in zip-top bags (one set per student)
- Precut triangles, squares, rectangles, and circles
- Tape

Organization (physical)

- **Getting Started:** Distribute a bag of geometric solids to each student; place a tray of precut shapes and a tape dispenser in the middle of each table (make sure the precut shapes all have the same dimensional units along the edges).
- **Winding Down:** Ask students to count the solids into their bags prior to putting them away; ask students to tidy up the tray of precut shapes and return them to the appropriate location.

Mathematical Purpose

Students use two-dimensional figures to compose three-dimensional figures.

Activity 9.3 Resources

Composing Geometric Solids Activity Video

 To access resource visit resources.corwin.com/ MasteringMathManips/K-3

Manipulative Illustrated

Geometric Solids (available from multiple sources)

Steps

1. Ask each student to take the cube out of the bag. Ask the students to use the precut paper shapes in the tray to create a pattern (net) that will fold into a geometric solid. Ask guiding questions to facilitate students' thinking such as the following:

   - *What shape do you see on the faces?*
   - *How many squares are there altogether?*
   - *How might you tape the pieces together to make a pattern that will fold up into a cube?*

2. Provide ample time for each student to complete this task. Then, when all students are finished, set aside the paper cube and move on to the rectangular prism. Revise the guiding questions from Step 1 each time.

3. Once a student is successful with the rectangular prism, move on to the triangular prism and pyramids. Omit the solids with curved surfaces for this exercise.

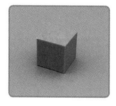  

4. After all students have completed at least one paper solid, bring the class together to discuss their strategies for composing three-dimensional solids from two-dimensional figures. To facilitate this conversation, you might use guiding questions such as the following:

   - *What did you find simple as you composed your geometric solids?*
   - *What was challenging?*
   - *How did you discover which edges could touch?*
   - *What were some of the ways in which you could put squares together to make a pattern that would fold into a cube?*
   - *How did you use the small geometric solids to help guide your work?*
   - *How did you think about the geometric solids as you were taping the two-dimensional shapes together?*

Why This Manipulative?

Geometric solids allow students to explore the attributes of both two- and three-dimensional figures. For this activity, using commercial geometric solids allows students to see standard figures that can be easily replicated. And because the two-dimensional figures that appear on the faces of the solids consist of two-dimensional shapes with which most young children are familiar, this manipulative provides ample opportunity for students to develop their understanding of two-dimensional shapes while working with three-dimensional solids.

Over time, you will want to take care that students do not overgeneralize commercial geometric solids. For example, you will want to provide students with opportunities to see that rectangular prisms can have squares on the ends but that there are also such things as pentagonal prisms and hexagonal prisms. You may also want to provide students with opportunities to view cones that are not perpendicular or pyramids that have incongruent triangular faces.

Developing Understanding

When talking with students about two- and three-dimensional figures, be sure to model precise vocabulary, descriptions, and definitions. For this activity, students may need support in using correct terminology and precise vocabulary. You may want to reference the Table 9.1 descriptions in Activity 9.1.

In particular, this activity provides students with the opportunity to compose and decompose three-dimensional figures using two-dimensional shapes. Although creating "nets" is typically an activity reserved for students in the middle grades, this activity provides a simple structure for younger children to explore the attributes of three-dimensional geometry. By taping together the paper shapes, students can see, for example, how edges and vertices are formed.

Featured Connection

In this activity, students are using a modified version of the Caption Your Picture strategy to connect verbal language to the manipulatives they are using. Although students are not asked to sketch or draw the geometric solids, they are asked to describe the shapes they composed using increasingly precise language. So, in essence, they are really captioning their actions and observations. As an extension, you may ask students to create sketches of their figures to the best of their abilities.

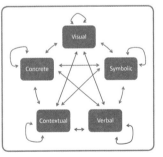 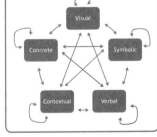

Source: Lesh, Post, & Behr (1987).

Students might also make further connections by using the Name Your Model strategy. Although this strategy is slightly modified for geometry, it's important for students to connect the geometric terminology with the geometric solids they created from the two-dimensional shapes. As students create increasingly sophisticated solids, they may begin to see how the names of the shapes correspond to the faces. For example, when making prisms, they may begin to see the patterns for creating a triangular prism, rectangular prism, pentagonal prism, hexagonal prism, and so on.

Materials

- Plastic or wooden three-dimensional solids
- Book or other flat surface that can be propped up to create a ramp
- Real-life objects that are shaped like spheres, cones, and cylinders
- Activity sheet (modify the recording sheet if the solids being used differ from the ones listed on the table)

Organization (physical)

- **Getting Started:** Distribute a bag of geometric solids to each pair of students; help students prop a book or other flat surface up so that it creates a ramp.
- **Winding Down:** Ask students to count the solids in their bags prior to putting them away.

Mathematical Purpose

In this activity, students compare solids with curved surfaces and solids with only flat surfaces.

Activity 9.4 Resources

Solids With Curved Surfaces Activity Sheet.

 To access resource visit resources.corwin.com/ MasteringMathManips/ K-3

Manipulative Illustrated

Geometric Solids (available from multiple sources)

Steps

1. Ask students to sort their solids into two groups: those that they think will roll down a ramp and those that they think will not. To guide students' thinking, ask guiding questions such as the following:
   - *Why do you think these will roll?*
   - *Why do you think these will not?*
   - *How many did you place in the "rollable" category?*
   - *How many did you place in the "not rollable" category?*

2. Ask students to work together to test their hypotheses. Help them create a ramp with a book or other flat surface, as needed.

3. Ask students to record the results of their experiment using the activity sheet. Continue asking guiding questions as listed in Step 1.

Solid	Does this Shape Roll?		If yes, why does this shape roll?
	Yes	No	
Cone			
Cube			
Cylinder			
Rectangular Prism			
Sphere			
Square Pyramid			
Triangular Prism			
Triangular Pyramid			

4. After students are finished, bring the group together, asking guiding questions such as the following:
   - *Which solids rolled down the ramp?*
   - *Which solids did not roll down the ramp?*
   - *Were there any solids that sometimes rolled down the ramp and sometimes did not?*
   - *What did you need to do to make sure the "sometimes rollable" solids would roll?*

5. As a group, physically sort the geometric solids into two categories, those that roll and those that do not roll. Ask students to verbalize the sorting rule (e.g., "shapes that roll" vs. "shapes that don't roll"), as well as the generalized reason that some shapes roll (e.g., "they have a curved surface").

6. *Extension:* Ask students to each select one geometric solid that has a curved surface and do a "treasure hunt" around the classroom, finding an object that has a shape similar to the solid they chose. In pairs, have students discuss how the objects they found are similar and how they differ from their selected geometric solid.

Why This Manipulative?

Geometric solids allow students to explore the attributes of both two- and three-dimensional figures. For this activity, using the geometric solids rather than real-life objects (such as cylinder-shaped cans or cone-shaped cups) allows students to focus on the defining attributes of the solids without extraneous features such as labels, lips, or seams.

Developing Understanding

When talking with students about two- and three-dimensional figures, be sure to model precise vocabulary, descriptions, and definitions. For this activity, students may need support in using correct terminology and precise vocabulary. You may want to reference the Table 9.1 descriptions included in Activity 9.1.

For this activity, students may need support in using correct two- and three-dimensional terminology and descriptions as they compare solids with curved surfaces and solids with only flat surfaces. Once students have sorted their solids into categories—rollable and not rollable—ask them to think about and discuss the attributes of each group and to design a hypothesis that could be generalized to all geometric solids. For example, they might state that geometric solids that roll must have a curved surface and that the type of curved surface determines how those shapes roll.

Finally, as students describe their selected objects during the extension, support them with realizing that most objects are close to the geometric solids, but not exact. For example, if students selected a cylinder and then found a can that has a similar shape, they should recognize that the lip of the can sticks up a bit, whereas a cylinder is smooth along the edges where the curved and flat faces meet. Although the can resembles a cylinder, it also has physical features that "get in the way."

Featured Connection

In this activity, students use the Create a Diagram strategy to connect the concrete objects (geometric solids) to the visual and symbolic representations included on the activity sheet. As students complete the chart with the data they collect during the rolling experiment, students should also record their general ideas for why certain shapes will roll down the ramp. This second step is partially associated with the Caption Your Picture strategy, although the students do not actually draw a picture but are, rather, describing the concrete objects.

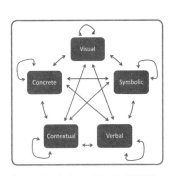

Source: Lesh, Post, & Behr (1987).

Materials

- Plastic or wooden geometric solids
- Recording sheet (modify the recording sheet if the solids being used deviate from the ones listed on the table)

Organization (physical)

- **Getting Started:** Distribute a bag of geometric solids to each student or pair of students.
- **Winding Down:** Ask students to count the solids into their bags prior to putting them away.

Mathematical Purpose

In this activity, students formally explore the attributes of geometric solids by completing a description table.

Activity 9.5 Resources

Attributes of Geometric Solids Recording Sheet

 To access resource visit resources.corwin.com/ MasteringMathManips/ K-3

Manipulative Illustrated

Geometric Solids (available from multiple sources)

Steps

1. Ask students to remove one shape at a time from their bags and review the names and attributes of the geometric solids. Be sure to review vocabulary included on the recording sheet such as *face*, *vertex*, and *edge*.

Solid	Number of...						
	Edges	Vertices	Square Faces	Rectangle Faces (non-square)	Triangle Faces	Circle Faces	Curved Surfaces
Cube							
Rectangular Prism							
Triangular Prism							
Triangular Pyramid							
Square Pyramid							
Cylinder							
Cone							
Sphere							

10.5 Attributes of Geometric Solids Recording Sheet

2. Ask students to remove one geometric solid from the bag. They should locate the name of that solid on the recording sheet and record the attributes listed across the top of the table.

3. As students work, support their learning by asking guiding questions such as the following:

   - *What is the difference between a vertex and an edge?*
   - *Why does the "Rectangle Faces" header say "non-square"?*
   - *How are you going to make sure you don't double-count the faces or the vertices?*

   Ask students to continue taking out one geometric solid at a time, completing the table for that solid, and then replacing it and selecting another until the table is completed. Continue asking guiding questions, and ask students to discuss their findings with one another as they go.

4. When students have completed the task, bring them back to together to share what they noticed and anything they're still wondering about the geometric solids. Ask guiding questions such as the following:

- *Was there anything that surprised you as you completed this task?*
- *What did you notice about the faces [vertices, edges, curved surfaces] as you were counting and recording?*
- *Did you notice anything that some of the shapes had in common?*
- *What are you still wondering about any of these geometric solids?*

Why This Manipulative?

Geometric solids allow students to explore the attributes of both two- and three-dimensional figures. For this activity, the precision of the geometric solids allows students to explore the attributes of the geometric solids such as the flat faces, curved surfaces, faces, edges, and vertices. If students were using real-life objects such as cylinder-shaped cans or prism-shaped boxes, extraneous features such as flaps and lips might get in the way of students' focus on the geometric attributes.

Developing Understanding

When talking with students about two- and three-dimensional figures, be sure to model precise vocabulary, descriptions, and definitions. For this activity, students may need support in using correct terminology and precise vocabulary, especially when it comes to the names of the shapes and their attributes. You may want to reference the Table 9.1 descriptions included in Activity 9.1.

For this activity, students may need support in using precise terminology and descriptions as they focus on specific attributes. For example, students may find the distinction between edges and vertices challenging. You may want to embed descriptive language into your question, such as "How many pointy vertices did you count?" or "How many flat faces does this shape have?" Encourage students to do the same.

Featured Connection

Use the Create a Diagram strategy as they connect the concrete objects (geometric solids) to a graphical representation (the table on the recording sheet). As students learn to transfer their observations to a table with rows and columns, getting everything into the correct space may be difficult for some. Although using tables to represent collected data may be difficult in the primary grades, mastery of this method will prove helpful as students progress within and across grade levels.

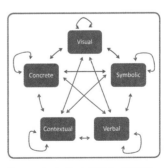

Source: Lesh, Post, & Behr (1987).

CLOSING REFLECTION: GEOMETRIC SOLIDS

How do I use geometric solids in my classroom now? What concepts do I use them to teach?

_____

_____

_____

_____

_____

_____

_____

_____

_____

_____

_____

_____

What new ways have I found to use geometric solids to better support student understanding?

_____

_____

_____

_____

_____

_____

_____

_____

_____

_____

_____

What are my goals to make geometric solids a more regular part of my instruction?

_____

_____

_____

_____

_____

_____

_____

_____

_____

_____

Chapter 10
Continuing the Journey

You, like the teachers in our introductory chapter, have been on a journey of discovering ways to use manipulatives more intentionally. We hope that you've had powerful conversations and found some new favorite activities, and that you feel more comfortable with these tools as part of your mathematics tool kit.

Using manipulatives is not a new instructional strategy, although new manipulatives are being developed and virtual manipulatives have become another resource for teachers and students. Remember that the power of manipulatives as tools for learning mathematics is in the connections you develop between these concrete representations and other representations of mathematics. The deep learning is in translation from one representation to another.

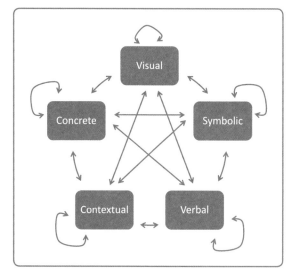

Source: Lesh, Post, & Behr (1987).

As you continue on your journey, we hope you will keep these important ideas in mind:

1. Manipulatives are tools for learning mathematics, for making sense of abstract ideas. As students develop understanding and confidence, they will naturally use manipulatives less and less because the tools become inefficient. Their early work with manipulatives grounds their experiences and serves as a cognitive support for their more efficient work with abstract symbols. The pace of this fading away will vary from student to student.

2. Context is always important. Students can and should connect physical representations, visual representations, and symbolic representations to experiences in their everyday lives. Context is not limited to working with concrete objects.

3. Manipulatives provide students with an opportunity to act out, think about, and talk about mathematics. That active engagement with the math is our goal, and manipulatives are a tool for creating student engagement. If students can act out a situation, they can talk about it. If they can talk about it, they can write about it. If they can write about it, they can develop an equation for it. *That* is how we move from concrete to abstract.

4. While we talk about concrete-pictorial-abstract as if it is a tight sequence of fixed steps, the reality is that learners move back and forth across the phases. They might start building and have an insight about an equation. They write that down and begin working abstractly, only to find a picture helps clarify their thinking. Then, back to the equation they go. Furthermore, students may be thinking abstractly when using concrete tools, or they may be thinking concretely when using pictorial representations (Kamii, 2006).

5. Mathematics is best learned by using and connecting *all* forms of representation. While this book is grounded in physical representations, we have shared a number of strategies for connecting the concrete with the visual, the symbolic, the verbal, and the abstract.

6. Encourage students to use materials creatively and flexibly. If a commercial manipulative is not available, what everyday objects might you substitute? Can you use a manipulative not designed for the problem at hand? What new insights do you gain by thinking about how to use these tools flexibly? What do you get by running up against the limits of the tools?

7. Challenge your students (and yourself) to think deeply about how these tools represent the mathematics and what we can learn from the tools. Learning to represent binomial multiplication with algebra tiles can push your own understanding of the distributive property and what it really means. While you may be quite good at using FOIL (first, outer, inner, last), what new learning happens when you build a model and sketch a picture?

8. Be open to digital tools and think about how they best support learning. Learners benefit from working with tangible objects to represent important mathematics. Just because this is beneficial does not mean it is always possible. When you use virtual tools, choose carefully to be sure the math is well represented. Push yourself to develop tasks that truly reimagine the work and take advantage of digital features like endless supplies of pieces.

SUGGESTIONS FOR SUPPORTING FAMILIES AND CAREGIVERS

Now that you and your students have more experience with manipulatives, we encourage you to support families and caregivers in becoming more comfortable with these important tools. The adults in students' lives will need time to explore and understand the tools, both digital and physical versions. Where possible, demonstrate a manipulative activity for them so they can see the power of learning this way. Provide basic tips for navigating and using virtual manipulatives for them so they can support their children at home. You might consider making *brief* video clips (2–3 minutes) that introduce them to the manipulatives and other visual strategies their children will be working on in the coming days.

Families and caregivers will likely share some of your questions about teaching with manipulatives. In the following section, we've addressed just a few of the major concerns we often hear from those supporting students' learning at home. One of the most important things you can do is relate to them, validate their concerns and frustrations, and ease them into realizing that we are not ignoring the ways they learned math in elementary school; we are simply delaying the standard procedures a bit in order to first develop understanding.

This is too complicated and takes too long. Why are you teaching this way?

Do you remember hearing that rhyme, "Mine is not to question why, just invert and multiply"? Many of us learned math by watching our teachers and then copying what they did. We did not focus on understanding, and we certainly weren't invited to ask them "why" questions. Rather, we focused on getting the right answer, and many of us had no idea what kind of magic had just taken place. Unfortunately, 60%–80% of adults in North America have some kind of aversion toward mathematics, and we can't afford to let the next generation fall into that same category.

Much of mathematics is very abstract, and making sense of the symbols is hard. Manipulatives provide us with a way to show students what the symbols represent and ensure that math makes sense to them. While we know it sometimes takes a little longer when we first use manipulatives, our patience is repaid in the long run with greater student understanding. Simply put, time spent helping students understand the math is always time well spent, and manipulatives play a huge role in developing that understanding.

Is it okay if I show my child the way I learned to do it instead?

Please know that the most efficient strategies, known as the standard procedures or standard algorithms, are part of our end game—they are simply not where we begin. One of the things we value in math is that there are many different ways to solve most problems. Having multiple solution pathways helps students become more flexible thinkers. Furthermore, it is so helpful when students become comfortable with many strategies before they learn the most efficient strategies (aka the procedures you and I learned in school). We encourage families and caregivers to wait to show traditional algorithms or shortcuts until students are learning about them in the classroom.

I don't know how to help my child with this kind of math. What can I do?

We encourage you to help your child with math by asking questions rather than providing answers. With manipulative activities, the questions are often about how the students represent the math. Here are some general questions you might use to support your child when learning math with manipulatives:

- *Show or tell me the problem you're working on. What parts of the problem make sense to you?*

- *How can you show those parts with your manipulatives?*

- *If this manipulative isn't working for you, is there another one you'd prefer to use?*

- *Where is each part of the problem in the representation you've created?*

I don't have any manipulatives at home, and my child needs help now. What should I do?

Many math problems can be represented with makeshift manipulatives you have in your home, especially in your kitchen. Here are just a few ideas to get you started (Wills, 2021).

- Counters: beans, dry pasta, cereal bits, buttons, beads, bottle caps

- Tens and ones: O-shaped cereal on dry spaghetti noodles, paper clips, beads, and string

- Area and perimeter: cheese crackers, small square bathroom tiles

- Fractions: egg cartons, muffin trays, toys with different attributes

- Measurement: paper clips, cubes, or other equal-sized objects; string; measuring tape; measuring cups; rice, sand, and water for filling containers

- Games: cards, dice, paper clip spinners, coins, game pieces

Additional Resources

On the website supporting this book, you will find the following:

- Resources for conducting your own school-wide manipulative inventory.

- A list of virtual manipulative sites along with the models available on each site, current as of late 2021. If you are looking for a particular tool, this can help you find some good options. Remember, the digital world is always changing, so the site may not look as it did when we first made the list.

- Black-line masters for the activities in this book.

 To view and download resource, please visit resources.corwin.com/ MasteringMathManips/K-3

Continuing the Journey

While we've shared many ideas for teaching with manipulatives, there is much more these tools can do. We encourage you to continue exploring these powerful tools as resources in your mathematics classroom. Make manipulatives freely available to your students for their mathematics work. Explore new uses for manipulatives at professional conferences or from other sources. And, like the teachers at the beginning of this book, dig deep into your closets and bookshelves to discover what treasures lie in wait. Bring them to the light of day, explore new ways of bringing math to life for students, and find renewed excitement in teaching for understanding. Your students will thank you ... and you'll so enjoy the journey.

GLOSSARY

Term Definition

Addend One of the quantities being added in an addition expression

Addition To combine or join together; related words: *add, and, plus (+), join, put together.* Addition is useful in situations where something arrives, where there are groups with a total, and where values are compared with constant difference

Analog Clock A clock with the numbers 1–12 around the face and rotating hands to show hours, minutes, and seconds

Angle Two rays that share an end point

Array/Area Model of Multiplication A model for multiplication (or division) in which items are arranged in rows and columns

Associative Property When three or more numbers are added (or multiplied), the result is the same regardless of the way the terms are grouped for computation

Attributes (of Shapes) Characteristics such as color, size, thickness, and number of sides or angles

Bar Model A representation of a word problem or mathematical situation where bars or boxes are used to represent the known and unknown quantities; also known as a *tape diagram*

Bundle To put individual units together to make a larger unit; for example, connecting 10 individual linking cubes to make a ten

Cardinality The number of objects in a set or group

Column A vertical arrangement of objects

Commutative Property Reversing the order of terms does not change the outcome; this property applies to addition and multiplication

Compare To look for similarities or differences

Compose To put a number or shape together using other numbers or shapes

Data Information in numerical form that can be processed

Data Analysis The interpretation of data; a process of assigning meaning to the collected information and determining conclusions

Decompose To separate a number or shapes into parts using other numbers or shapes

Denominator The number of equal-sized pieces in a whole; the number of members of a set with an identified attribute; the bottom number in a fraction

Difference The amount by which one number is greater or less than another number; can be found by subtracting, comparing, or finding a missing addend

Distributive Property Multiplying a sum by a given number is the same as of Multiplication Over Addition multiplying each addend by the number and then adding the products

Division The inverse of multiplication. When using an "equal groups" interpretation, the divisor may indicate either the group size or the number of groups, depending on the situation

Edge A straight side (two-dimensional figures); the place where two faces of a solid figure meet (three-dimensional figures)

Equal Having the same value or size

Equal Groups Multiplication Situation A multiplication situation where there are a number of groups and each group is the same size

Equation A mathematical sentence in which one part is the same amount as, or equal to, another part; statement using an equals sign (=) showing that two expressions have the same value

Expression A value expressed as numbers and/or variables and operation symbols (such as +, −, and ×) grouped together; one side of an equation; for example, 9y + 7, 3 + 5, or 8

Face A flat surface of a three-dimensional shape

Factor As a noun, a number (or expression) that divides without remainders into the number (or expression); as a verb, to break down into terms that multiply to make the quantity to be factored

Fewer Less than

Figure A closed shape in two dimensions or three dimensions

Five Frame A graphic representation in the form of a 1 x 5 array that is useful to help students to count, see number relationships, and learn basic facts

Fractions Equal parts of a whole, of a set, or of a length (e.g., a number line)

Greater More than

Groupable vs. Pre-grouped Models for which each group of ten can be made or grouped from the single pieces are "groupable" (e.g., 10 beans in one cup, 10 linking cubes in one tower, 10 straws in one bundle); models for which the ten is already grouped and must be exchanged for 10 single pieces are "pre-grouped"

"Groups of" Interpretation See equal groups multiplication situation of Multiplication

Half One of two equal parts (e.g., half-circles, halves of, two halves)

Hundred A group or bundle of 10 tens or 100 ones

Iterate To repeatedly cover a surface with no gaps and no overlaps

Lesh Translation Model Suggests that mathematical ideas can be represented in five different modes: manipulatives, pictures, real-life contexts, verbal symbols, and written symbols

Manipulatives Physical objects teachers and students can use to discover and illustrate mathematical concepts

More Greater than

Multiplication Multiplication is an operation that combines or scales groups of equal size. See *equal groups multiplication situation* or *array/area model of multiplication*—these are the most common interpretations of multiplication used in Grades K–3; in upper grades, multiplication is also used for scaled comparison, such as "half as many" or "twice as long"

Nonstandard Unit s A unit used to measure that is made up of informal objects such as cubes, straws, or paper clips

Number A count or measurement

Number Line A line used to show the position of a number in relation to other numbers

Numeral A symbol that represents a number (e.g., 3 is the numeral that represents a count of three objects)

Numerator The number in a fraction that indicates the number of parts of the whole that are being considered; the top number in a fraction

One-to-One Correspondence The act of counting each object in a set once and only once

Open Number Line A number line with no numbers or partitions used as a visual representation for recording and sharing strategies for adding, subtracting, multiplying, or dividing numbers

Order To arrange in a particular sequence based on a specified attribute

Parallelogram A quadrilateral with two pairs of parallel sides

Part-Part-Whole Model A visual model for showing the relationship among numbers in addition and subtraction situations where there are groups and a total quantity

Partition To divide equally

Perimeter The distance around a polygon

Place Value The value represented by a digit based on its position in a given number

Polygon A many-sided, closed, simple figure whose sides are line segments

Prism A three-dimensional figure with parallel congruent polygons for bases and parallelograms for faces

Product The result of or answer to a multiplication problem

Proportional Manipulatives Materials whose components are "true to scale"; they have a deliberate mathematical relationship

Pyramid A polyhedron with a polygon for the base and triangular faces that meet at the apex

Quarter One-fourth, a quarter-circle, a quarter of, fourths

Quotient The result of or answer to a division problem

Rectangle A parallelogram with four right angles

Rectilinear Figure A figure composed of multiple, non-overlapping rectangles

Representation A description or model that demonstrates or presents a mathematical concept or idea

Right Angle A 90° angle, sometimes called a "square" angle

Row A horizontal arrangement of objects

Side A line segment of a many-sided figure, also known as an *edge*

Sort To arrange or group by a given attribute such as size, shape, or color

Sphere A three-dimensional figure with all points equally distant from the center

Square A parallelogram with four congruent sides (equal length) and four right angles (also, a special category of rectangles)

Subitizing The instant and accurate recognition of a quantity without pausing to count

Subtraction Taking one number away from another; finding the difference between two numbers; related words: *subtract, minus (−), take from, take apart, compare*

Sum The answer in an addition problem; see also *total*

Surface The faces and curved surfaces of a three-dimensional figure

Tape Diagram A representation of a word problem or mathematical situation where bars or boxes are used to represent the known and unknown quantities; also known as a *bar model*

Ten A group or bundle of 10 ones

Ten Frame A graphic representation in the form of a 2 x 5 array that is useful to help students to count, see number relationships, and learn basic facts

Thirds Thirds of a circle, one-third, three thirds

Thousand A group or bundle of 10 hundreds, 100 tens, or 1,000 ones

Total The result when two or more numbers are added together; see also *sum*

Unit Fraction A fraction with 1 in the numerator; the basic unit for a fractional amount

Unitizing Combining or forming into one unit (one group of ten, one stack of three, one bundle of one hundred, etc.)

Unknown In an equation, the variable to be solved

Vertex In a two-dimensional figure, the point at which two line segments meet to form an angle; in a three-dimensional figure, the point at which three or more edges meet; both are often referred to as *corners*, though this term lacks mathematical precision

Note: Some glossary entries are used with permission from the *Common Core Mathematics Companions*, Grades K–2 (Gojak & Miles, 2015), 3–5 (Gojak & Miles, 2016), and 6–8 (Miles & Williams, 2016).

REFERENCES

Bruner, J. (1960). *The process of education.* Harvard University Press.

Center for Applied Special Technology. (2018). *The UDL guidelines* (version 2.2). http://udlguidelines.cast.org

Dienes, Z. P. (1971). *Building up mathematics* (4th ed.). Hutchinson Educational.

Fetter, A. (2011, April). *Ever wonder what they'd notice?* [Ignite session]. National Council of Teachers of Mathematics Annual Conference, , Indianapolis, IN.

Gojak, L. M., & Miles, R. H. (2015). *The Common Core mathematics companion: The standards decoded, grades K–2.* Corwin Mathematics.

Gojak, L. M., & Miles, R. H. (2016). *The Common Core mathematics companion: The standards decoded, grades 3–5.* Corwin Mathematics.

Hattie, J., Fisher, D., Frey, N., Gojak, L. M., Moore, S. D., & Mellman, W. (2017). *Visible learning for mathematics, grades K–12: What works best to optimize student learning.* Corwin Mathematics.

Kamii, C. (2006, April). *Why many second graders think they can't pay for a 6¢ item with a dime* [Session presentation]. National Council of Teachers of Mathematics Annual Meeting and Exposition, , Saint Louis, MO.

Karp, K. S., Dougherty, B. J., & Bush, S. B. (2021). *The math pact: Achieving instructional coherence within and across grades.* Corwin Mathematics.

Lesh, R. A., Post, T., & Behr, M. (1987). Representations and translations among representations in mathematics learning and problem solving. In C. Janvier (Ed.), *Problems of representations in the teaching and learning of mathematics* (pp. 33–40). Lawrence Erlbaum Associates.

Magiera, J. (2016). *Courageous edventures.* Corwin.

Marshall, A. M., Superfine, A. C., & Canty, R. S. (2010). Star students make connections. *Teaching Children Mathematics, 17*(1), 39–47.

Miles, R. H. & Williams, L. A. (2016). *The Common Core mathematics companion: The standards decoded, grades 6–8.* Corwin Mathematics.

Morrow-Leong, K., Moore, S. D., & Gojak, L. (2020). *Mathematize it! Going beyond key words to make sense of word problems, grades K–2.* Corwin Mathematics.

National Council of Supervisors of Mathematics. (2013, Spring). Improving student achievement in mathematics by using manipulatives with classroom instruction [Position statement]. *Improving Student Achievement Series,* 11. https://www.mathedleadership.org/position-papers/

National Council of Teachers of Mathematics. (2020). *Catalyzing change in early childhood and elementary mathematics.* https://www.nctm.org/Standards-and-Positions/Catalyzing-Change/Catalyzing-Change-in-Early-Childhood-and-Elementary-Mathematics/

Piaget, J. (1971). *The psychology of intelligence.* Routledge & Kegan.

Vygotsky, L. S. (2012). *Thought and language* (E. Hanfmann, G. Vakar, & A. Kozulin, Eds.; A. Kozulin, Trans.; Rev. and expanded ed.). MIT Press. (Original work published 1934)

Wills, T. (2021). *Teaching from a distance.* Corwin Mathematics.

INDEX

Supporting TEACHERS | *Empowering* STUDENTS

PETER LILJEDAHL

14 optimal practices for thinking that create an ideal setting for deep mathematics learning to occur

Grades K–12

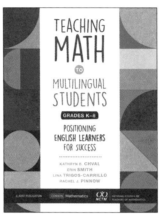

KATHRYN B. CHVAL, ERIN SMITH, LINA TRIGOS-CARRILLO, RACHEL J. PINNOW

Strengths-based approaches to support multilingual students' development in mathematics

Grades K–8

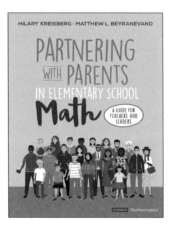

HILARY KREISBERG, MATTHEW L. BEYRANEVAND

Guidance on building productive relationships with families about math education

Grades K–5

BETH MCCORD KOBETT, FRANCIS (SKIP) FENNELL, KAREN S. KARP, DELISE ANDREWS, TRENDA KNIGHTEN, JEFF SHIH, DESIREE HARRISON, BARBARA ANN SWARTZ, SORSHA-MARIA T. MULROE

Detailed plans for helping elementary students experience deep mathematical learning

Grades K–1, 2–3, 4–5

BETH MCCORD KOBETT, KAREN S. KARP

Your game plan for unlocking mathematics by focusing on students' strengths

Grades K–6

JOHN J. SANGIOVANNI, SUSIE KATT, KEVIN J. DYKEMA

Empowering students to embrace productive struggle to build essential skills for learning and living—both inside and outside the classroom

Grades K–12

JENNIFER M. BAY-WILLIAMS, JOHN J. SANGIOVANNI

Because fluency is so much more than basic facts and algorithms

Grades K–8

KAREN S. KARP, BARBARA J. DOUGHERTY, SARAH B. BUSH

A schoolwide solution for students' mathematics success

Elementary, Middle School, High School

MARGARET (PEG) SMITH, VICTORIA BILL, MIRIAM GAMORAN SHERIN, MICHAEL D. STEELE

Take a deeper dive into understanding the five practices—anticipating, monitoring, selecting, sequencing, and connecting—for facilitating productive mathematical conversations in your classrooms

Elementary, Middle School, High School

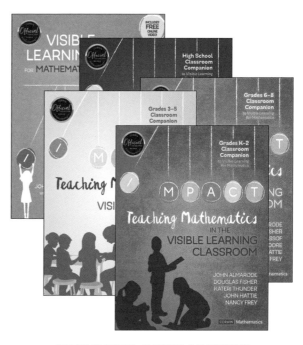

JOHN HATTIE, DOUGLAS FISHER, NANCY FREY, JOHN ALMARODE, LINDA M. GOJAK, SARA DELANO MOORE, WILLIAM MELLMAN, JOSEPH ASSOF, KATERI THUNDER

Powerful, precision teaching through intentionally designed, guided, collaborative, and independent learning

Grades K–2, 3–5, 6–8, 9–12

A SAGE Publishing Company

Helping educators make the greatest impact

CORWIN HAS ONE MISSION: to enhance education through intentional professional learning.

We build long-term relationships with our authors, educators, clients, and associations who partner with us to develop and continuously improve the best evidence-based practices that establish and support lifelong learning.

NATIONAL COUNCIL OF
TEACHERS OF MATHEMATICS

The National Council of Teachers of Mathematics supports and advocates for the highest-quality mathematics teaching and learning for each and every student.